This book is the first to offer a comprehensive history of child labor reform in early
industrial France, and as such it comple-
ments recent works of a more general
nature. Weissbach provides important insights into the fundamental nature of social
reform in nineteenth-century France.
Through his analysis of child labor legislation, he helps to explain how the dominant
classes of French society confronted the
complex question of the relationship between liberty and social welfare.

LEE SHAI WEISSBACH is associate professor of
history at the University of Louisville.

Child Labor Reform in Nineteenth-Century France

Child Labor Reform in Nineteenth-Century France

Assuring the Future Harvest

Lee Shai Weissbach

Louisiana State University Press
Baton Rouge and London

Designer: Patricia Douglas Crowder
Typeface: Linotron 202 Baskerville
Typesetter: G & S Typesetters, Inc.
Printer: Thomson-Shore, Inc.
Binder: John H. Dekker & Sons, Inc.

LIBRARY OF CONGRESS CATALOGING-IN-PUBLICATION DATA
Weissbach, Lee Shai, 1947–
    Child labor reform in nineteenth-century France: assuring the
future harvest / Lee Shai Weissbach.
        p.   cm.
    Bibliography: p.
    Includes index.
    ISBN 0-8071-1483-9 (alk. paper)
        1. Children—Employment—France—History—19th century.
    2. Children—Employment—Law and legislation—France—History—19th century.   I.
    Title.   II. Title: Child labor reform in 19th-century
    France.
    HD6250.F82W45   1989
    331.3'1'0944—dc19   88-30349
                                                                        CIP

The paper in this book meets the guidelines for permanence and durability
of the Committee on Production Guidelines for Book Longevity of the
Council on Library Resources.♾

In memory of my father,
in honor of my mother

Contents

Tables

Preface

This book tells the story of child labor reform in early industrial France. It recounts the history of the factory and apprenticeship legislation that was enacted during the middle decades of the nineteenth century, and it examines the various influences that shaped France's child labor reform movement in a period of ideological ferment and economic transformation. This study considers how attitudes and theories interacted with structural factors to determine not only the nature and timing of French child labor reform efforts but also the actual impact of those efforts on the nation's working children. It examines the beliefs of nineteenth-century child labor activists, and it reveals how their movement was shaped more by their humanitarian and ideological concerns than by either the specific realities of child labor abuse or its exact extent. This book also endeavors to convey some sense of the experience of the children laboring in the factories and workshops of France during the middle of the nineteenth century, though it does not aspire to be either an exhaustive study of the condition of laboring children or a complete account of working-class family life in early industrial society. In this sense, it is intended to complement rather than to replicate the excellent work that has recently been done by historians interested in the life experiences of working-class children, especially of girls.[1] This book is as

1. See, for example, Louise A. Tilly and Joan W. Scott, *Women, Work, and Family* (New York, 1978); Mary Lynn McDougall, "Working-Class Women During the Industrial Revolution, 1780–1914," in Renate Bridenthal and Claudia Koonz (eds.), *Becoming Visible:*

much a political history and a study of upper-class *mentalité* as it is a social history.

The campaign for child labor legislation was among the very first reform movements of post-Napoleonic France, and its fundamental nature derived from the fact that throughout the period of its ascent the movement was dominated by an informal coalition of religious traditionalists and paternalistic middle-class liberals who, while disagreeing on many other matters, agreed on the need for legislation to curb the abuse of working children. The child labor reform movement of the nineteenth century was led to advocate factory legislation because its supporters assumed the moral and social superiority of the privileged classes and inferred from this assumption the responsibility of the elite to protect and influence the nation's youth. Their solicitude, they believed, would make it possible for young people not only to grow up healthy and productive but also to adapt themselves to the kind of stable, hierarchical society the elite envisioned. The reformers frequently fell back upon an agricultural analogy: the tender seedlings of the nation had to be protected in order to assure a future harvest of effective citizens, able workers, and mighty warriors.

The reformers who championed child labor legislation in France were pioneers in their advocacy of government interventionism. Nonetheless, the campaign they mounted reflected the attitudes and ideologies of a large segment of the privileged elite. For this reason, the study of child labor reform provides a window on the mentality of those who dominated French public life and government throughout the early industrial era. It reveals a great deal about the vision of society shared by many within the privileged classes, about their concern with the condition of the working population, and about their role in the evolution of state intervention for the protection and guidance of children.

Indeed, the history of child labor reform suggests a rather precise chronology for the development of several critical features of nineteenth-century French social, political, and intellectual life, and serves as something of a barometer for the social policy of the various French governments of the central decades of that century. It reveals, for example, that the close association between the physical and moral regeneration of the nation's youth and their preparation for the defense of

---

Women in European History (Boston, 1977); and Lenard R. Berlanstein, "Vagrants, Beggars, and Thieves: Delinquent Boys in Mid-Nineteenth Century Paris," *Journal of Social History*, XII (Summer, 1979).

the motherland, often characterized as a development of the years after the traumatic defeat of 1870–1871, had its roots in the 1820s and 1830s.[2] It suggests, too, that the new understanding of childhood as a period to be prolonged and devoted to nurturing and education was a normative feature of the mentality of the comfortable classes in France by the late 1860s. The history of child labor reform also demonstrates that the practice of campaigning for social action through intense lobbying at the highest levels of government, which has been described as a feature of the politics of the 1860s and after, actually began early in the nineteenth century.[3]

The half-century-long debate over how child labor legislation should be framed and how it should be implemented served as a sort of apprenticeship for the French nation as it grappled with the complex issue of state regulation in a society that was undergoing modernization and industrialization. All the fundamental political and philosophical issues revolving around government intervention and its relationship to parental authority and to entrepreneurial prerogative were thrashed out in the context of child labor reform. Thus the national consensus on child labor legislation that was reached by the 1870s paved the way for a widening array of regulatory measures touching upon the child and his family and upon the industrial worker.

Of course, the story of child labor reform in nineteenth-century France has an inherent interest aside from its importance as a window on the larger issue of early industrial reform. It is a story with its own narrative and its own cast of characters, and it is a story that has remained largely untold until now. There are some older works dealing with child labor legislation in nineteenth-century France (a 1927 article by Louis Gueneau on France's first factory law, for example, and a dozen or so law theses produced at the turn of the century), but, for the most part, these studies are superficial and unscholarly.[4] The more recent

2. See, for example, David B. Ralston, *The Army of the Republic: The Place of the Military in the Political Evolution of France, 1871–1914* (Cambridge, Mass., 1967), 34–35.

3. See, for example, Robert J. Bezucha, "The Moralization of Society: The Enemies of Popular Culture in the Nineteenth Century," in Jacques Beauroy, Marc Bertrand, and Edward Gargan (eds.), *The Wolf and the Lamb: Popular Culture in France* (Palo Alto, 1977).

4. Louis Gueneau, "La Législation restrictive du travail des enfants: La Loi du 1841," *Revue d'histoire économique et sociale*, XV (1927); examples of late nineteenth- and early twentieth-century law theses are Louis Duval-Arnould, *Essai sur la législation français du travail des enfants* (Paris, 1888), Cyr. van Overbergh, *Les Inspecteurs du travail* (Paris, 1893), Emile Durand, *L'Inspection du travail en France de 1841 à 1902* (Paris, 1902), Benjamin Bec, *La Législation de l'inspection du travail* (Rennes, 1907), and Suzanne Touren, *La Loi de 1841 sur le travail des enfants dans les manufactures* (Paris, 1931).

works that touch upon the history of child labor reform tell only a small part of the story. The work of Peter Stearns studies entrepreneurial attitudes, for example, while that of A. J. Tudesq analyzes the replies of French notables to early government inquiries and that of Katherine Lynch considers the 1841 factory law in the context of family policy.[5] Moreover, there has been almost nothing of substance written on the child labor issue in the period after 1848 (Colin Heywood's recent work is a notable exception here), and as yet little has been said about the relationship of child labor reform to the changing political situation in France or to changing attitudes toward the family and childhood.[6]

This book is thus intended to serve a two-fold purpose. On the one hand, it fills a considerable gap in the literature of modern French history by providing a comprehensive account of child labor reform and early factory legislation in France. On the other hand, by examining why child labor became an issue when it did, how ideological and practical considerations interacted to influence the form of the nation's early child labor legislation, and what factors determined the actual impact of reform on working children, this study provides some insights into the fundamental nature of social reform in early industrial France.

This book is the result of research on child labor, apprenticeship, and social reform that I have been pursuing for well over a decade, and I have acquired a great many debts of gratitude in the course of preparing it. I first became interested in the issue of child labor while a graduate student at Harvard, and the advice and guidance I received there from David Landes benefited my early work on the subject tremendously. This book has also benefited from the insights and suggestions of many friends and colleagues with whom I have discussed my work in more recent years; in this connection, Rachel Fuchs deserves my special thanks. Also to be thanked are the several manuscript reviewers who commented on this study (or parts of it) in one of its various incarnations. Their suggestions were always carefully considered and often proved extremely useful.

5. Peter N. Stearns, *Paths to Authority: The Middle Class and the Industrial Labor Force in France, 1820–1848* (Urbana, Ill., 1978), *passim*; André-Jean Tudesq, *Les Grands Notables en France (1840–1849)* (Paris, 1964), II, 581–98; and Katherine A. Lynch, *Family, Class, and Ideology in Early Industrial France: Social Policy and the Working-Class Family, 1825–1848* (Madison, 1988), Chap. 5.

6. Colin Heywood, "The Market for Child Labour in Nineteenth-Century France," *History*, No. 216 (1981); Colin Heywood, *Childhood in Nineteenth-Century France: Work, Health, and Education Among the Classes Populaires* (Cambridge, Eng., 1988).

While conducting my research on child labor reform and factory legislation, I made use of a number of research collections both in France and in the United States. Although it is not feasible to name the many individual librarians and archivists upon whose help I relied, I do want to acknowledge the assistance of the staffs of the Archives nationales, the Bibliothèque nationale, and the Bibliothèque historique de la ville de Paris in Paris and the staffs of the Widener Library at Harvard University and of the Ekstrom Library at the University of Louisville. Sincere thanks are due also to all those who helped with the preparation of the manuscript for this book and its final editing. I am grateful for the conscientious work of Sharon Mills, Karen Richardson, Sandy Hartz, and their staff in the Academic and Professional Development Service at the University of Louisville. I also very much appreciate the assistance I received from Margaret Fisher Dalrymple, Catherine Barton, Catherine Landry, and the many others at the Louisiana State University Press who helped with this project at various stages. For the excellent job she did in editing the final copy of my manuscript, Christine Cowan deserves special recognition. My colleague Wendy Pfeffer graciously helped translate the passages of poetry contained in this book. Two institutions are to be thanked for providing some of the funding that facilitated my research on child labor and factory legislation over the years: the Committee on West European Studies (now the Center for European Studies) at Harvard University and the College of Arts and Sciences at the University of Louisville.

Finally, a word of thanks to my wife Sharon, who has been the perfect companion throughout the many years of my research and writing on child labor. She has given me useful criticism and practical support, and she has encouraged me in my scholarship by enriching my life in innumerable ways. Thanks also to my children, Jacob and Maya, who arrived while this book was in the making and who have helped me keep my work in perspective by bringing me joy beyond measure.

Abbreviations

AN	Holdings of the Archives nationales, Paris
BSIM	*Bulletin de la Société industrielle de Mulhouse*
BSPA	*Bulletin de la Société de protection des apprentis et des enfants des manufactures*
CD	Proceedings of the Chamber of Deputies
CP	Proceedings of the Chamber of Peers
JE	*Journal des économistes*
NA	Proceedings of the National Assembly
RDM	*Revue des deux mondes*

Child Labor Reform in Nineteenth-Century France

ONE

Child Labor in France
Before Midcentury

In the traditional society of preindustrial France, as in traditional societies throughout Europe, the use of children in productive labor was an accepted practice, essential to the maintenance of virtually every household. The full integration of children into society seemed to come only when they became economically integrated into their families. From infancy until the age of seven or thereabouts, children were given a great deal of freedom to do as they wished, and they interacted only minimally with their parents.When they ceased their physical dependence on parents and caregivers, however, children entered the world of adults. They would be dressed in adult clothing, they would be initiated into adult gender roles, and unless their families had unusual wealth and status, they would begin to assist in the productive activities of the household. An extended period of formal schooling was a luxury reserved for the privileged few.

For most children in traditional society, the beginning of work meant the beginning of agricultural labor or perhaps an introduction to handicraft manufacturing in the home or in the workshop. Even before age ten, most children had been initiated into some of the simpler tasks essential to the working of the soil and to the practice of the handicraft trades. As one recent study of the European family observes, "Identity of family, occupation, life and work inevitably blended childhood into working youth."[1] It was often very young children who fed the poultry

1. Michael Mitterauer and Reinhard Sieder, *The European Family*, trans. Karla Oosterveen and Manfred Hörzinger (Chicago, 1982), 105.

and fetched the water, who herded the cows and gleaned in the fields, who cleaned the wool and carded it for spinning.

Children generally continued to labor under the tutelage of their elders through their early and middle teens, and as their strength and ability increased, they were given greater responsibilities. By the time they were twelve or thirteen, it was not uncommon for children to be living away from their own homes as domestic servants, as supplementary agricultural laborers, or as resident industrial workers in the handicraft trades. In those crafts with a structured apprenticeship, the period of formal training also generally began in the early teens.[2]

In the second quarter of the nineteenth century, as France began on the road toward industrialization, the practice of setting children to productive labor from a very early age remained largely unchallenged. Traditional child-rearing attitudes and customs persisted in nearly every French household.[3] Although the notion that childhood and adolescence should be an extended period of protection, nurturing, and education had been advanced at least as early as the eighteenth century (most notably by Jean-Jacques Rousseau), that notion was by no means universally accepted, and what influence it had was only upon families of the upper and middle classes.[4] Certainly until the middle of the nineteenth century, it was assumed that the children of the working classes at least would begin their economic productivity well before they reached their middle teens.

The statistics on school attendance in the second quarter of the nineteenth century reflect the persistence of a dependence on children's la-

2. On traditional childrearing and early work experience in France, see, for example, Maurice Crubellier, *L'Enfance et la jeunesse dans la société française, 1800–1950* (Paris, 1979), 117–19, 123ff; Georges Duby and Armand Wallon (eds.), *Histoire de la France rurale* (Paris, 1975–76), II, 280, 480, III, 340–42; John R. Gillis, *Youth and History* (New York, 1981), 5–9; Tilly and Scott, *Women, Work, and Family*, 32–37; Edward Shorter, *The Making of the Modern Family* (New York, 1975), 26–28, 169ff; Olwen Hufton, "Women and the Family Economy in Eighteenth-Century France," *French Historical Studies*, IX (Spring, 1975); Laura S. Strumingher, "The Artisan Family: Traditions and Transition in Nineteenth-Century Lyon," *Journal of Family History*, II (Fall, 1977). See also Ivy Pinchbeck and Margaret Hewitt, *Children in English Society* (London, 1973), II, 347ff.

3. On the persistence of traditional child labor in peasant households, see Eugen Weber, *Peasants into Frenchmen* (Stanford, 1976), 170–71, 321–23. See also Yves Lequin, *Les Ouvriers de la région lyonnaise (1848–1914)* (Lyon, 1977), II, 4–6.

4. See Frank Musgrove, *Youth and the Social Order* (Bloomington, Ind., 1965), 33–57; A. D. Tolédano, *La Vie de famille sous la Restauration et la Monarchie de juillet* (Paris, 1943), 42ff; Philippe Ariès, *Centuries of Childhood*, trans. Robert Baldick (New York, 1962), 329, 403–404; and Jacques Gélis, Mireille Laget, and Marie-France Morel, *Entrer dans la vie: Naissances et enfances dans la France traditionnelle* ([Paris?], 1978), 218.

bor in households throughout France. Although primary education was available almost universally after François Guizot, the minister of public instruction, sponsored a new education law in 1833, many French families failed to send their children to school nonetheless. One important reason for this fact was that children were needed for work at home. In 1840, for example, some 1.1 million of the approximately 4 million children aged six to twelve in France were receiving no schooling whatsoever. Even more telling is the fact that a large percentage of those children who were sent to school were withdrawn during those times of the year when their labor was most needed at home. It appears that most French schoolchildren actually attended classes only three to five months out of the year, and attendance figures for summer were invariably lower than those for winter. For instance, whereas the number of boys in communal primary schools in 1840 was reported as 756,464 in winter, their number dropped by 38.8 percent, to 463,464, in summer.[5] So taken for granted was the use of child labor in most French families that the government's Bureau of Public Assistance reduced the subsidies paid to foster parents when their charges turned seven, reasoning that by then the children's service to the households in which they were placed was sufficient recompense in lieu of payments. Subsidies to foster families ceased completely when the children in their care turned twelve.[6]

The key reason that traditional child rearing included an early introduction to labor was that the family economy demanded it. Child labor was an economic necessity in most French households. This had been true in preindustrial society, and it was still true in the early industrial society developing during the era of the July Monarchy. Most of the families that depended on industrial labor for their income, like most families in the older sectors of the economy, simply could not survive without the economic productivity of their children. For working-class couples, the most difficult years were those when there were very young children in the household, for these children not only were incapable of contributing to their own upkeep but also commanded the attention of their mothers and kept them from income-producing labor. Some relief came only when a couple's eldest child could begin to work, and thus

5. See Edouard Ducpétiaux, *De la condition physique et morale des jeunes ouvriers* (Brussels, 1843), I, 237, 245; and P. Lorain, *Tableau de l'instruction primaire en France . . . à la fin de 1833* (Paris, 1837), 20–23.
6. Rachel G. Fuchs, *Abandoned Children: Foundlings and Child Welfare in Nineteenth-Century France* (Albany, N.Y., 1984), 240–41.

many families were compelled to hasten their children's entry into the labor force.

The dilemma of many early nineteenth-century families is illustrated by the data on family income reported by Louis Villermé, perhaps the most important observer of early industrial society in France. Villermé reported that in the town of Rouen, for example, a husband and wife working as weavers could together earn 861 francs per year in the 1830s. Since the minimum income they needed to sustain themselves in normal times was only about 761 francs per year, a newly married, childless couple could probably subsist quite nicely. A couple with an infant child, however, needed about 879 francs to subsist for a year, and a couple with three children under the age of thirteen would need some 1,274 francs. It is no wonder that a couple with children would put them to work as soon as possible.[7]

So crucial were children's earnings to working-class parents that children who could not contribute to their own upkeep sometimes had to be abandoned. Because total dependence is inherent in infancy, mothers with limited resources often had to give up their babies. In Paris, babies were abandoned at the rate of three thousand to five thousand annually throughout most of the nineteenth century.[8] Older children as well were sometimes abandoned for economic reasons. Two cases from the records of the Paris police court in 1842 are illustrative. One is that of Louis Vacher, the fifteen-year-old son of a laborer. Sent to work in a printing shop, he was released when there was not enough work for him, and he had to resort to begging. When he was arrested for vagrancy, Louis did not even know where his father was living. The other case is that of Frédéric Valentine, a fourteen-year-old "who appeared to be barely ten." This child had been sent to labor turning the wheelwork in a mercer's shop but had quit because he was unable to meet the physical demands of his job. He, too, turned to begging when his mother found she could not possibly support him.[9]

Because working families in early industrial society continued as they had done in traditional society to depend on economic contributions from all their members, they readily accepted the new factories as alternative settings in which children could earn an income. The children who worked in industry would certainly have been obliged to labor else-

---

7. Louis Villermé, *Tableau de l'état physique et moral des ouvriers* (Paris, 1840), I, 144ff. See also Gillis, *Youth and History*, 16.

8. Fuchs, *Abandoned Children*, 64ff; Gillis, *Youth and History*, 44–45, 48–49.

9. Ducpétiaux, *Condition*, I, 43–45.

where had factory work not been available. The observation of a contemporary Belgian notwithstanding, the children who were sent to work in industry were seldom "torn away from their games, from their school desks, from the arms of their mothers."[10] In essence, the participation of children in factory labor was the consequence of the persistence of traditional child-rearing practices, based on the existence of a family economy. For working-class families not to have sent their children to work in industrial manufacturing would have been a revolutionary act; sending them into the factories was not.

Textile manufacturing was the keystone of early industrialization, and it was in this sector of the industrial economy that children were employed most extensively. In virtually every branch of the French textile industry and at every stage of the production process, they had a role to play. Typically, children in textile factories worked in teams of two or three as assistants to adult workers, and they were frequently hired and paid by those who supervised their work. Girls did much of the cleaning and carding of raw materials in the procedures preliminary to spinning; in the spinning process itself, both boys and girls served as piecers (*rattacheurs*), tying broken threads, and as bobbin-minders, keeping bobbins clean and replacing them when necessary. In weaving, children assisted with the preparation of the yarn, and in some advanced mills with more modern equipment, they also helped with the warping. At times, adolescents were even given the responsibility of operating some of the smaller spinning frames and some of the more manageable looms. In the mechanized process of cloth printing, teams of two adult printers aided by three children were common. The children helped prepare both dyes and machinery, and the responsibility of keeping the printing chase charged with color was sometimes left to children as young as six years old. The tremendous importance of children in the textile industry is illustrated in Villermé's account of the composition of the work force in a woolens mill in Louviers in 1838. Alongside 97 adult men, the mill employed 107 children (72 as assistants in carding and 35 as assistants in spinning), and 40 women, 18 of whom were themselves only twelve to twenty years old.[11]

Although children most often found factory employment in the increasingly industrialized textile industry, they also found work in metal-

10. Ducpétiaux, *Condition*, I, 9.
11. Villermé, *Tableau*, I, 4–5, 10; Ducpétiaux, *Condition*, I, *passim*; Katherine A. Lynch, "The Problem of Child Labor Reform and the Working-Class Family in France during the July Monarchy," *Proceedings of the Annual Meeting of the Western Society for French History*, V (1977), 230–31; Villermé, *Tableau*, I, 174–76.

lurgical and chemical factories, in sugar refineries, in glass and pottery works, in mining enterprises, and in the shops of countless other industries.[12] In the glassworks of early nineteenth-century France, for instance, the essential team of glassworkers commonly consisted of a master glassblower and three children: two apprentices, who had begun their formal training at the age of twelve or thirteen and who were at different stages of their apprenticeship, and a bottle carrier, nine or ten years old and usually the son of a glassworker.[13] In the period before the assembly line was introduced, transporting materials from one station to another was a task commonly assigned to children in many kinds of factories.

By and large, early French manufacturing entrepreneurs, like working-class parents, accepted child labor in factories as a natural outgrowth of traditional child-rearing practices. These entrepreneurs relied on long-standing precedents in establishing hiring and firing procedures, in setting work schedules, and in determining wage rates, and they saw the hiring of youngsters without restriction as simply a continuation of established employment patterns. Ultimately, the demand for child labor in industry, like the supply of children, was economically motivated. Children were welcomed into factory labor because they, like women, commanded a much lower wage than did adult men. According to figures recorded by Villermé, for example, young *rattacheurs* in the town of Elbeuf in 1837 were being paid the meager wage of 67 centimes per day, while the adult spinners with whom they worked were getting from 3.00 to 3.67 francs per day. Similarly, in the textile mills of Sedan, where some adult male spinners earned up to 2.80 francs per day, young bobbin-minders made as little as 40 centimes per day.[14]

An industrial survey conducted by the government in the early 1840s showed that the average daily wage of a man in French industry was 1.94 francs, whereas the average wage of a woman was 91 centimes (46.9 percent of the man's wage), and the average wage of a child was only 66 centimes (34.0 percent of the man's wage).[15] The wide gap between the

12. See Ministre de l'agriculture et du commerce, *Statistique de la France* (Paris, 1847–52), series 1, X–XIII.

13. Joan Wallach Scott, *The Glassworkers of Carmaux: French Craftsmen and Political Action in a Nineteenth-Century City* (Cambridge, Mass., 1974), 23–33.

14. Villermé, *Tableau*, I, 169, 264.

15. Ministre de l'agriculture, *Statistique*, series 1, X–XIII, *passim*. The national average wage reported in 1845 was apparently computed incorrectly and is given as 2.07 francs for men, 1.02 francs for women, and 72 centimes for children; the average wage given in the text has been recomputed from departmental data.

wages paid adult men and those paid women and children had been established by custom in preindustrial society, where men had always been viewed as the principal breadwinners in their families. Traditional wage differentials were never seriously challenged in the early industrial era, so even where children were in demand for factory labor, their wages remained extremely low. Manufacturers would have considered it a waste of money to employ adult workers to do the tasks usually assigned to children, for they reasoned that these tasks required neither more skill nor more strength than children possessed.[16]

Children were employed in the early factories also because they were perceived as especially well suited for certain jobs. Defenders of child labor argued that the small fingers of children suited them for tying threads, that their small frames suited them for cleaning the recesses of machinery, and that their nimbleness suited them for fetching and carrying. In addition, children were considered easier to discipline than adults. They were conditioned to accept the authority of their elders, and even their corporal chastisement was accepted. There is at least one example, from the Department of the Ain, of children being bound to their factories: they not only labored there but ate and slept there as well. Where factory owners secured foundlings for use in their shops, they could go so far as to require them to wear uniforms and to remain on the job under threat of arrest and punishment.[17]

Finally, manufacturers employed children because youngsters who were brought into the work routine at an early age might gradually learn the more complex aspects of factory labor and be prepared to step into skilled jobs as they matured. Because the skilled jobs these children might be able to secure paid a higher wage than unskilled labor, parents had an added incentive for sending their children to work early, in the hope that they would be trained on the job.[18]

16. Compare responses to the government inquiry of 1837 from the Department of the Aisne and from the town of Rouen, in AN, F12–4705.

17. Leonard Horner, *On the Employment of Children in Factories and Other Works in the United Kingdom and in Some Foreign Countries* (London, 1840), 27; Heywood, "Market," 47; Stéphane Douailler and Patrice Vermeren, "Les Enfants des hospices, remède contre l'instabilité des ouvriers," *Les Révoltes logiques*, III (1976), 8–12. See also Sidney Pollard, "Factory Discipline in the Industrial Revolution," *Economic History Review*, 2nd ser., XVI (December, 1963), 260–61.

18. The motivation of manufacturers in employing children is discussed in Heywood, "Market," *passim*, and in Stearns, *Paths*, 61ff. On training for skilled labor in factories, see also Yves Lequin, "Apprenticeship in Nineteenth-Century France: A Continuing Tradition or a Break with the Past?," in Steven Laurence Kaplan and Cynthia J. Koepp (eds.), *Work in France: Representations, Meaning, Organization, and Practice* (Ithaca, 1986), 468–71.

It is very difficult to know if industrial employment took a higher toll in actual physical suffering than did more traditional forms of child labor. One of the best available measures of the general physical condition of youngsters in any given region of nineteenth-century France is the rate at which young men were rejected for military service. Comparisons of rejection rates for agricultural areas and for industrial areas have been used since the early nineteenth century in attempts to measure the effects of industrial employment. The most sophisticated studies of these data, however, reveal no significant correlation between the level of industrialization of a region and the suitability of its twenty-year-old men for military service. A recent study of the statistics for 1819–1826 found that there was no correlation at all between the proportion of the conscript population involved in agriculture and the proportion of recruits rejected on medical grounds.[19]

An examination of the data for the period 1837–1839, when industrialization had a firmer hold in at least a few departments, suggests a similar lack of correlation. In the late 1830s, for example, the highest rejection rate of conscripts (53.1 percent of potential recruits) was in the Dordogne, France's thirty-fifth most industrialized department. At the same time, the lowest rejection rate (20.6 percent) was in the Morbihan, France's fifteenth most industrialized department. So, too, although the highly industrialized departments of the Seine-Inférieure and the Nord had rejection rates for this period substantially above the national average of 38.3 percent, with rates of 49.8 and 44.9 percent respectively, the industrial Haut-Rhin had a rejection rate of only 35.4 percent, slightly below the national average, and the rejection rate in the Seine was only 31.7 percent.[20]

Despite the absence of any clear-cut relationship between departmental levels of industrialization and military rejection rates, however, the extremely high rates of rejection in several specific cities do suggest that life in an urban industrial environment may have had an unusually strong negative effect on the health of industrial child laborers. Rejec-

19. Colin Heywood, "The Impact of Industrialization on the Health of Children in Nineteenth-Century France" (Typescript in possession of Colin Heywood, Nottingham, Eng., 1982).

20. Data on 1837–39 rejection rates for military service is in AN, F12–4706. The level of industrialization here is measured in terms of the value of industrial goods produced and is computed from early 1840s data in Ministre de l'agriculture, *Statistique*, series 1, X–XIII, *passim*. According to the available data, the Nord was France's most highly industrialized department, the Seine-Inférieure was third, the Haut-Rhin was ninth, and the Seine was fifth.

tion rates have been reported at 52.4 percent for early industrial Mulhouse, 53.9 percent for Lille, 62.4 percent for Rouen, 66.6 percent for
Elbeuf, and an astonishing 83.3 percent for Bolbec.[21]

The ambiguity of the results obtained from an examination of the
available statistical information on recruitment is, unfortunately, matched
by the problematic nature of the narrative accounts produced in the
early decades of industrialization describing the conditions of child labor. Nearly all of the available information on industrial conditions in
France before midcentury comes from the accounts of observers from
the privileged classes, such as Louis Villermé, or from various local
notables who prepared reports in response to government inquiries.
Because these individuals did not have much direct contact with the
working classes, they probably had little understanding of traditional
working-class life, and their perceptions were often influenced by their
own ideological commitments or personal sentiments. Almost all the
early accounts of child labor in France were produced in the context of
highly politicized philosophical debates over working-class misery and
depravity, so much of what was written about child labor in the second
quarter of the nineteenth century is of questionable objectivity.[22]

Still, it is possible to gain some impression of children's experiences in
the factories from the various sources of information available. The accounts of those who observed industrial conditions in the 1830s and
1840s suggest strongly, for example, that whether or not the hardships
encountered by factory children were more severe and debilitating than
those suffered by other working children, many of those hardships were
of a quite new variety. Indeed, it was the novelty of child labor conditions in the factory, together with their conspicuousness, that attracted
the attention of outside observers.

Many things about industrial labor marked it as different from the
more traditional economic activities of youngsters. Although there is
perhaps a tendency to romanticize the experiences of workers and apprentices in the preindustrial era, it is true that child labor in agriculture

21. Charles Dupin, *Du travail des enfants qu'emploient les ateliers, les usines et les manufactures* (Paris, 1840), 25; Villermé, *Tableau*, I, 17; Jean-Pierre Thouvenin, "De l'influence que
l'industrie exerce sur la santé des populations," *Annales d'hygiène publique et de médecine
légale*, XXXVI (1846), 17.
22. On the problem of biased reporting about industrial conditions, see William M.
Reddy, *The Rise of Market Culture: The Textile Trade and French Society, 1750–1900* (Cambridge, Eng., 1984), 169–82; William Coleman, *Death is a Social Disease: Public Health and
Political Economy in Early Industrial France* (Madison, 1982); and William H. Sewell, Jr., *Work
and Revolution in France: The Language of Labor from the Old Regime to 1848* (Cambridge,
Eng., 1980), 223–32.

and in the handicraft trades had always taken place under the relatively close supervision and tutelage of parents or masters. Whether young workers were the offspring, the servants, or the apprentices of those under whom they worked, their relationship with their elders was one of personal dependence. This relationship involved a wide range of mutual obligations and allowed for a certain flexibility in the work routine. The new types of industrial labor, on the other hand, were conducted under conditions that were virtually unknown in preindustrial society. Industrial labor presented new hardships that had never been of major concern in agricultural labor or in preindustrial manufacturing.

One of the greatest hardships faced by young workers in the new factories of France (as in early factories everywhere) was that they were required to work very long hours doing monotonous tasks at a pace they could not control. The average workday in early French factories was reported to be anywhere from twelve to sixteen hours long, and the pace imposed by factory machinery, together with the discipline enforced by the factory system, allowed little or no respite. During the workday, periods for rest or meals totaled one and a half or two hours at most. Even where the physical strength required of young workers was less, the stamina required was greater. The work that children did was not necessarily more difficult, but it was more intense, and it especially taxed the youngest of the child laborers. Eight or nine was the age at which children commonly entered the factories, but in 1837, for example, there were reports from at least eleven departments indicating that children of six and seven were engaged in factory labor.[23]

Another major new hardship encountered by factory children stemmed from the environments in which they were put to work in early industrial establishments. These factories were liable to be ill designed and poorly ventilated. As a result, many of them were overheated by the machinery they contained. In mechanical trimming works, for instance, the temperature could be 34° to 40°C (93° to 104°F), and Louis Villermé reported the temperature in one textile shop he visited to be a stifling 50°C (122°F). So too, many early factories were saturated by the dust created in various industrial processes. It was only in the 1840s, for example, that vented batting machines were introduced in the most modern cotton spinning works of Alsace. Until then, all the particles

23. See the responses to the 1837 government inquiry in AN, F12–4705, and also the summary of those responses: *Rapport du Bureau des manufactures sur les réponses à la circulaire du 31 juillet relative à l'emploi des enfants dans les fabriques* (Paris, 1837); Villermé, *Tableau*, I; and Heywood, "Market," 36–37.

produced in the batting process were shut inside the factory with the workers.

As a result of the conditions under which they labored, factory children were frequently tired and sleepy. Their fatigue was caused not only by the monotonous and often harried pace at which they worked but also by a lack of sleep at night. At least some young workers, like those employed seasonally from the environs of the textile town of Mulhouse, lived so far from their places of employment that they had to awaken in the wee hours of the morning in order to arrive at work by six o'clock. When they returned home, they were so exhausted that though they went to bed immediately, they invariably went off to work the next day "without being completely refreshed."[24] For children employed in nighttime labor, as they were in industries such as glassmaking, which depended on the maintenance of a continuous fire, the normal sleep routine was even further frustrated. Perhaps the most common motive for the beating of factory children was to keep them at their work despite their weariness. One manufacturer's wife tremblingly explained in 1835 that "in times of pressure, when the workers keep laboring through the night, the children must also stay awake and work, and . . . when these poor creatures, succumbing to sleep, stop working, they are aroused by any means necessary, including the lash."[25]

As factory labor could leave children exhausted, it could also make them sick. Youngsters working in the cotton dust of spinning mills came down with newly labeled diseases such as "cotton phthisis" and "cotton pneumonia." The children who sharpened the equipment used in carding breathed in metal filings, and those who worked with dyes inhaled acetic acid vapors. In dusty flax-spinning mills, the child laborers were "subject to indigestion, vomitting, chronic bronchial and pulmonary inflammations, and pulmonary consumption."[26]

Above and beyond all the problems of fatigue and illness associated with factory labor, there were also problems inherent in working with

24. Villermé, *Tableau*, I, 27; see also II, 91. On Villermé's exaggeration of this problem, see Reddy, *Market Culture*, 178–80.

25. *Industriel de la Champagne* (1835), quoted in Ducpétiaux, *Condition*, I, 29. The responses to the 1837 government inquiry also indicate that factory children were sometimes beaten, usually by parents or siblings; see *Rapport du Bureau des manufactures*, and Villermé, *Tableau*, II, 115–16.

26. Ducpétiaux, *Condition*, I, 50. 53. On factory environments, see, for example, Ducpétiaux, *Condition*, I, 49–53; "Une Politique de la force de travail," *Les Révoltes logiques*, III (1976), 18–22; Marie-Madeleine Kahan-Rabecq, *La Classe ouvrière en Alsace pendant la Monarchie de juillet* (Paris, 1939), 161–62; and P. Pierrard, "Le Patronat et le travail des enfants en 1848," *Economie et humanisme*, XVIII (1959), 57.

complex machinery. Workers were unprotected from most of the shafts, belts, and wheels of early factories, and these took a toll of victims both young and old, though it must be suspected that youngsters were more careless and thus more vulnerable. The fact that children were often expected to clean and service spinning machinery and other equipment while it was in motion only added to the risks they faced.

There was yet another set of costs associated with the use of children in factory labor as that practice became increasingly common in France in the second quarter of the nineteenth century. These were the costs resulting from missed opportunities for education and socialization. Children who began factory labor at age six or seven, and even those who began at eight or nine, had virtually no opportunity for formal schooling, and even their opportunities for informal socialization were truncated. Children in traditional work situations, on the one hand, were able to remain closely tied to their parents or masters in the early stages of their productive lives. They were provided with appropriate role models, and they were taught a variety of practical and social skills. Because of the flexibility of their positions as laborers in their childhood years, they might well have received some formal education, at least at the primary level. Factory children, on the other hand, were frequently thrown into situations where normal interaction with adults and with peers was severely restricted, where opportunities for the acquisition of artisanal skills were limited, and where provisions for even a minimal level of formal schooling were lacking. As one commentator in the mid-1830s concluded, "when a factory, a spinning mill, an arsenal or a workshop is about to open, the school may as well close down."[27]

Some French parents may have been inclined to keep their working children under their own watchful eyes in the factories, as they had in traditional work settings (this was apparently the case in early industrial England), and some entrepreneurs attracted workers by offering employment to entire families.[28] But increasingly parents and children found themselves separated from each other in industrial labor. Although the frequency with which parents and children worked together

27. Lorain, *Instruction primaire*, 31–35, esp. 32.
28. William M. Reddy, "Family and Factory: French Linen Weavers in the Belle Epoque," *Journal of Social History*, VIII (Winter, 1975), 102–103; Michelle Perrot, "The Three Ages of Industrial Discipline in Nineteenth-Century France," in John M. Merriman (ed.), *Consciousness and Class Experience in Nineteenth-Century Europe* (New York, 1979), 153–54; Leslie Page Moch and Louise A. Tilly, "Joining the Urban World: Occupation, Family, and Migration in Three French Cities," *Comparative Studies in Society and History*, XXVII (1985), 33–34. See also Neil J. Smelser, *Social Change in the Industrial Revolution* (Chicago, 1959), 182ff.

apparently varied greatly from place to place, observers of the child labor situation in the late 1830s concluded that only about one-third of
factory children worked alongside their mothers or fathers. There were
reports that parents sometimes purposely placed their children in shops
other than the ones in which they themselves worked in order to protect
at least a part of the family income in case a plant closed.[29] Thus a great
many factory children were deprived of the parental attention that could
have mitigated some of the ill effects of labor in the perverse environments of the factories.

Children who worked alongside strange adults in large factories were
frequently privy to the vulgar conduct and language of their elder co-
workers. Although children had never been rigorously sheltered from
adult behaviors in traditional society and young women had always been
vulnerable to seduction by their co-workers and employers, observers of
factory conditions were troubled nonetheless by the exposure of youngsters to immoral influences in the semipublic arena of the shop floor.
Manufacturers complained that the vulgarities children overheard they
soon repeated "with a revolting satisfaction" and that the children frequently came to "understand things of which they should remain ignorant."[30] It was also feared that factory workshops served as places where
girls were molested and young prostitutes recruited. The girls in the
shops could do little to escape a persistent procurer, and there were
reports of factory girls of thirteen and younger in Reims and in Sedan
supplementing their income with prostitution. Louis Blanc wrote in
1840 that the working arrangements of factories led to "the innoculation
of youth with vice"; and the Belgian observer of child labor Edouard
Ducpétiaux lamented that the typical young industrial worker had
"taken off the robe of innocence, and cast it far from him."[31]

Moreover, it was not just in the factories of France that new forms of
child labor were appearing and that new working conditions were being
imposed during the second quarter of the nineteenth century. The advent of industrial society also meant the transformation of craftshop
manufacturing. Already in the late eighteenth century, many craftshops
were being influenced by the new organizational concepts of industrial
capitalism, especially by the idea of division of labor. During the early
nineteenth century, small, unmechanized shops increasingly became

29. See *Rapport du Bureau des manufactures* and Reddy, *Market Culture*, 172–73.
30. Quoted in Villermé, *Tableau*, I, 31; see also Ducpétiaux, *Condition*, I, 323.
31. Villermé, *Tableau*, I, 226–27, 258–59; Ducpétiaux, *Condition*, I, 325; Louis Blanc,
Organisation du travail (Paris, 1841), 31; Ducpétiaux, *Condition*, I, 37.

sweatshops, and this radically transformed child labor in these shops. The conditions under which children labored in small shops came to resemble those under which they worked in early French factories in several ways. Child labor in small shops was no longer supervised by a system of guild control and no longer subject to traditional standards of organization and production. The intensity and the monotony usually associated with factory labor were coming to characterize craftshop production as well. Even though they generally retained the title of apprentices, the children working in small shops were looked upon no longer as artisans or craftsmen in training but rather as cheap laborers to be exploited in the present with little concern for the future. The strictly regulated apprenticeship system of the Old Regime, like French industry's corporate structure itself, had vanished with the French Revolution, and the training of apprentices in the traditional fashion was seldom a concern of the newer breed of entrepreneur.

There had always been some negative consequences associated with craftshop production. The ill effects of labor on children in the Lyon silk trade were notorious, and children in metal working could be greatly deformed from the constant hammering they did. The lot of the young girls employed in such trades as lacemaking, tailoring, and artificial flower making was not a happy one either. But as the middle of the nineteenth century approached, the situation was clearly deteriorating. In the best of circumstances, apprentices were still taught many of the skills they would need to carry on the practice of their craft. Increasingly, however, even well-meaning shop owners were unable to provide the complete and well-rounded training that apprenticeship had once implied, and apprentices learned and performed only a limited number of routinized tasks. More and more, long hours, boredom, and insalubrious surroundings came to characterize small-shop production for adults and children alike.[32]

32. Crubellier, *Enfance*, 123–30; Lequin, *Ouvriers de la region lyonnaise*, II, 7–9; Christopher H. Johnson, "Economic Change and Artisan Discontent: The Tailors' History, 1800–1848," in Roger Price (ed.), *Revolution and Reaction* (London, 1975), 87–114; Lee Shai Weissbach, "Artisanal Responses to Artistic Decline: The Cabinetmakers of Paris in the Era of Industrialization," *Journal of Social History*, XVI (Winter, 1982), 67–81. On Old Regime apprenticeship, see Julien Hayem, *Histoire de l'apprentissage* (Paris, 1868); Eugène Dolfus-Francoz, *Essai historique sur la condition légale du mineur, apprenti, ouvrier d'industrie, ou employé de commerce* (Paris, 1900), 5–21; Paul Merlet, *Les Lois sur l'apprentissage et leurs consequences économiques et sociales* (Paris, 1912), 5–14; Emerand Bardoul, *Essai sur l'apprentissage industriel en France* (Paris, 1919), 5–8; and Robert Darnton, "Workers Revolt: The Great Cat Massacre of the Rue Saint-Séverin," in Robert Darnton, *The Great Cat Massacre and Other Episodes in French Cultural History* (New York, 1984), 75–104.

In the worst of circumstances, apprentices became nothing more than domestic servants: exploited, ill treated, and at times physically abused. Seldom was there a written contract to protect apprentices from the whims of their employers. One story that came to light in the late 1830s provides an excellent example of the abuse of apprenticeship in its most extreme manifestation. The story is that of a Paris shop owner and his wife who took on thirty-two apprentices, all of whom were from outside Paris and all of whom were virtual prisoners of their master. These apprentices were put to work under the most abominable conditions, and they were disciplined in the most inhuman fashion. Their workday lasted from five in the morning until eleven at night, and they were subjected to frequent beatings to keep them at their labor. As punishment, the shop owner's wife once branded a child "on one of the most sensitive parts of his body" and forced another to eat his own excrement. At night, the apprentices slept on a garret floor covered with decomposing straw. For their meals, they were fed little more than black bread and rotten vegetables. When their stomachs would no longer tolerate this vile diet, the children were beaten and forced to eat their own vomit.[33]

Just as it is difficult to construct a complete and totally accurate picture of the work experience of young laborers, it is also quite difficult to determine exactly how pervasive industrial child labor was by the second quarter of the nineteenth century. The earliest systematic account of child labor on a national basis comes from an industrial survey completed by the French statistical service in 1845, and even the data reported then present several problems. First, the data were collected over a period of half a decade, during which time France's first child labor law was enacted. It is not clear how the passage of the law affected the data, and this is a drawback. Second, there is evidence that the enumerators who collected the data on child labor were not careful to follow the directions they were given. Although they were instructed to survey only those establishments employing ten or more workers, they apparently counted smaller shops as well, at least in some places. Thus, some child laborers in small workshops were included in the survey, but what percentage of the total they represented remains unknown. Nevertheless, the figures from the 1845 survey are the most complete available, and it

33. *Gazette des tribunaux*, September 26, 1839, quoted in Ducpétiaux, *Condition*, I, 38–39. See also Villermé, *Tableau*, II, 116–17; and Michelle Perrot, "A Nineteenth-Century Work Experience as Related in a Worker's Autobiography: Norbert Truquin," in Steven Laurence Kaplan and Cynthia J. Koepp (eds.), *Work in France: Representations, Meaning, Organization, and Practice* (Ithaca, 1986), 302–303.

is worth considering what they show even if they cannot be considered exact.[34]

The 1845 data indicate that just before midcentury, French industrial enterprises employed 143,665 children under the age of sixteen and that these children constituted 11.7 percent of the total industrial work force. As Table 1 indicates, the departments in which the greatest number of children were employed were the Seine-Inférieure and the Nord. All told, there were six departments in each of which over 5,000 children were employed in industry. There were an additional thirty departments in each of which between 1,000 and 5,000 children were employed in industry. Although in general in the 1840s there seems to have been no correlation between the level of industrialization of a department and the percentage of its work force composed of children (r = .08), those departments most heavily involved in textile production did employ a relatively high percentage of children.[35] Children constituted 21.4 percent of the work force in the Eure, 21.3 percent in the Haut-Rhin, 17.5 percent in the Seine-Inférieure, and 13.4 percent in the Nord. The 1845 data indicate that 72.6 percent of France's industrial child laborers were employed in one of the textile industries and that they constituted a relatively large percentage of the total work force in several of those industries. In the French cotton textile industry, children constituted 18.3 percent of the work force, and in woolen textiles they constituted 20.0 percent. In the manufacture of cotton blends, the percentage of children in the work force rose to 24.5.[36] Overall, there were fifteen industries that employed over 1,000 children each, as Table 2 indicates.

In the first half of the nineteenth century, no attempts were made to determine the exact number of child laborers working as apprentices in the smaller workshops of France, but some idea of the scope of apprenticeship before midcentury does emerge from a study of industrial conditions conducted by the chamber of commerce of Paris in 1847

---

34. For a contemporary critique of the statistical service's data, see Alexandre Moreau de Jonnès, *Statistique de l'industrie de la France* (Paris, 1856). Moreau de Jonnès claims that there were some 208,398 child laborers in France at midcentury.

35. The symbol *r* (which may be positive or negative) represents the Pearson correlation coefficient; when r = 1.00, a perfect correlation exists, and when r = 0.00, no correlation exists. The level of industrialization here is measured by the annual value of industrial goods produced.

36. Ministre de l'agriculture, *Statistique*, series 1, X–XIII, *passim*. See also J. Rolley, "La Structure de l'industrie textile en France, en 1840–1844," *Histoire des entreprises*, IV (November, 1959), 20–48.

Table 1
Industrial Child Labor by Department, ca. 1845

Department	Children Employed	Children as Percentage of Work Force	Industrial Ranking of Department*
Seine-Inférieure	15,240	17.5	3
Nord	14,313	13.4	1
Haut-Rhin	12,977	21.3	9
Ardennes	6,693	19.5	4
Rhône	6,330	4.7	2
Aisne	5,235	24.2	21
Eure	4,968	21.4	10
Loire	4,304	8.5	8
Calvados	3,558	18.0	14
Hérault	3,410	16.2	13
Gard	3,083	12.0	23
Orne	2,674	17.0	24
Somme	2,558	14.9	16
Marne	2,532	12.3	12
Loire-Inférieure	2,048	6.9	6
Bas-Rhin	1,960	18.1	48
Pas-de-Calais	1,953	9.5	26
Moselle	1,883	13.9	47
Aube	1,851	14.7	56
Oise	1,714	13.4	22
Vosges	1,597	15.2	52
Vaucluse	1,586	20.5	33
Ardèche	1,566	17.5	31
Puy-de-Dôme	1,529	7.8	28
Haute-Saône	1,528	18.3	43
Isère	1,459	10.6	32
Drôme	1,439	19.3	17
Basses-Pyrénées	1,393	11.6	38
Ille-et-Vilaine	1,315	6.5	30
Seine, without Paris	1,304	14.7	5
Bouches-du-Rhône	1,281	9.9	7
Seine-et-Oise	1,281	15.3	19
Haute-Vienne	1,277	12.0	57
Tarn	1,065	13.8	60
Charente	1,056	14.2	42
Meurthe	1,024	5.7	44
Finistère	987	9.3	72

continued

Department	Children Employed	Children as Percentage of Work Force	Industrial Ranking of Department*
Haute-Garonne	980	16.1	29
Manche	938	12.6	49
Maine-et-Loire	902	9.0	45
Charente-Inférieure	880	5.0	55
Aude	877	14.7	62
Doubs	831	12.0	63
Mayenne	810	9.3	54
Meuse	786	10.4	59
Gironde	730	8.8	18
Sarthe	725	4.0	20
Seine-et-Marne	723	15.6	39
Haute-Marne	681	9.4	46
Vendée	676	6.2	25
Indre-et-Loire	638	13.6	50
Côte-d'Or	637	14.0	36
Creuse	621	17.6	69
Ariège	606	11.9	74
Loir-et-Cher	564	15.8	68
Eure-et-Loir	540	12.4	27
Allier	521	8.7	40
Indre	464	9.7	64
Aveyron	451	7.1	70
Ain	424	18.3	67
Nièvre	419	6.7	61
Loiret	416	7.2	34
Lot-et-Garonne	394	6.3	41
Landes	381	6.4	65
Deux-Sèvres	380	9.9	71
Morbihan	378	3.2	15
Tarn-et-Garonne	335	13.1	66
Var	325	8.0	76
Saône-et-Loire	316	3.4	11
Basses-Alpes	284	20.3	81
Vienne	244	8.8	51
Cher	210	9.1	77
Dordogne	208	4.4	35
Lozère	189	16.8	85
Côtes-du-Nord	179	2.6	37
Gers	175	4.3	53
Hautes-Pyrénées	157	9.7	58

Department	Children Employed	Children as Percentage of Work Force	Industrial Ranking of Department*
Jura	156	10.5	78
Haute-Loire	139	25.0	84
Corrèze	123	3.7	73
Hautes-Alpes	100	14.8	82
Yonne	89	6.3	80
Lot	42	6.6	83
Cantal	34	1.6	75
Pyrénées-Orientales	16	9.0	79

*Determined by annual value of industrial goods produced.
Source: Ministre de l'agriculture et du commerce, *Statistique de la France* (Paris, 1847–52), ser. 1, XIII, 362–67.

Table 2
French Industries Employing over One Thousand Children, ca. 1845

Industry	Children Employed	Children as Percentage of Work Force	Percentage of All French Child Laborers
Cotton textile	44,828	18.3	31.2
Woolen textile	26,800	18.6	18.7
Iron	12,300	9.8	8.6
Cotton blend textile	11,038	23.9	7.7
Silk	9,326	5.6	6.5
Hemp and flax textile	7,232	12.8	5.0
Wool and silk blend textile	4,765	12.5	3.3
Clay products	3,899	14.1	2.7
Coal mining	2,927	12.5	2.0
Grain milling	2,571	3.3	1.8
Sugar production	2,198	13.1	1.5
Paper manufacturing	1,873	11.3	1.3
Glassmaking	1,784	10.5	1.2
Quarrying	1,660	5.6	1.2
Fishing and seafood	1,456	11.2	1.0
Salt production	1,316	6.1	0.9

Source: Ministre de l'agriculture et du commerce, *Statistique de la France* (Paris, 1847–52), ser. 1, XIII, 283–361.

and 1848. Paris was France's primary center of small-shop production: though the city employed 342,530 industrial workers when the study took place, only 11.0 percent of its industrial establishments had over 10 workers, and fully 50.3 percent of its shops provided work for only 1 or 2 people. What the chamber of commerce study showed was that there were some 24,714 working children under sixteen in Paris around 1848 and that these children constituted 7.2 percent of the work force. Of the working children in Paris, 2,118 (8.6 percent) were under twelve, and fully 19,078 (77.2 percent) were described as apprentices. Of all the apprentices, however, only 21.4 percent were known to have had written apprenticeship contracts. The clothing trades had the largest single body of apprentices (5,392), whereas spinning and weaving occupied 3,783 apprentices, and the furniture trades occupied 3,594. Most of the child laborers not classified as apprentices were employed in spinning and weaving (almost certainly in the larger shops). There were also substantial numbers of such children in cloth printing and in wallpaper manufacturing.[37]

Even before midcentury, then, the new forms of industrial child labor, whether in factories or in workshops, represented a significant and widespread phenomenon. Already in the first quarter of the nineteenth century some references were being made to the new issue of child labor abuse in industry, as the problems of working-class poverty, morality, and family life began to draw the attention of the privileged classes. They were troubled by the misery of the growing working population in their midst but perhaps even more by the implications of that misery for the stability and safety of the society at whose pinnacle they stood. As they developed a concern with what was often called the *question sociale*, some within the dominant classes came to view the exploitation of child labor as one of the most disconcerting features of the industrial society emerging in France. They recognized the profound differences between the employment of youngsters in manufacturing and the traditional employment of children in agriculture or domestic production, and they voiced the first misgivings about industrial child labor.

As early as 1819, the Franco-Swiss economist Jean Simonde de Sismondi published a work in political economy that criticized the employ-

37. Chambre de commerce de Paris, *Statistique de l'industrie à Paris . . . 1847–48* (Paris, 1851), Pt. 1, pp. 36, 48–49, 56–57. For a discussion of this study and its biases, see Joan W. Scott, "Statistical Representations of Work: The Politics of the Chamber of Commerce's *Statistique de l'Industrie à Paris, 1847–48,*" in Steven Laurence Kaplan and Cynthia J. Koepp (eds.), *Work in France: Representations, Meaning, Organization, and Practice* (Ithaca, 1986), 335–63.

ment of young children in industry. Sismondi argued that the practice was damaging to the children and in the long run counterproductive even for their parents, since child labor tended to drive down adult wages. The conservative Louis-Gabriel, vicomte de Bonald also revealed a concern over the problem of child labor. In an address to the Restoration legislature concerning primogeniture, Bonald compared the well-being of the agricultural family to that of the family dependent upon industrial labor for its livelihood. He noted that "in the industrial family . . . the members work in isolation, often in different industries, and without knowing their master except by the demands of his orders and the insufficiency of their pay," and he complained that though industry, like agriculture, provided employment for the young, the children involved were "often too young to have acquired strength and health and any education." Then industry, he said, "abandons them when they are old and can no longer work."[38]

In 1821, one group of officials in the Alsatian town of Colmar severely criticized several local manufacturers for their "cupidity" in "making children of either sex and of any age work day and night in their workshops to keep their machines going all the time." The officials decried the fact that "the poor children and young people, handed over to this new species of slave labour, lose their health and hardly retain a human appearance," and they worried aloud that this situation was producing a generation "that shows no physical growth and displays unexampled moral corruption." Similarly, in 1826 a M. Brunot wrote from the Nord to the minister of ecclesiastical affairs that "the greed of the manufacturers knows no limits; they sacrifice their workers to enrich themselves. . . . The children employed in [their] workshops become stunted and weakly, and the men—deprived of wholesome air—lose all their vitality."[39] There were even some isolated instances of attempts to control certain aspects of child labor very early in the century. A Napoleonic decree of 1813 forbade the work of children under ten in underground mines, for example, and in 1821 the mayor of Amiens decreed that spinners could not hire children of the opposite sex as aids.[40]

Despite the fact that some within the French sociopolitical elite recognized very quickly that the new varieties of child labor were fundamen-

38. Jean Simonde de Sismondi, *Nouveau Principes d'économie* (Paris, 1819), I, 353–54; Louis de Bonald, "De la famille agricole, de la famille industrielle," in *Oeuvres complètes de M. de Bonald* (Paris, 1859), I, 238.

39. The examples from Colmar and from the Nord are both quoted in William Otto Henderson, *The Industrial Revolution in Europe, 1815–1914* (Chicago, 1961), 107–108.

40. Paul Louis, *L'Ouvrier devant l'état* (Paris, 1904), 214; Villermé, *Tableau*, I, 292.

tally different from earlier forms, there was no sense of alarm over child labor in society generally, nor was there any call for a basic change in the way children were being employed. Although industrial child labor was an important element in the new working-class culture that was beginning to trouble those who dominated French social and political life, it was a problem of relatively small proportions in the early years of the nineteenth century, one that was, for the most part, ignored. No one in France took an overriding interest in the specific problem of industrial child labor, and no one was yet thinking of the need to control the employment of the young in any far-reaching, systematic way. The first recognition of a serious need to reform the child labor situation in France came only in the late 1820s. Even then, those who raised the possibility of restricting the participation of children in industry were an isolated few who found themselves defying the prevailing attitude toward the employment of the young. Nonetheless, it was these individual child labor reformers of the late 1820s and 1830s who were ultimately responsible for the adoption of a factory law in France, and the story of their campaign is an essential element in the history of nineteenth-century child labor reform.

TWO

The Earliest Champions
of Reform

Allusions to the idea that it might be beneficial to legislate a minimum age for factory employment first appeared only as the second quarter of the nineteenth century began. J. Gerspach of Thann in the Haut-Rhin suggested such a minimum age in his 1827 doctoral thesis, and Jean-Baptiste Say, in his 1828 course in political economy, argued (as Sismondi had before him) that child labor legislation could be legitimated even in a free market, since children were inherently incapable of dealing with their employers as equals.[1] The earliest champion of a comprehensive program of child labor reform in France, however, was Jean-Jacques Bourcart, the scion of an important Alsatian manufacturing family. He appears to have been the first individual in France to argue for a complete system of factory legislation.

Bourcart's initial appeal for action came in a talk he gave before the Société industrielle de Mulhouse in November of 1827, when he was twenty-six years old. In his talk, the young Bourcart laid out a plan for legislation that would institute a maximum workday, a minimum age, and standards of sanitation for all spinning-mill workers. What he sought before going further with his ideas was the support of his colleagues. Bourcart was among the small but growing number of business and industrial leaders concerned with the condition of the emerging working classes, and he made it clear in his presentation that he believed

1. Victor Mataja, "Les Origines de la protection ouvrière en France," *Revue d'économie politique*, IX (June, 1895), 531; Villermé, *Tableau*, II, 96; Jean-Baptiste Say, *Cours complet d'économie politique* (Paris, 1840), II, 50.

manufacturers had a "duty" to "look after the happiness and well-being of the workers, as well as the advancement of industry." He observed that though the development of industry had already eased the misery of the working classes considerably by providing employment opportunities, industry had to concern itself also with workers' "betterment in moral and physical respects." What was unusual about Bourcart's concern with the condition of the working classes was that it led him to propose a specific system of factory legislation.[2]

Although his proposal addressed the condition of spinning-mill workers generally, Bourcart stressed its importance for the laboring young. Indeed, the arguments that he presented to bolster his appeal for factory legislation in 1827 were ones that would be employed repeatedly as the campaign for child labor reform intensified in later years. The ideas that lay behind Bourcart's arguments were not necessarily original, but he was the first to articulate them systematically and to use them to justify a national factory act. For this reason, it is worth considering his presentation before the Société industrielle de Mulhouse in some detail.

Bourcart began with what was perhaps the most basic argument against industrial child labor: the ill-effects of factory work on the youngsters who engaged in it. He alluded to the physical hardships child laborers faced, but he was equally concerned with the effects of factory labor on their characters. "Children employed indoors for too long a time are weakened in body and health," he declared, "and . . . having no time to see to their education, they are unable to develop morally." Bourcart had struck at the heart of the problem, and the image he painted here of frail, ignorant, morally debased children would become a most familiar one, as it was conjured up again and again in the course of the campaign for child labor reform.

Bourcart continued his appeal by assuring his audience that steps taken on behalf of young workers would in no way harm industrial production. This, too, was a point that later advocates of reform liked to emphasize. A shorter workday, Bourcart said, would mean greater efficiency. Less fatigued laborers would certainly produce goods of higher quality and perhaps would even be able to keep the quantity they produced from declining. To those who would insist that decreased output was bound to come on the heels of restrictive legislation, Bourcart an-

2. For Bourcart's entire speech, quoted here and in the following paragraphs, see Jean-Jacques Bourcart, "Proposition . . . sur la necessité de fixer l'âge et de reduire les heures de travail des ouvriers des filatures," *BSIM*, I (1827–28), 373–76.

swered that the cotton textile industry, which would be the most seriously touched by his proposed restrictions, was in any event producing more than was justified by the level of demand and that manufacturers "should want a diminution of production, as long as the reduction is equally distributed and affects all equally." This last proviso is the kernel of the argument for a reliance on national legislation rather than on local regulations or voluntary restraint. No matter how well-intentioned individual industrialists might be, the advocates of legislation would always reason, entrepreneurs could not afford to injure their businesses for the sake of humanitarianism. As long as some factories employed children in order to keep labor costs low, all their competitors would be forced to do the same. In order to allow those who would voluntarily restrict child labor to do so, those who would not act alone would have to be coerced.

But even more than the welfare of children and that of industry was involved in the child labor issue, Bourcart insisted. The welfare of France itself was being jeopardized by the employment of children. The protection of the physical and moral well-being of the young was intimately tied to the national interest. This was Bourcart's most powerful argument, for it spoke to the mounting concern of the privileged classes about the stability of their society and the future of their country. Bourcart wanted to project the idea that working-class youngsters deprived of proper surroundings and moral influences could not possibly grow up to become productive workers, peaceful citizens, and able soldiers. He warned that the nation, if it were not more careful with its youth, would soon find as "defenders of the homeland . . . only the miserable, the feeble, the depraved, those incapable of recalling the glory of their country." Thus, for the sake of the children in the shops, but perhaps even more for the sake of industrial progress and for the sake of the nation itself, a labor law was mandatory. In case these arguments were not sufficient, Bourcart added an appeal to precedent. England, he observed, had already proven that child labor legislation was workable. He closed his presentation with a specific proposal that the society petition the legislature in Paris for a factory law "as in England."

Bourcart's appeal to the English precedent, like his basic arguments in favor of a factory law, was to be echoed frequently by later champions of child labor reform. The first to industrialize, the English were also the first to confront the problem of industrial child labor, and what they did on this score was watched carefully on the continent. Britain, with about

half the total population of France, had at least as many child laborers
in the early decades of the nineteenth century as France had, and England had begun its experiment with child labor legislation as early as
1802, when a child labor measure was adopted as a reform of the Poor
Law.[3] Since the seventeenth century, the Poor Law had provided for the
apprenticing of pauper children, but after a government inquiry revealed blatant abuses of that practice, a reform bill was passed to afford
a modicum of protection to young workers in those enterprises where
the situation was worst: the larger cotton and woolen mills. Limited as
the measure adopted in 1802 was, however, it proved to be unenforceable, for it left many types of exploited child laborers unprotected and
it contained no provisions for the effective inspection of factories. Because the 1802 law was so inadequate, there arose a call for further reform, and the advocates of revised legislation met with some success in
1819, when Parliament enacted a new child labor law, this time applicable to all children employed in textile works. The new act made nine
the minimum age for employment and allowed a workday of no more
than twelve hours for those children under sixteen, but it was still a very
unsatisfactory measure: its applicability remained extremely limited and
its provisions for enforcement weak. Despite these drawbacks, the law
was a step forward in controlling the abuse of child labor, and it served,
to Bourcart's mind, as a model for suitable legislation. Indeed, the *Bulletin de la Société industrielle de Mulhouse* published the 1819 English factory act (as slightly amended in 1825) as a supplement to Bourcart's
appeal for a French child labor law.[4]

The members of the Société industrielle before whom Bourcart spoke
in 1827 had a long-standing involvement in social issues. From a very
early date, the factory owners of the Mulhouse region, often acting

3. In the mid-1840s, while French textile factories employed about 104,000 child laborers under sixteen, British textile factories employed about 206,000 children under eighteen. For the British data, see B. R. Mitchell, with Phyllis Deane, *Abstract of British Historical
Statistics* (Cambridge, Eng., 1962), 188, 199, 204, 211. In 1834 there had been about
167,000 factory children under eighteen in Britain and Ireland; by 1851 there were some
600,000 English children between the ages of three and fifteen "at work" generally. See
Charles Wing, *Evils of the Factory System* (1837; rpr. New York, 1967), clxxxv, and J. F. C.
Harrison, *The Early Victorians, 1832–1851* (New York, 1971), 136.

4. On apprenticeship as a device of poor relief, see O. Jocelyn Dunlop, *English Apprenticeship and Child Labour* (London, 1912), 248ff. On early English factory legislation, see
Overbergh, *Inspecteurs*, 21ff; B. L. Hutchins and A. Harrison, *A History of Factory Legislation*
(London, 1926), 1ff; Maurice W. Thomas, *Young People in Industry, 1750–1945* (London,
1945), 1ff; or the more detailed Maurice W. Thomas, *Early Factory Legislation* (Leigh-on-
sea, Eng., 1948).

through their local Masonic lodge, had supported such institutions as savings banks, sick funds, relief committees, and charity societies to aid the working classes. When the Société industrielle was founded in 1825, the philanthropic concerns of its members began to influence the work of that organization as well. The society was particularly interested in efforts to aid in the education of the lower classes.[5]

All the philanthropic endeavors with which the entrepreneurs of the Société industrielle were routinely involved, however, were of the traditional, paternalistic, and voluntary type. Bourcart found that in 1827 his colleagues still shared the nearly universal hesitancy of early nineteenth-century manufacturers to see government intervene directly in industrial affairs. Although they had long striven to ameliorate the lot of the local working population, the industrialists of Mulhouse balked at the idea of tampering with the basic conditions of employment. Bourcart's speech prompted the formation of a committee to study his proposal, but when the committee issued its report on December 27, 1827, the resistance to his suggestions became evident.

The study committee established at Bourcart's behest refused to recommend that the government be petitioned to enact a factory law. Still, the members were uneasy about appearing to ignore the problems Bourcart had so graphically brought to the society's attention. "Although the report does not recommend the immediate adoption of the proposition," the committee apologized, the society was asked to "take care not to infer from this that the committee does not concur with the honorable and humanitarian sentiments before it." The committee was predictably worried about the problems of legislative interference with personal liberty, with parental authority, and with industrial freedom. Unable to resolve for itself the philosophical doubts that had arisen, it turned for advice to outside experts on social questions. The society was to withhold its judgment until it could hear the responses of the experts polled.[6]

5. See Eugène Véron, *Les Institutions ouvrières de Mulhouse et des environs* (Paris, 1866); Kahan-Rabecq, *Classe ouvrière*, 301ff; and Paul Leuilliot, *L'Alsace au début de XIXe siècle* (Paris, 1959), II, 494ff. Leuilliot, who tries to make a case for support of child labor legislation in Alsace as early as the 1820s, states incorrectly that the Société industrielle de Mulhouse supported Bourcart's proposed plan in 1827. See also "Règlement de la société," *BSIM*, I (1827–28), 10–11, and the early volumes of *BSIM* generally. Although studies such as Adrien Dansette, *Religious History of Modern France*, trans. John Dingle (New York, 1961); and Agnès de Neufville, *Le Mouvement social protestant en France depuis 1880* (Paris, 1927), suggest that the Protestant faith of the Mulhouse industrialists helped motivate their interest in social problems, the evidence for this is only circumstantial.

6. For the report of the committee, see [Zickel], "Rapport de la commission spéciale, concernant la proposition de M. Jean-Jacques Bourcart," *BSIM*, I (1827–28), 376–86.

It appears that only one of the experts contacted showed enough interest in the society's inquiry to respond. The liberal economist Charles Dunoyer, one of those writers who consistently blamed the plight of the working classes on their own intemperance, lack of foresight, and depravity, communicated the opinion that the legitimate limits of legislation did not include interference in any way with a person's ability to sell his own labor. Dunoyer conceded, however, that there was perhaps room to submit the labor of children to restrictions, since children were never free to act as they wished, and he hinted that there was some precedent also for limiting paternal authority.[7]

Prompted by Dunoyer's communication, by recent visits to manufacturing towns where he witnessed abuses even greater than those in Alsace, and by the society's obvious reluctance to act on his initial ideas, Bourcart presented a new proposal to his colleagues in December of 1828, a full year after the tabling of his earlier suggestion. Although obviously he would have liked a broader approach, Bourcart restrained himself and this time asked the Société industrielle to endorse a resolution calling for limitations only on the labor of children, not on that of all workers. Again a committee was formed to examine Bourcart's proposal, and this time its deliberations ended on a note of greater commitment. On January 20, 1829, it recommended that the society demand the enactment of a law prohibiting parents and factory owners from allowing children employed in spinning mills to work more than twelve hours a day. The enforcement of the proposed legislation, the committee further concluded, should be left in the hands of local officials, and violations should be punished by fines levied against both parents and manufacturers. The recommendation of the committee was a greatly diluted version not only of Bourcart's 1827 proposal but even of his more recent suggestion. However, the committee did advise that the Société industrielle take a stand as a body in favor of some sort of factory legislation.

Because it called for government action, even the revised version of Bourcart's proposal met with opposition when it was introduced before a plenary session of the society. Frédéric Reber, for example, insisted that the misery of the working classes was due to causes unrelated to work in factories, such as housing conditions, undernourishment, and

7. See [Zickel], "Rapport de la commission spéciale," 383–86, and Charles Kestner-Rigau, "Rapport fait au nom de la commission spéciale chargée d'examiner les questions relatives au travail des jeunes ouvriers des fabriques," *BSIM*, VI (1832–33), 342–43.

moral laxity. This point was heard often from opponents of any measure that would interfere with an entrepreneur's complete control over his shop. A reduction of working hours would not contribute effectively to the improvement of the young workers' condition in any way, Reber concluded. Another member of the society argued that in the present depressed state of industry, it would be inappropriate to begin experimenting with innovative labor legislation. In the end, a decision was made to table the committee's proposal indefinitely. Thus, even after compromise and dilution, Bourcart's proposals could not win the support of the Société industrielle as a whole. But the seeds had been sown, the problem had been debated and publicized, and the stage had been set for later developments.[8]

It was in response to a circular questionnaire from the Ministry of Public Instruction that the Société industrielle finally did present its views on child labor legislation to the administration. The minister of public instruction, François Guizot, had a long-standing interest in issues of public welfare, including the care of orphans and of the insane, relief for the poor, and public hygiene. His chief passion, however, was educational reform, and in that area he achieved his greatest success with the passage of the 1833 law that bears his name.[9] It was apparently in formulating his education law that Guizot encountered the related issue of child labor, and in approaching that issue, he circulated a questionnaire designed to elicit the opinions of those most closely involved with the employment of youngsters.

Respondents to the circular from Guizot's office were asked to communicate their views concerning the age at which children should be admitted to factory work, the length their workday should be, and the days on which they ought to be free from work. Speaking more to the issue that was Guizot's primary interest, the questionnaire asked respondents to react to the idea of having manufacturers provide schooling for their young employees. Those who thought this practice advisable were asked also to suggest how much schooling should be required. Another question posed in the circular dealt with the desirability of in-

8. Bourcart's second attempt at getting the society to act is described in Kestner-Rigau, "Rapport," 345ff, and in Achille Penot, "Rapport de la commission chargée d'examiner la question relative à l'emploi des enfans dans les filatures de coton," *BSIM*, X (1836–37), 490. The report by Penot was also published as a separate pamphlet in Mulhouse.

9. See, for example, Elizabeth Parnham Brush, *Guizot in the Early Years of the Orleanist Monarchy*, vol. XV of *University of Illinois Studies in the Social Sciences* ([Urbana?], Ill, ca. 1927), 37, 145ff.

stituting health inspections. Finally, the questionnaire sought opinions about supervision and penalties in the event child labor restrictions became a reality.

The members of the Société industrielle appointed a committee, as was their custom, to study the questions posed in the ministerial circular. After hearing the committee report, they discussed their response in two subsequent plenary sessions. The document they eventually dispatched to Paris provides the first firm indication that the Société industrielle de Mulhouse, as a body, had been won over to the advocacy of child labor reform. Some five years after the issue of factory legislation had first been raised by Bourcart, his views were finally dominant in the society, and he now had some like-minded allies in his crusade for government action. The society went on record in support of the admission of children to industrial labor only at the age of eight and in support of a workday graduated from ten to thirteen hours for children between the ages of eight and sixteen. The Alsatian industrialists also indicated that they wanted children's work at night and on Sundays and holidays restricted.

Concerning education, the consensus reached by the members of the society was that manufacturers should not be required to provide schools, since the anticipated education law would fill that need, but that following an interval of four years after the enactment of factory legislation, literacy should be required of children under sixteen seeking employment. The members judged advisable the establishment of cantonal commissions to supervise sanitary conditions in factories, and they insisted that what was called for was specific legislation on child labor and not some sort of less authoritative action by chambers of commerce or by a government ministry. The legislation, they said, should carry a requirement that factory owners keep records of their young workers and that these records be open to inspection by local authorities. They also suggested that fines be imposed upon both parents and entrepreneurs in cases of contravention and that the proceeds from the fines be contributed to some local charitable institution established to aid workers. Unfortunately, there is no available evidence of any other responses to Guizot's circular, but if there were other responses, they apparently did not match the reasoned opinions expressed by the Société industrielle de Mulhouse.[10] While the minister's education reform saw fruition, the

10. Although evidence of Guizot's inquiry is not available in the series of cartons concerning child labor in the Archives nationales, its existence is apparent from Kestner-Rigau, "Rapport," which includes a chart showing the questions posed and the responses

general lack of concern over child labor stifled any talk there might have been in administration circles about factory reform, at least for the time being.

In 1834, the Société industrielle went on record yet a second time as favoring factory legislation when it reacted to the new, and far more forceful, child labor law adopted in England the previous year. Although the English Factory Act of 1833, like the legislation it superseded, still applied only in the textile industry, it reduced the workday of children under the age of thirteen to a maximum of nine hours and required that they receive some schooling. The new law also extended the provision for a twelve-hour day to young people between the ages of sixteen and eighteen, and, most important, it provided for an effective system of enforcement. Having finally realized that local control of enforcement was tantamount to no enforcement, Parliament broke with the long English tradition of localism and organized a centralized system of inspection.[11] The statement of the Société industrielle published in 1834 simply and succinctly proposed that the new English law be the point of departure in formulating French legislation on child labor. Soon after the society made its position known, its proposal was seconded by both the chamber of commerce of Mulhouse and the *conseil général* (the departmental council) of the Haut-Rhin, two bodies that were undoubtedly influenced by the newly manifested enthusiasm for reform generated locally by Bourcart and his associates.[12]

The region of Alsace in the 1830s was an unusually industrialized area, with many innovative manufacturers, and in the early years of the July Monarchy, it appeared that the Alsatian advocates of child labor reform existed in virtual isolation. By the mid-1830s, however, some evidence of support for child labor legislation from beyond Alsace was beginning to appear as well. One voice raised in favor of reform was that of the conservative Catholic writer and activist, Alban de Villeneuve-Bargemont.

Villeneuve-Bargemont's initial interest in the child labor issue, like Jean-Jacques Bourcart's, dates from the late 1820s. His experience in the

---

of the Société industrielle. Penot, "L'Emploi des enfans," 492, refers to this inquiry as related to "a law to reconcile the interests of industry and those of popular education."

11. See David Roberts, *Victorian Origins of the British Welfare State* (New Haven, 1960), 22ff.

12. "Des enfans et des jeunes ouvriers employés dans les fabriques," *BSIM*, VIII (1834–35), 51–52; Penot, "L'Emploi des enfans," 496–97; Touren, *Loi de 1841*, 34; Horner, *Employment*, 24.

course of an administrative career that stretched back to 1811 had slowly brought him to question the wisdom of laissez-faire economics in light of the poverty and suffering he encountered. In 1828, as prefect of the Department of the Nord, he issued a wide-ranging document concerning the administration of poor relief and the improvement of social conditions in his jurisdiction. In the section of the document dealing with education, Villeneuve-Bargemont indicated clearly that he realized the negative effects factory labor had on the development of children. He noted that "one of the principal obstacles to the education of working-class children is that, from the tenderest age, their parents require them to do productive labor," and he concluded that the "premature employment of . . . these feeble beings has the serious two-fold fault of jeopardizing the development of their physical strength, . . . and of keeping them from acquiring either education or moral training."[13]

In his administrative instructions, Villeneuve-Bargemont's suggestions for combating the problems of child labor did not go beyond urging an increase in facilities to educate children during their nonworking hours and asking factory owners to refrain from employing illiterate children under the age of ten or twelve. A few months after issuing his guidelines on poor relief in the Nord, however, he carried his ideas significantly further. He outlined a general program of social reform and submitted his ideas to Paris for consideration. The program demanded that laissez-faire had to be compromised, and it included a call for legislative action to protect working children. Arguing that interference with both parental and entrepreneurial authority was justified by "considerations of the general interest" and by "motives of public health and social order," Villeneuve-Bargemont suggested a number of regulations for governing child labor. These regulations would deny factory employment to anyone under twelve and to illiterate youngsters, would require the imposition of standards of cleanliness in both home and factory, and would force parents and employers alike to see to the educational needs and moral development of the children in their charge. Villeneuve-Bargemont also wished to see some sort of governmental authority instituted to enforce compliance.[14]

The program submitted by Villeneuve-Bargemont caught the attention of Jean-Baptiste Gay, vicomte de Martignac, Charles X's minister of

13. Villeneuve-Bargemont's 1828 instructions are described and quoted in Alban de Villeneuve-Bargemont, *Economie politique chrétienne* (Paris, 1834), II, 613–14.
14. Villeneuve-Bargemont, *Economie*, II, 73–80.

the interior, but the Revolution of 1830 thwarted any chance the program had of immediate implementation and abruptly halted Villeneuve-Bargemont's administrative career as well.[15] The revolution did not, however, curtail his interest in the welfare of factory children. As a private citizen, he continued his investigations of poverty in all its aspects and extended them in scope to cover all of France and later all of Europe. The result of his studies was a three-volume work published in 1834 under the title *Economie politique chrétienne*.

The ideas on economics and society that Villeneuve-Bargemont developed in the course of his investigations and put forth in *Economie politique chrétienne* were based to some extent on the thoughts of earlier economists such as Sismondi, but they also drew heavily on the author's own traditional Catholic background. Among the earliest Social Catholics, Villeneuve-Bargemont built his theory on the application of Christian morality to economic questions. He contrasted his own philosophy with the predominant contemporary systems, which, he believed, looked at human beings simply as commodities. "Laissez-faire," he wrote, "has more efficiently taught man the art of producing wealth than that of equitably distributing it."[16] Concerned primarily with poverty, he saw much hope in a return to agrarianism, but he also gave his attention to industrial life. He wanted to see a more sympathetic and humane attitude on the part of employers toward their workers, one that would lead to the eventual elimination of urban misery, but he knew that factory owners would not go far enough on their own. At the same time, he realized that charitable efforts to help the poor were of only immediate and temporary value. Thus, he reasoned, it was only realistic to expect government to play a part in improving social conditions.

Like others concerned with the future of industrial society, Villeneuve-Bargemont saw the children of the working classes as the most unfortunate victims of economic inequity but also as those most susceptible to relief.[17] It was natural therefore that among his concerns should have been the abuse of child labor. *Economie politique chrétienne* carried the same basic ideas on child labor reform that its author had expressed when he was prefect of the Nord, though he had refined some of his specific suggestions. Villeneuve-Bargemont now believed, for example,

---

15. See Villeneuve-Bargemont, *Economie*, II, 19–20, and Mary Ignatius Ring, *Villeneuve-Bargemont, Precursor of Modern Social Catholicism* (Milwaukee, 1935), 200.
16. Quoted in Ring, *Villeneuve-Bargemont*, xv.
17. See, for example, Villeneuve-Bargemont, *Economie*, II, 338, III, 68ff, 82ff.

that only manufacturers with over fifty employees should be compelled to conform to legislated standards. So too, he now called for literacy and a minimum age of fourteen or a medical certificate of fitness as requirements for employment. As in his earlier proposal, he suggested action to enjoin workshop cleanliness, a separation of the sexes in factories, and the oversight of moral and religious conformity.[18] By presenting all these ideas in print, Villeneuve-Bargemont established himself as an important advocate of child labor reform.

Villeneuve-Bargemont had arrived at his conclusions about the need for child labor reform by a route somewhat different from that taken by Jean-Jacques Bourcart and his colleagues in Alsace. As a bourgeois liberal industrialist, Bourcart was concerned with the perfection of France's emerging industrial society, but he believed that most of the problems of working-class misery and corruption were due to factors other than industrial working conditions. In fact, most of the philanthropic activities of Bourcart and his peers were aimed at influencing the way workers behaved outside the factory. The Alsatian entrepreneurs considered industrial production a system that functioned well, and they viewed child labor abuse as but a minor flaw in that system, one that was susceptible to correction. Villeneuve-Bargemont, on the other hand, as a traditionalist aristocrat with a bias toward agrarian society, was fundamentally concerned with the preservation of a preindustrial social system that he viewed as preferable to the industrial society developing around him. He saw child labor abuse as part of a larger problem brought on by industrialization: the breakdown of the traditional economic and familial structures he idealized.[19] What is critical for the history of the factory reform movement in France, however, is not that Bourcart and Villeneuve-Bargemont approached the problem of child labor abuse from different perspectives but that they both saw children as blameless victims of industrialization who, because they were the hope of the future, had to be protected by a national program of child labor legislation. Their agreement on the harmful nature of child labor and on the need for legislation to control it presaged the coalition of convenience between humanitarian liberals and religious conservatives that would evolve to form the basis of the child labor reform movement in France for over half a century.

18. Villeneuve-Bargemont, *Economie*, III, 168–69; Ring, *Villeneuve-Bargemont*, 191–92.
19. Compare Lynch, "Problem of Child Labor Reform," 228–36; Jacques Donzelot, *The Policing of Families*, trans. Robert Hurley (New York, 1979), 56–57.

By the mid-1830s, as the industrialist community and the Social Catholic movement were producing their first advocates of factory reform, the first proponents of a national child labor law were emerging from within the ranks of liberal intellectuals as well. Emile Bères, for example, issued a call for factory legislation in his book *Les Classes ouvrières*, which won the prestigious prix Montyon in 1836. Bères' appeal was based on his perception that the working child was treated as a mere cog in the machinery of industry: "To make one go, you grease it," he wrote emotionally, "to make the other go, you whip it."[20] Far more influential as an advocate of reform was Louis Villermé, whose observations about the child labor situation in the 1830s have already been examined.

Villermé was a physician by training and had practiced medicine, but he apparently had a poor bedside manner and in the second decade of the nineteenth century had turned his attention to social questions. He became a researcher and statistician and during the 1820s involved himself extensively with investigations of prison conditions and public hygiene. When the previously suppressed Académie des sciences morales et politiques was revived in 1832, Villermé was one of the first persons elected to that body. The academy followed the practice of periodically commissioning persons from within its ranks to undertake and report upon fieldwork. In 1835, the opportunity to conduct research into social conditions in France under the auspices of the academy fell to Villermé. The task he undertook was an investigation of the condition of textile workers in the North and the Midi. After two years spent visiting many industrial centers, interviewing people connected with manufacturing in various ways, and even living with working-class families, Villermé was prepared to present an interim report. That report, delivered before the annual public session of the Académie des sciences morales et politiques on May 2, 1837, and subsequently published as a pamphlet, concerned only one matter—the one that seems to have struck Villermé as the most urgent—the problem of child labor.[21]

Villermé's public remarks revealed the direction of his thinking and the nature of the conclusions he would reach concerning child labor legislation in his completed study. His report reflected the influence of

20. Emile Bères, *Les Classes ouvrières* (Paris, 1836), 92–93.
21. On Villermé's career, see Maurice Deslandres and Alfred Michelin, *Il y a cent ans* (Paris, 1939), 9ff; Coleman, *Death is a Social Disease*; Hilde Rigaudias-Weiss, *Les Enquêtes ouvrières en France* (Paris, 1936); and Léon Duvoir, *Recherche des tendances interventionnistes chez quelques économistes libéraux français de 1830 à 1850* (Paris, 1901), 9ff.

his contact with the factory owners of the Société industrielle de Mulhouse and also the impact of the extreme conditions he himself had witnessed.[22] His documentation provides an extensive and graphic (if sometimes exaggerated) account of child labor in the French textile industry of the 1830s. His descriptions of youngsters who had to awaken in the middle of the night and trek miles to the factory because there was no nearby housing for their families and of children who made the trip in the rain with their clothes waterproofed only by the machine oil with which they were covered are now classic. In Villermé's mind, the regulation of child labor by legislation along the English model had become an obvious necessity, and by 1837 he was calling unequivocally for its institution.[23] It is impossible to know the specific reaction of Villermé's audience to his ideas, but the airing of those ideas before a gathering of numerous influential intellectuals and legislators was in itself significant.

The spring of 1837 was an important time for the child labor reform movement in France. Not only did Villermé make his appeal for government action before the prestigious gathering of his academy, but the Société industrielle de Mulhouse issued at that time its most forceful demand ever for a child labor law. Disappointed that no action had been taken in the more than four years since it had first petitioned the government to enact child labor legislation and prompted by a letter of concern from "several young men" of the city, the society again took up the issue on May 31, 1837. On that date, Achille Penot reported on the work of a committee charged with examining anew the question of factory reform.

Penot's address to the membership was, in the main, a description of the evils of child labor much like the one that Bourcart had presented ten years earlier. Penot reviewed the English handling of the child labor problem and reminded the society of its own past efforts to pressure the French government on this issue. The resolution proposed by Penot's committee and adopted by the association called for the dispatch of yet another appeal. Every member of both the upper and lower chambers of the legislature in Paris, as well as the ministers of the interior, of commerce, and of public instruction, was to get a copy of a letter restating the case for reform and demanding a child labor law.

The Société industrielle summarized in the letter the standard arguments in favor of legislation. The industrialists spoke of the employment

22. See Penot, "L'Emploi des enfans," 494–95; letter in AN, F12–4704.
23. Louis Villermé, *Discours sur la durée trop longue du travail des enfants dans beaucoup de manufactures* (Paris, 1837).

of children in factories for fifteen and sometimes seventeen hours a day as a "very grave abuse" and insisted that the labor imposed on youngsters "inhibits their proper physical development and tends to stunt and weaken the species." Moreover, they continued, long workdays "preclude the least intellectual and moral instruction" of the "unfortunate children" who labor in the mills, and they warned that "society finds itself facing the threat of a population becoming pitiful and unprincipled." The industrialists further proclaimed the inadequacy of voluntary efforts to limit the participation of children in industry, noting that such efforts, though "praiseworthy," were "isolated and soon abandoned." They also asserted that the need for controls would only grow over time, "as the increasingly extensive use of machines permits the replacement in factories of a growing number of men, by children." The industrialists of Mulhouse concluded that it was thus their "duty" to demand a factory law "like that which has been promulgated in England"; they hoped that those to whom their letter was addressed would act to remedy the child labor problem before it produced "the most unfortunate results." [24]

By the summer of 1837, then, there had been several rather pointed appeals for child labor reform, and each had come from an individual or a small group within a different, highly influential segment of society. The elimination of child labor abuse had been linked to the regeneration of the working classes, to the promotion of industrial progress, and to the establishment of a truly Christian society, and factory legislation had been touted as essential to the well-being of the nation. The administration, however, was decidedly reluctant to act. The government of the July Monarchy was dominated by a *haute bourgeoisie* that drew its wealth and power primarily from large-scale landholding. Its members were traditionalist in their general outlook and though most of them were disinclined to concern themselves with the affairs of industry at all, they tended to respect the vested interests of the business and commercial middle classes when they did. The government's bias in favor of the middle classes was only reinforced by the labor unrest with which it had had to contend during and after the Revolution of 1830, and the Orleanist administration had managed effectively to ignore the child labor issue ever since it had come to power. [25]

24. Penot, "L'Emploi des enfans," 499–501.
25. For a brief account of the composition and policy of the government under the July Monarchy, see Alfred Cobban, *A History of Modern France* (Baltimore, 1965), II, 114ff. For more detailed accounts, see E. Beau de Loménie, *Les Responsabilités des dynasties bourgeoises* (Paris, 1948), I, and Jean Lhomme, *La Grande Bourgeoisie au pouvoir (1830–1880)* (Paris, 1960).

On the other hand, the demand for child labor reform was coming from extremely well placed individuals, and it was being voiced just at the time a somewhat wider concern over the new industrial working class was beginning to emerge, and just at the time the concept of limited government interventionism was beginning to gain legitimacy, even in some liberal circles. Some concerned observers of society from the late 1820s to the mid-1830s who could not bring themselves to advocate a French factory law (such as Sismondi) nonetheless worried about the evils of child labor. Others, such as Charles-Marie, comte Duchâtel, Ange Guépin, and Alexandre Parent-Duchâtelet, were writing about such issues as working-class poverty, education, and health, all of which were in some way related to the issue of child labor.[26] The perception that working-class children had to be subjected to a more "supervised freedom" was growing.[27] In this environment, even though there was no substantial support for government intervention to control child labor per se and even though men such as Bourcart, Penot, Villeneuve-Bargemont, and Villermé represented only an isolated handful of individuals championing the cause of factory legislation, the insistent appeals of these few could not be ignored by the government indefinitely. Although the government remained unwilling to commit itself to take any action (in his reply to the Société industrielle de Mulhouse, the minister of commerce emphasized the relative mildness of the child labor problem in France), it did nonetheless decide to undertake its first extensive inquiry into the child labor situation.[28] That inquiry would produce a wealth of information and, at the same time, move forward the campaign for a child labor law.

26. See Michelle Perrot, *Enquêtes sur la condition ouvrière en France au 19e siècle* (Paris, 1972); Duvoir, *Recherche*; Guy Frambourg, *Le Docteur Guépin* (Nantes, 1964), esp. 67ff, 132ff; Jean Simonde de Sismondi, *Du sort des ouvriers dans les manufactures* (Paris, 1834), 10. On Sismondi, see also Albert Aftalion, *L'Oeuvre économique de Simonde de Sismondi* (Paris, 1899), 149; Jean-R. de Salis, *Sismondi* (Paris, 1932), 418ff; and Mao-Lan Tuan, *Simonde de Sismondi as an Economist* (New York, 1927), esp. 118ff.
27. Donzelot, *Policing*, xxi, 9–47.
28. Letter from Minister of Commerce Martin du Nord, in AN, F12–4704.

THREE

Government Involvement
and Its Consequences

The first extensive governmental inquiry into the child labor situation in France was initiated on July 31, 1837, when the minister of commerce, Martin du Nord, circulated a two-part questionnaire to all the country's prefects. The first part of the questionnaire posed questions about the actual state of child labor at the local level. It asked at what age children normally entered the work force, how long their workday was, how much they earned, and how much money was saved by manufacturers who employed them. It also requested information about the education and the moral condition of working children. The second part of the government questionnaire asked not for factual information but for opinions concerning reasonable standards for the employment of youngsters: At what age should children be admitted to factory labor? Should they be forbidden to work at night? Should the length of their workday be graduated according to age? Until what age should children be subject to employment restrictions?

The Ministry of Commerce questionnaire instructed the prefects to solicit responses to the questions it posed from various interested parties in their regions and to forward those responses to Paris. Replies were sought primarily from chambers of commerce, *chambres consultatives des arts et manufactures* (the equivalents of chambers of commerce in smaller towns), and *conseils des prud'hommes* (industrial arbitration boards), for these were the bodies in which local entrepreneurial interests were best represented. Martin's covering letter provided some background for the questionnaire and, at the same time, revealed the reluctance of the administration to associate itself with the cause of child labor reform.

The inquiry he was conducting, Martin explained, had been instigated by the Chamber of Peers, which itself had been prompted to act by pressure from the members of the Société industrielle de Mulhouse and others. He reminded the prefects that similar pressure in England had forced the adoption of child labor legislation across the channel, and he outlined the basic provisions of the Factory Act of 1833. He cautioned the prefects, however (as he had the industrialists of Mulhouse earlier), that the problem of child labor was much more severe in England than in France, and he observed also that public agitation for the protection of working children was far more extensive in Britain. Indeed, Martin asserted, the extent and exact nature of the child labor problem in France was still very much in question. The manuscript draft of his letter suggests that he had originally intended to say more about the evils inherent in industrial child labor, but this material was edited out of the final version of the letter, perhaps to avoid the appearance of too great a concern.

Throughout the latter months of 1837, responses to the government's inquiry arrived at the Ministry of Commerce from the various bodies that the prefects had contacted, as well as from the prefects themselves.[1] By December, it was possible for the ministry's Bureau of Manufactures to compile a report summarizing the information that had been gathered.[2] The 1837 inquiry provided a broad overview of the child labor situation early in the period of industrialization. Although the account it presented was incomplete and somewhat biased, it remains one of the richest sources of information available about the nature of child labor in early nineteenth-century France. It was this inquiry that established, for example, that the average age of entry into the work force was eight or nine and that children commonly worked twelve to fourteen hours a day. It was this inquiry also that revealed much of what is known about the nighttime employment of children, their corporal punishment, and

1. Materials concerning the preparation of the ministerial circular of July 31, 1837, are in AN, F12–4704, and the manuscript responses to the 1837 survey are in AN, F12–4705. Approximately 19 percent of the responses to the survey were from chambers of commerce, 28 percent from *chambres consultatives*, 16 percent from *conseils des prud'hommes*, 28 percent from prefects, and 10 percent from other individuals or bodies.

2. *Rapport du Bureau des manufactures* is the printed summary of the 1837 inquiry, and a translation of much of this document appears in Horner, *Employment*, 26–38. The Bureau of Manufactures was within the division of Domestic Commerce, one of several divisions of the Ministry of Commerce.

their work environment. The responses to the inquiry showed that the laboring young were considered degenerate almost everywhere; respondents cited the frequent use of obscene language and the high incidence of drunkenness, sexual misconduct, and criminal behavior among factory children.

Important as the 1837 inquiry is for the broad picture it paints of child labor in the second quarter of the nineteenth century, it is at least as important for its revelations about general attitudes toward child labor reform within the French commercial and entrepreneurial bourgeoisie. Essentially, the inquiry revealed that there was very little support for factory legislation in this period. Indeed, the most striking thing about the response to the 1837 child labor inquiry is the widespread apathy about child labor reform that it suggests. The available evidence shows that there was no response whatsoever to the inquiry from a third of France's eighty-six departments. From at least seven other departments came nothing more than perfunctory communications declining for one reason or another to comment on the issues raised. The prefect of the Pyrénées-Orientales, for example, wrote simply that "the questions with which the circular deals are inapplicable in [this] department . . . which, being essentially agricultural, has no industry"; and the prefect of the Saône-et-Loire responded to the 1837 inquiry with the curt observation that "there exist in my department neither *chambres consultatives*, chambers of commerce, nor *conseils des prud'hommes* to which I can communicate your excellency's circular."

Several prefects who made attempts to solicit responses to the government survey were forced to report frustration. In December of 1837, for example, the prefect of the Calvados wrote to the minister of commerce that despite repeated requests, neither the chamber of commerce of Caen nor the five *chambres consultatives* and *conseils des prud'hommes* in his department had been concerned enough to respond to the government questionnaire. Similarly, the prefect of the Jura, in a letter that reached the Ministry of Commerce a year and a half after the child labor questionnaire was circulated, complained that he had encountered great difficulty in gathering information in his department. He explained that he had solicited information from his subprefects and from several industrial establishments in his jurisdiction but that initially only one subprefect had written in response. It took a second appeal to get the other subprefects to respond, and it seems that not one manufacturer in the department was willing to furnish information or advice on the matter of child labor. The prefect of the Tarn also complained that though he had presented the child labor questionnaire to the *chambres consultatives* of both Castres and Albi and to the *conseil des prud'hommes* of Castres, none of those bodies had responded.

Several of those polled declined to reply to the 1837 questionnaire on the pretext that there were no instances of industrial child labor in their areas, but this excuse does not sufficiently explain the silence of so many of those contacted. As the minister of commerce pointed out to the head of the *chambre consultative* at Grenoble when that official declined to respond, not only had the inquiry appealed for information on the child labor situation, which may or may not have been forthcoming depending on local conditions, but it had also solicited comments on what minimum standards for child labor there ought to be. This second subject could well have been addressed by anyone with an interest in the social and economic well-being of France. The Ministry of Commerce had anticipated so many more responses than it actually received that the Bureau of Manufactures' summary of the child labor study was prefaced with a lament about the regrettable paucity of replies.

As a general apathy about child labor reform was reflected in the failure of so many to respond to the government inquiry, so too was indifference to the issue reflected in many of the replies that were returned to Paris. Many respondents offered only cursory remarks on the state of child labor in their regions and said nothing at all on the subject of minimum standards. Others offered some thoughts on minimum standards but did not go beyond the very specific questions posed by the government into the larger and more fundamental question of the need for national legislation to impose those standards.

Precious few responses contained an outright advocacy of child labor legislation, and the most important of these, such as the ones from the chambers of commerce of Mulhouse, Rouen, and Orléans, reflected in their language the influence of the few crusaders for reform who had been active before 1837. Moreover, even those respondents willing to go so far as to suggest legislated restrictions on child labor made it clear that they did not want to see any significant limitations placed on the employment of the young. In large part, this unwillingness stemmed from the belief of factory owners that child labor was economically indispensable. Several respondents repeated the assertion that children were absolutely essential for the performance of certain tasks, and the Bureau of Manufactures concluded that "the employment of children in industrial workshops is an absolute necessity; there is unanimous agreement on this point." Furthermore, even the more positive responses to the inquiry reflected the traditionalism and the paternalism of most manufacturers. They still assumed that nothing was unusual about child labor, since it was based on longstanding precedents, and they still believed that because successful industrial enterprises provided employment opportunities, the interests of owners and of workers naturally coincided. Most entrepreneurs wanted to control their own shops without external regulation and tended to blame the pervasive wretchedness of factory children on working-class parents rather than on anything inherent in industrial labor.

The specific suggestions that came from some members of the entrepreneurial bourgeoisie illustrate their unwillingness to take responsibility for the abuse of working children or to propose any but the most innocuous limitations on the employment of the young. Some of those polled suggested that the hiring of children under nine or ten years of age might be prohibited, for example, and that the use of child labor at night might be limited, but they felt free to make these suggestions because such practices were already rare. Moreover, some respondents believed that there should be exceptions to even the most basic limitations on the employment of the young. So, too, even though nearly all the respondents of 1837 agreed that the moral condition of working children was extremely debased and many cited the specific problem of employing children of both sexes in the same workshop and in close contact with adults, there was no call for a reorganization of industrial workshops or a segregation of the sexes, for this would have involved radical departures from prevailing industrial practices. Similarly, while entrepreneurs generally accepted the desirability of education for working children and generally recognized that workdays of twelve hours and more precluded its pursuit, they did not want to take responsibility for this problem or to see children educated at the expense of their participation in the work force.

The faith of entrepreneurs in the idea that their welfare and that of their workers coincided and their conviction that they knew what was in the best interests of their employees were echoed in the stand manufacturers took on the issue of medical certification for factory children. Although they were aware of the stipulation in the English Factory Act of 1833 that a physician could be asked to verify the fitness of any youngster who applied for factory employment, the French business leaders polled in 1837 overwhelmingly adopted the view that the medical examination of young workers was unnecessary, since it was in a manufacturer's own interest not to force children to work beyond their physical capacity.

Clearly, there were elements within the business and manufacturing community that were willing by 1837 to accept the most innocuous child labor regulations if they themselves would be neither blamed for the abuse of children nor asked to countenance a major change in industrial practices, but there was just as clearly no active advocacy of meaningful child labor legislation among the entrepreneurial bourgeoisie as a group. On the contrary, a significant minority among those polled in 1837 unequivocally condemned the prospect of child labor legislation.

Some who expressed opposition to child labor regulations denied the existence of a child labor problem, whereas others protested against the very concept of limitations on the use of any labor, whether abuses existed or not. The *chambre consultative des arts et manufactures* at Sedan claimed that factory children were treated with "humanity and good will," for example, and the *chambre consultative* of Sommières dismissed the child labor problem as "chimerical." Respondents from Elbeuf and from Louviers argued that nothing should be allowed to upset the existing system of production. A few bodies that responded in 1837 actually defended the use of youngsters in factory labor as a way of keeping potential problem children under control. The chamber of commerce of Paris recognized that a child labor problem existed in the capital but concluded that limitations on the hiring of children would be "not only useless, but detrimental," since such limitations would release previously employed youngsters to roam the streets unattended.[3] The chamber of commerce of Nantes expressed a similar view.

Perhaps the most violent attack on the prospect of child labor legislation came from a member of the chamber of commerce of Lille, the spinning-mill operator T. Barrois. His report contained most of the standard arguments against factory reform heard in entrepreneurial circles in the early part of the century. He protested the exaggeration of the negative aspects of working-class life and asserted that where bad conditions existed, they were the fault of the home environment, not of the factory. Children were never really overworked, he argued, and to prove his point he offered that "the labor of those young people who attend the university . . . tires them much more." Barrois objected to legislating compulsory education, for he believed that even if compul-

---

3. There is no response from the Paris Chamber of Commerce among the other manuscript responses to the 1837 inquiry, but Touren, *Loi de 1841*, 54, reports on its opinion. On street children in Paris, see Louis Chevalier, *Classes laborieuses et classes dangereuses à Paris pendant la première moitié du XIXe siècle* (Paris, 1958), 120–30, and Berlanstein, "Vagrants," 531–52.

sory education were effective (which he doubted), it would serve only to raise unduly the expectations of the working classes. He argued further that labor kept youngsters out of trouble and that, in any case, the government had no right to interfere with the private affairs of the factory and the household.[4]

It is not possible to produce an exact quantitative analysis of the results of the 1837 child labor inquiry, since any interpretation of attitudes is bound to be somewhat subjective. Nonetheless, it can be said that of the roughly 125 responses received by the Ministry of Commerce, nearly half avoided expressing a clear opinion on the necessity of child labor legislation, either by failing to comment on the advisability of legislating minimum child labor standards or by declining altogether to supply information or answer questions about standards. Within the other half of the body of responses, expressions of outright hostility toward child labor legislation clearly outnumbered expressions of support. For example, among the twenty-four chambers of commerce that responded to the government questionnaire, nine remained uncommitted on the issue of child labor legislation, ten registered opposition to such legislation, and only five expressed some measure of support. Of the five chambers that came out in favor of a child labor law, moreover, three claimed to be doing so even though there was no child labor problem in their own cities.

It is very difficult to discern any pattern of correlation between the opinions on child labor expressed by local leaders and actual industrial conditions at the local level, though it is true that the various councils in France's more industrialized regions were more likely to express their views on child labor than were their counterparts in less industrialized regions. About 40 percent of all the responses to the 1837 inquiry came from France's thirteen most industrialized departments; two-thirds of the responses from these departments expressed a clear opinion either for or against the introduction of child labor legislation.

Nonetheless, the level of industrialization of a department did not seem to bear any relationship to the specific opinions held by its local notables and manufacturers. For instance, in five of France's thirteen most highly industrialized departments (the Rhône, the Seine-Inférieure, the Haut-Rhin, the Eure, and the Hérault), most local councils seemed inclined to support a factory law, but in another three of these departments (the Nord, the Ardennes, and the Bouches-du-Rhône), most were

---

4. On entrepreneurial attitudes in Lille, see also Pierrard, "Patronat," 56–57. The Barrois report has been published in *Les Révoltes logiques*, III (1976), 45–58.

inclined to oppose a law. Even a department's actual reliance on child labor did not seem to influence the responses of local bodies to the government inquiry of 1837. In three of the six departments with the most child laborers in France (five thousand or more just a few years after the government's inquiry), there was significant support for child labor legislation in 1837 and little or no opposition; in the other three departments, there was significant opposition and no support.

The geographic distribution of support for child labor reform and of opposition to it also defies generalization. In the north along the Belgian border, child labor legislation was opposed in the Nord and the Ardennes, but there was much support for a factory law in the Meuse. In the east, respondents in the Haut-Rhin tended to favor a child labor law, but respondents in the neighboring Doubs and some in the neighboring Bas-Rhin opposed it. Opinions often differed within a department or even within a town. In Strasbourg, for example, the *conseil des prud'hommes* supported a factory law whereas the chamber of commerce noted that most local manufacturers were opposed to it and the prefect contended that there was no child labor problem in his department in the first place. Even in Mulhouse, the primary center of agitation for child labor reform at the time, there was no unanimity of opinion. The *conseil des prud'hommes* there went on record as opposing factory legislation. In the final analysis, it appears from the evidence that the opinions expressed in the responses to the 1837 child labor inquiry were determined primarily by the personal philosophies and the individual perceptions of the people who prepared the responses.

The great divergence of opinion among the middle-class groups that reacted in 1837 to the concept of factory legislation reflected the ambivalence within bourgeois circles about the advantages of a child labor law. Not only was there some controversy over the exact nature of industrial child labor, but even among those who recognized its potential hazards there were mixed opinions about the wisdom of barring young children from the factory. Some manufacturers thought that the risks inherent in child labor were outweighed by the benefits that came from having working-class children under the control and influence of middle-class employers. Furthermore, although many bourgeois entrepreneurs were highly critical of working-class households, they still held out some hope for the strengthening of working-class family life, and this implied that laboring children should be left under the complete control of their parents. The liberal bias against government interventionism only strengthened this point of view.[5] Overall, then, the child labor inquiry of 1837 revealed some qualified acceptance of the prospect of child labor legislation, some adamant objection to that prospect, and a great deal of indifference, especially in less industrialized regions. Despite the fact that by the 1830s some manufacturers were beginning to express concern about the condition of the working classes generally, the government inquiry of 1837 did not reveal anything that could be taken to indicate widespread support for child labor legislation within the French entrepreneurial community.[6]

With the results of the 1837 inquiry tabulated by the end of the year, the Ministry of Commerce set about digesting its findings and considering what to do next on the question of factory legislation. To aid in its deliberations, the ministry had available to it not only the results of its own investigation but also a wealth of information about the child labor situation in England. The files of the Ministry of Commerce reveal that it was amassing a huge collection of documents from across the channel: everything from translations of factory inspectors' reports and communications from Frenchmen in England to county-by-county data on factory act violations and examples of the forms used in record keeping. Furthermore, the ministry solicited advice on child labor from its intermittently convened general councils of agriculture, commerce, and manufacturing. These three councils, each composed of leading figures in their respective fields, considered the results of the 1837 inquiry, and two of the bodies suggested their own composite schemes for factory reform. The suggestion of the General Council of Commerce was based on a minimum age of eight and a twelve-hour day for child laborers, whereas the General Council of Manufacturing proposed a minimum age of seven, with an eight-hour day for children up to age ten, a twelve-hour day for children ten to twelve, and a thirteen-hour day for children between twelve and thirteen. The General Council of Agriculture sug-

5. Compare Georges Snyders, *Il n'est pas facile d'aimer ses enfants* (Paris, 1982), 135–41; "Les Enfants du capital," *Les Révoltes logiques*, III (1976), 3–5.

6. Previous analyses of the 1837 child labor inquiry, such as those in Louis Gueneau, "Législation restrictive," and in Stearns, *Paths*, have all de-emphasized or even ignored the significance of missing, incomplete, or equivocal responses in judging the climate of opinion on child labor legislation among manufacturers. The analyses in Tudesq, *Notables*, II, 581–98, and in André-Jean Tudesq, "Comment le grand patronat considère le travail des enfants en 1840," in *VIIIe colloque d'histoire sur l'artisanat et l'apprentissage* (Aix-en-Provence, 1965), 25–37, are perhaps the most accurate to date, but they are distorted because in these works the 1837 inquiry is considered together with another conducted in 1840 under significantly different circumstances.

gested that a system of incentives rather than restrictions be devised to curb the abuse of working children.[7]

As the early months of 1838 passed, however, the administration seemed to retreat into silence and inaction with regard to the problem of laboring children. The results of the 1837 inquiry, even as they were interpreted by the reform-minded head of the Bureau of Manufactures, Delambre, did not impress the ministry with the need for action, and the failure of the general councils of commerce and manufacturing to pursue implementation of their own suggestions, coupled with the general paucity of appeals for child labor reform from the public, apparently convinced the ministry that there was no reason to move forward with any sense of urgency. The government's hesitation was often explained in terms of its need to consider the many variations in industrial practices and needs. This was the contention of the conservative deputy Jean-Claude Fulchiron (an important manufacturer of Lyon), of the minister of finance, and of Martin du Nord himself.[8]

When the question of child labor reform was raised in the 1838 legislative debate on the budget of the Ministry of Commerce, the dominant mood in official circles was expressed by Martin, who still insisted that the child labor problem was no cause for alarm. The deputy Laurent Cunin-Gridaine, who would soon become minister of commerce himself, echoed this conviction. Going even further, he proclaimed that the child labor issue had been studied sufficiently and that it was now clear there was no need for factory legislation. As late as January of 1840, one proponent of legislation could still complain that whenever the issue of child labor was discussed in the Chamber of Peers, virtually all those who addressed it could be considered "defenders of the status quo."[9] It soon became apparent to the committed few that if the idea of a child labor law was to be kept alive, it was incumbent upon them to continue and even to intensify the campaign for its adoption, and this they did.

Louis Villermé of the Académie des sciences morales et politiques, for example, remained an active advocate of reform. He was completing his massive study of industrial conditions in the final years of the 1830s, and he published his findings in his highly influential, two-volume *Tableau de l'état physique et moral des ouvriers* just as the decade drew to a close.[10]

7. AN, F12–4704; CD, June 15, 1839.
8. CD, May 11, May 28, 1838; CP, June 1, 1839.
9. CD, May 28, 1838; Gillet, *Quelques réflexions sur l'emploi des enfans dans les fabriques et sur les moyens d'en prévenir les abus* (Paris, 1840), 11.
10. Although the publication date of Villermé's work is 1840, internal evidence indi-

Villermé's completed study confirms that his overriding concern with child labor persisted; there was no other problem he considered more essential to confront. Two chapters of the *Tableau* deal almost exclusively with the child labor issue, and references to this issue abound throughout the entire text. Villermé's consideration of child labor in the *Tableau* takes advantage of the information gathered during the government's 1837 inquiry, adding it to the data he had personally amassed.

The opinions on child labor reform that Villermé had allowed the academy to preview in 1837 were repeated and amplified in his completed study. As before, Villermé painted a vivid picture of the pitiful factory children he had encountered during his travels. In a passage that would come to be frequently quoted, he described these children: "All pale, nervous, slow in their movements, quiet at their games, they present an outward appearance of misery, of suffering, of dejection that contrasts with the rosy color, the plumpness, the petulance and all the signs of glowing health that one notices in children of the same age each time that he leaves a manufacturing area to enter an agricultural canton."[11] Villermé was still adamant about the need for generalized child labor legislation that would benefit young workers both by limiting the length of their workday and by providing for their education and moral development. In support of his position, he again described the precedent set by England and again cited the failure of voluntary efforts to better the working conditions of the young.

Villermé recognized that there was, of course, another side to the argument. He agreed that enacting a child labor law would reduce the income of some working-class families, would impose regulations where they should perhaps be avoided, and would present both manufacturers and workers with a law they might try to evade. But he concluded that to allow the existing state of affairs to persist would be a far greater evil.[12] His insistence is often couched in very forceful language: "The remedy for the wasting of children in industry, for the homicidal abuse to which they are subjected, can be found only in a law . . . that will establish . . . a *maximum* length for the workday." A child labor law, he wrote, "is necessary, [nay] indispensible."[13]

The activists from Alsace were also at work in the period after the

cates that it was completed in 1839, and it is clear that its contents were already known before the book appeared in print; compare Horner, *Employment*, 20–23.

11. Villermé, *Tableau*, II, 88.
12. Villermé, *Tableau*, II, 358–59.
13. Villermé, *Tableau*, II, 93, 107. See also Coleman, *Death is a Social Disease*, 250–55.

completion of the government's 1837 inquiry, and in mid-1839 the administrative council of the Société industrielle de Mulhouse dispatched yet another in its series of pleas for legal controls on child labor. The substance of the petition sent to Paris was familiar, and little was new in what was said in the rather lengthy debate it generated on the floor of the legislature.[14] Nonetheless, the appeal from the Mulhouse industrialists indicated that they would not allow the government's inaction to go unchallenged. The largely Protestant factory owners of the Société industrielle apparently influenced the Société pour l'encouragement de l'instruction primaire parmi les protestants de France to prepare a petition to the legislature at this time as well.[15]

Moreover, the earliest crusaders for reform were no longer so alone in their campaign. By provoking the government to raise the child labor issue in a national inquiry, the reformers had discovered that there was potential for at least tacit acceptance of factory legislation in France. Just as important, however, they had prompted a few previously uninvolved individuals to join the effort to promote reform. The very fact that an inquiry was conducted seems to have raised the consciousness of some who had never before seriously considered the specific issue of child labor legislation. Thus, in the years immediately after 1837, the ranks of the crusaders for a factory law were augmented by several new advocates of legislation. Some of these spoke out only on a single occasion, whereas others became engrossed in the entire campaign for legislation, but all of them helped to foster the perception that the child labor issue was one aspect of the more general *question sociale* that could and should be addressed immediately. Although the advocates of reform remained few in number, they were able to enhance their efforts to promote the cause of factory legislation.

Among those who joined men such as Bourcart, Villeneuve-Bargemont, and Villermé in the front ranks of the child labor reform movement was Daniel Legrand, an industrialist from the Department of the Vosges. Legrand had adopted a variety of humanitarian practices in his own mill, and he now began to argue for the generalization of child labor restrictions through a series of pamphlets directed to those in authority.

14. CD, June 15, 1839.
15. CD, June 15, 1839. The petition of the Société pour l'encouragement de l'instruction primaire was brought to the attention of the Chamber of Peers by the comte de Tascher; see CP, May 31, 1839. See also the manuscript petition in AN, F12–4704, and Horner, *Employment*, 1. It was the agitation of the Mulhouse industrialists that must have also prompted a series of articles favoring factory legislation in *L'Industriel alsacien* late in the decade; see Kahan-Rabecq, *Classe ouvrière*, 185.

His first communication on the child labor issue came in 1838 in the form of a letter addressed to the heads of an Alsatian firm that, like his own, had adopted voluntary child labor restrictions. In this letter, which was circulated among members of both houses of the legislature in Paris, Legrand pointed to the inadequacy of voluntary restrictions and to the consequent need for reform through legislation. In 1839, he aimed an appeal directly at Paris. In two letters intended for general dissemination in the highest echelons of government, he called for a prompt remedy to the child labor problem and indicated the provisions he thought a child labor law should embody. Legrand suggested that a minimum age of ten be established initially and that it be raised eventually to eleven or twelve. For children ten to twelve years old, he wanted a ten-hour workday that would allow for a required two hours of daily schooling. For children thirteen to eighteen years old, he envisioned a twelve-hour workday. Legrand's recommendations also included suggestions that education be compulsory for children seven to ten years old and that physicians verify the physical capacity of the working young.[16]

Emerging as another important proponent of child labor reform in this period was François Delessert. A banker by profession, Delessert was a past president of the Paris Chamber of Commerce, a friend of the English factory inspector Leonard Horner, and deputy for the Pas-de-Calais. It was he who had questioned the inaction of the administration in the budgetary debates half a year after the conclusion of the 1837 inquiry, and it was he who had insisted on the need for swift action in the face of governmental equivocation. It was Delessert who had circulated Legrand's early appeals for child labor reform among France's political elite, and he soon came to be recognized as the foremost champion of reform within the Chamber of Deputies.[17]

While the core of committed crusaders for factory reform was growing, the activists promoting legislation could also take courage from a variety of cursory comments that appeared in print in the late 1830s on the evils of child labor and on the desirability of controlling them. There were, for example, several French theorists who had long been concerned with social issues generally but who were moved to write favorably about child labor legislation for the first time only after 1837. Their

16. See [Daniel Legrand], *Lettre d'un industriel des montagnes des Vosges à M. le Baron Charles Dupin . . . suivie de plusieurs lettres et adresses* (Strasbourg, 1841), and [Daniel Legrand], *Nouvelle Lettre d'un industriel des montagnes des Vosges à M. François Delessert* (Strasbourg, 1839). On Legrand's activities in favor of child labor legislation throughout the period of its consideration, see Raymond Weiss, *Daniel Le Grand* (Paris, 1926), 99–181.

17. CD, May 28, 1838; Gillet, *Réflexions*, 11.

decision to comment on the need for a factory law indicated a changing perception of the immediacy of the child labor issue among those concerned with the *question sociale*. Again, it seems that the child labor inquiry of 1837 was the catalyst for this new perception, and the government's inaction in the years following the inquiry became a source of at least mild irritation to some.

For instance, the liberal economist Jérôme-Adolphe Blanqui, Jean-Baptiste Say's student and successor at the Conservatoire des arts et métiers, spoke out in this period in favor of limited government intervention to safeguard working children. In his 1837 study of European political economy, Blanqui noted with approval the recent factory act adopted in England, and in the course on the economics of industry he gave during 1838 and 1839, he expanded his thinking. Comparing large- and small-scale manufacturing, he pointed to the exploitation of child labor as one of the evils of the factory system, and citing the unsuccessful attempts to prevent the abuse of children through voluntary controls at Mulhouse and elsewhere, he proclaimed the necessity of legislation.[18]

Similarly, H. A. Frégier addressed the matter of child labor reform in a volume that was awarded a prize by the Académie des science morales et politiques in 1839. Frégier's work, *Des classes dangereuses de la population dans les grandes villes*, focuses on the problem of moral corruption in the working classes and emphasizes the importance of rescuing the young from those environments where they learn corrupt behavior. In discussing the plight of children in industry, Frégier made use of information derived from the 1837 government inquiry, and he pointed to the most glaring examples of degenerate behavior it revealed. He repeated, for example, the account from the Vosges of children as young as six who "try to follow in adult footsteps: smoking pipes, frequenting cabarets and choosing mistresses for themselves." Championing reform among the young for both their own sakes and the sake of society, Frégier called for the institution of strong child labor legislation. Although he concluded that locally enacted and variegated legislation would be sufficient, he was adamant about the need for laws that would keep youngsters away from the corrupting influences of the factory and provide them a chance for education.[19]

18. Jérôme-Adolphe Blanqui, *History of Political Economy in Europe*, trans. Emily J. Leonard (New York, 1880), 543; Jérôme-Adolphe Blanqui, *Cours d'économie industrielle, 1838–1839* (Paris, 1839), 55–56. On Blanqui, see also Duvoir, *Recherche*, 40ff.

19. H. A. Frégier, *Des classes dangereuses de la population dans les grandes villes* (Paris, 1840), II, 1ff, esp. 29.

The Social Catholic philosopher, teacher, and administrator Joseph-Marie de Gérando also spoke in favor of child labor reform for the first time in the period after 1837. The baron de Gérando had a longstanding paternalistic commitment to education and to the welfare of the young, and he had been aware of the problem of children in industrial labor for many years. As early as 1820, he had already commented on it in general terms, placing the blame for child labor abuse on both manufacturers and working-class parents:

The development of industry in certain countries has produced a great demand even for very young children who are employed in manual labor that requires neither much vigor nor much intelligence; but the avarice of certain manufacturers abuses the strength of these little creatures; they are exhausted by fatigue; they are left time neither for school, nor for rest; hardly enough to eat a hasty morsel or take hurried sleep. . . . Their health suffers as much as their character and education. Yet the pressing want of some parents, the cupidity of others, and the lack of foresight in many deliver up these young creatures to this fatal regimen.

By the late 1830s, Gérando was apparently convinced of the need for a child labor law, and in 1839 he wrote approvingly of the prospect of factory legislation in the pages of his treatise *De la bienfaisance publique*.[20]

Other references to the plight of child laborers appeared as well. Early in 1838 the abbé Ferry of Saint-Nicholas-du-Pont, near Nancy, addressed to the legislature an appeal favoring action to relieve the suffering of factory children. At about the same time, the mayor of Elbeuf, responding to an inquiry from England, indicated his advocacy of a minimum age of twelve and a literacy requirement for factory employment.[21] And an eloquent appeal came in the 1838 Lenten message of Cardinal de Croy, archbishop of Rouen. "Open your eyes and look! The parents and masters of these young saplings demand that they bear fruit in the season of flowers," cried the archbishop. "Poor young children!" he continued. "May the law hasten to extend its protection over your existence, and may posterity read with astonishment on the face of this oh so self-contented century: *In these days of progress and discovery, an iron law was needed to protect children from death by overwork.*"[22]

20. Joseph-Marie de Gérando, *The Visitor of the Poor*, trans. Elizabeth Palmer Peabody (Boston, 1832), 121; Joseph-Marie de Gérando, *De la bienfaisance publique* (Brussels, 1839), I, 119–23.

21. CD, May 11, 1838; Jelinger C. Symons, *Arts and Artisans at Home and Abroad* (Edinburgh, 1839), 103.

22. See Parker Thomas Moon, *The Labor Problem and the Social Catholic Movement in France* (New York, 1921), 19. The archbishop's statement is quoted in Ducpétiaux, *Condition*, I, i.

After 1837, there were even some expressions of support for child labor reform measures in the press. The liberal *Mémorial du commerce et de l'industrie*, for instance, undertook an analysis of the child labor problem in 1839. The journal asserted that entrepreneurs, who could gain nothing from overworking the young, could not be faulted for the abuse of child labor, but it suggested rather that children were overworked by those parents who were not satisfied with providing only "for the ordinary needs of a family." Thus, the *Mémorial* contended, legislation to protect factory children was acceptable, as it would compromise only the prerogatives of parents and not those of factory owners. A subsequent article in the *Journal de l'industriel et du capitaliste* dealt with child labor in a less obviously biased fashion, since it was primarily a report on the government survey of 1837. Nonetheless, the *Journal* did editorialize that though the right to work deserved protection, so too did the laboring young.[23]

By the end of 1839, the increasing interest in the child labor issue, coupled with the unrelenting pressure of the advocates of reform, finally bore fruit. Prompted by the various petitions addressed to them, both chambers of the legislature heard new committee reports on child labor, and in January of 1840, the government finally submitted a child labor bill to the Chamber of Peers for consideration.

Despite the apparent success of the advocates of reform, however, support for factory legislation in France on the eve of its discussion in the Chamber of Peers remained extremely narrow and superficial. The government itself had given ample evidence of its reluctance to pursue a course of forceful action, and public opinion generally was far from enthusiastic. There was no identifiable economic or political faction that, as a group, supported child labor legislation, nor was there any specific segment of society that backed it.

The 1837 inquiry among the notables of the business and manufacturing community had revealed little enthusiasm for meaningful child labor legislation, and this situation had not changed in the intervening years. In 1839, the Alsatian entrepreneur Nicholas Schlumberger could still explain to an English correspondent that government inaction on child labor legislation was due primarily to "the opposition of the great majority of the manufacturers."[24]

23. "Du travail des enfants dans les manufactures," *Mémorial du commerce et de l'industrie*, III (1839), legislation sec., 129ff; "Du travail des enfants dans les manufactures," *Journal de l'industriel et du capitaliste*, VIII (January, 1840).

24. Symons, *Arts and Artisans*, 39–40.

Liberals, whether they were directly involved in manufacturing or not, were inclined to reject government intervention in industrial affairs out of hand. Only a few liberal theorists had as yet been won over to the idea of limited government intervention in the name of social harmony, and none were interested in seeing a reinstatement of the type of economic regulations that had been imposed under the Old Regime.[25] French liberals before 1840 almost invariably considered social issues from a paternalistic or even a Malthusian perspective; thus, they could hardly be enthusiastic about factory legislation. The handful of liberal writers who did work for the adoption of child labor legislation were exceptional for their activism, and even they were willing to advocate regulation only on the assumption that children were not free agents to begin with and on the premise that a factory law would be a control more on working-class parents than on capitalist entrepreneurs.[26]

Nor was the climate of opinion regarding child labor reform any more encouraging among those, such as the utopian socialists, who argued for a radical redirection of France's emerging industrial society. Neither the Saint-Simonians nor the Icarians, for example, turned their attention to the specific problem of child labor, though both groups were concerned about such related issues as education and the structure of the family. Apparently, they assumed that the problem of child labor would simply disappear in their perfected societies, so its persistence in the contemporary world was of no real concern to them.[27] The followers of Charles Fourier seemed even less troubled than other utopians about the potential ill effects of child labor. Indeed, Fourier, unlike Henri de Saint-

25. On Old Regime regulations, see Franc Bacquié, *Les Inspecteurs des manufactures sous l'ancien régime: 1669–1792,* in Julien Hayem (ed.), *Mémoires et documents pour servir à l'histoire du commerce et de l'industrie,* 11th ser. (Paris, 1927).

26. Gueneau, "Législation restrictive," 459ff, Stearns, *Paths,* 160, and Sébastian Charléty, *La Monarchie de juillet* (Paris, 1921), 242, all suggest that the Académie des sciences morales et politiques, a bastion of liberalism, actively backed child labor reform. However, although many members of the academy were perhaps reconcilable to a factory law that would protect defenseless youngsters, the academy as a body did not become actively involved in support of child labor legislation before 1841. Most of the discussion of child labor legislation in the academy took place only after a law had been passed, and even then there was as much argument against factory reform as for it.

27. On the Saint-Simonians, see *The Doctrines of Saint-Simon: An Exposition—First Year, 1828–1829,* trans. George G. Iggers (Boston, 1958), 149ff; Mathurin Dondo, *The French Faust, Henri de Saint-Simon* (New York, 1955); Henry-Réné D'Allemagne, *Les Saint-Simonians, 1827–1837* (Paris, 1930), 130; Frank E. Manuel, *The Prophets of Paris* (New York, 1962), 151ff; and Alexander Gray, *The Socialist Tradition* (London, 1946), 136ff. On the ideas of the Icarians, see Etienne Cabet, *Voyage en Icarie* (Paris, 1848), esp. 72–82, and Christopher Johnson, *Utopian Communism in France: Cabet and the Icarians, 1839–1851* (Ithaca, 1974). Cabet's book first appeared in 1840.

Simon or Etienne Cabet, made the employment of children an integral part of his scheme for a new society. The education of the young in his ideal world would begin at age two, and as in traditional society, children would be prepared to act as productive members of the community by the time they were about seven years of age. Believing that in contemporary society, and especially in urban society, most children were useless parasites, Fourier suggested they be put to work at tasks for which he thought they had a natural penchant: stable cleaning, road work, garbage collection, and pest control. Although Fourier was not necessarily advocating industrial employment for youngsters, he was certainly far from being a critic of child labor.[28] In general, then, the early socialists and utopians were disinclined even to consider the need for child labor legislation.

The Catholic Church, too, remained essentially silent on child labor reform in the 1820s and 1830s. Within the Catholic community, the existence of working-class poverty and misery was generally accepted as inevitable, and child labor was simply treated as a fact of life. Indeed, the Church itself sponsored scores of workshops in which young children entrusted to its care were put to work at industrial tasks. Although there were some within the Catholic community who felt an obligation to aid those suffering under the conditions imposed by industrialization and urbanization, in general neither conservative nor progressive elements in the Church were moved to advocate legislated remedies to the child labor problem. The politically conservative among concerned Catholics occupied themselves almost exclusively with traditional charitable work, which aimed at ameliorating the suffering of the unfortunate but didn't attack its causes. Catholic charitable institutions such as the Société de Saint Joseph and the Société de Saint Vincent de Paul, established to aid the urban young, provided educational and welfare services for young workers but never attempted direct interference with working conditions. To the extent that conservative Catholics became caught up in Social Catholicism, they tended to look for a new society based on the revival of Old Regime institutions such as guilds, and they wanted nothing to do with such seemingly radical ideas as social legislation.

The politically more progressive elements within the concerned Catholic community also turned either to charitable work of a traditional nature or to some form of Social Catholicism. The Social Catholics of

28. See Gray, *Tradition*, 177, 188–190, and Manuel, *Prophets*, 229. On Fourier generally, see Nicholas V. Riasanovsky, *The Teachings of Charles Fourier* (Berkeley, 1969).

the left looked to the future rather than to the past for a model on which to reconstruct society. They worked for a completely new social order founded upon democracy or socialism and thus did not concern themselves with piecemeal legislation and reform. The journal of the most progressive element within the Catholic community, *L'Atelier*, kept silent on the issue of child labor legislation even when it finally came under debate in the legislature.[29] What the progressives and the conservatives, the Social Catholics and the traditionalists all had in common, moreover, was their insistence on changing social conditions by working with the laboring classes themselves rather than by attempting to influence the political policy of the notables who controlled business and government.[30]

Among prelates, only a very few spoke out on any labor questions at all before 1848; the 1838 appeal of the archbishop of Rouen was a glaring exception to a general silence.[31] Just as the opinions of Bourcart, Penot, and Villermé were manifest departures from the thinking of the entrepreneurs and intellectuals of the liberal bourgeoisie generally, so too were the opinions of Villeneuve-Bargemont, the abbé Ferry, and the Cardinal de Croy significant individual departures from the predominant attitudes of the Church's lay and clerical leadership.[32]

In order to appreciate fully the isolation in which the champions of child labor reform operated, it is important to realize that they lacked support not only among the leaders of French opinion but also among the very workers in whose interest they believed they were acting. Unfortunately, no government agency in France sought out working-class opinions on child labor in the 1830s as had the Sadler commission in England before the passage of the Factory Act of 1833, so the main existing evidence of working-class attitudes toward child labor reform in France comes from the rare accounts of workers' views that were left by

29. Eugène Fournière, *Le Règne de Louis Philippe* (Paris, *ca.* 1906), 358.

30. See Dansette, *Religious History*, I, 252ff; Alexander Roper Vidler, *A Century of Social Catholicism, 1820–1920* (London, 1964), ixff, 3ff; and Jean-Baptiste Duroselle, *Les Débuts du Catholicisme social en France* (Paris, 1951).

31. Paul Droulers, "Des évêques parlent de la question ouvrière en France avant 1848," *Revue de l'Action populaire*, No. 147 (April, 1961), *passim.* Tudesq, "Grand Patronat," 33, and Stearns, *Paths*, 142, both use Droulers' work to argue for clerical support for humanitarian efforts generally but seem to ignore the fact that Droulers found little or no clerical support for child labor legislation specifically.

32. Villeneuve-Bargemont had an ambivalent relationship with the Social Catholic movement in general; see Ring, *Villeneuve-Bargemont*, 38. Moon, *Labor Problem*, errs in arguing much too strongly for an early interest in reform legislation within the Catholic community on the basis of the activities of Villeneuve-Bargemont and a few others.

outside observers and from the actions of the workers themselves. The evidence that is available indicates that working-class families in the middle decades of the nineteenth century still considered the child labor issue from a traditional perspective. Child labor was still justified in those families by traditional child-rearing practices and by economic necessity. As the government's Bureau of Manufactures observed in 1837, "Under any circumstances, the operatives will not be pleased with a restriction either as to the age or hours of work of the children, because the result must be a reduction in the wages of the family." Furthermore, it should be recalled that some child labor in the early factories was viewed by working-class parents as having an educational value, a point that is often overlooked by modern scholars, and working-class parents were still frequently the ones who supervised the factory labor of their own children.[33] If English workers were taking up the cause of child labor reform by the 1830s because they saw in it a way to preserve traditional family work patterns and to benefit the industrial working class as a whole, French workers were not viewing child labor reform in the same way, and they remained uninvolved in appeals for its implementation.[34]

Perhaps nothing attests to the difficulty of mustering support for child labor legislation more strikingly than does the initial reluctance with which even the leaders of the campaign for factory legislation themselves arrived at their positions. The hesitancy of the members of the Société industrielle de Mulhouse to support child labor legislation has already been described. Bourcart's difficult position as the moving force behind the society's eventual endorsement of reform was recognized by at least some contemporaries and would even be cited in the legislative debates of 1840. In those debates the deputy Sigismond Dietrich, who owned an ironworks in the Haut-Rhin, observed that though Bourcart had spoken to the Société industrielle of the need for reform on several occasions, "for a long time it was impossible for him to obtain the agreement of the society," and that only "by dint of persistence" did he finally win it over.[35]

33. See *Rapport du Bureau des manufactures*, quoted in Horner, *Employment*, 29–30, and Colin Heywood, "Education and the Industrial Labour Force in Nineteenth-Century France" (Typescript in possession of Colin Heywood, Nottingham, Eng., 1980).

34. Compare Neil J. Smelser, "Sociological History: The Industrial Revolution and the British Working-Class Family," *Journal of Social History*, I (Fall, 1967), 28–29. Octave Festy, *Le Mouvement ouvrier au début de la Monarchie de juillet* (Paris, 1908), 145, suggests that the child labor issue was raised in response to worker agitation in the 1830s, but this claim is totally unsubstantiated.

35. CD, December 24, 1840. See also Jacques Bénet, *Le Capitalisme libéral et le droit au travail* (Neuchâtel, 1947), I, 194, 300–302.

In the case of Villeneuve-Bargemont as well, advocacy of legislation had come only haltingly. When he first proposed the restriction of child labor, Villeneuve-Bargemont had wanted it to be implemented solely on the basis of morally motivated volunteerism, and even when he first raised the possibility of a factory law to protect working children, he had wanted it applied only where fifty or more workers were employed. Only later did he see the need for a more generalized child labor law. The baron de Gérando also flatly rejected the idea of child labor legislation initially, though he was clearly concerned about the lot of factory children. Child labor abuse, he wrote in the 1820s, "has been carried so far in England that an express law was required for its suppression." But in France, he continued, "we hope legislative authority will not be necessary to restrain it."[36] His declaration in favor of a child labor law came only in 1839, when the passage of such a measure seemed imminent.

Even for Villermé, the decision to advocate a child labor law was a most painful one, for it flew in the face of his most basic beliefs. Villermé's position has been perceptively assessed in a scholarly commentary that appeared on the hundredth anniversary of the publication of his *Tableau de l'état physique et moral des ouvriers*. According to this commentary, it was "the problem of child labor in factories that alone placed the existing state of affairs in question for Villermé, that alone was open to serious criticism, that alone admitted the intervention of the State and of the law." The *Tableau* clearly reveals "the reluctance with which Villermé broke with the doctrine [of nonintervention]" and the amount of evidence of abuse he had to uncover in order "to justify his iconoclastic boldness."[37]

Despite the prevailing atmosphere of nonsupport, however, the advocates of child labor reform did have two things working in their favor. Both of these factors had facilitated their success in bringing the child labor question under discussion within the government, and both would continue to help the reformers promote their ideas. One of the factors working in favor of reform was the nature of the French political system. Political power in France was highly centralized and notably unresponsive to popular demands and public opinion. What the events of the decades before 1840 had seemed to demonstrate was that there were only two ways to achieve social change: through the decisions of top policy makers or amid the upheavals of revolution. Radical upheaval was

36. Gérando, *Visitor*, 121.
37. Deslandres and Michelin, *Il y a cent ans*, 196–97. See also Coleman, *Death is a Social Disease*, xix, 254–55.

of course anathema to the cautious reformers campaigning for child labor legislation, so, realizing the nature of the political system in which they were operating, they brought their case not into the forum of public opinion but directly into the halls of power. The champions of child labor legislation in France were themselves within the power elite, and several of them had seats in the legislature. Both before 1840 and after, they were thus able to lobby on an equal footing those who governed France and to influence the top policy makers of the country directly. Furthermore, the staunchest advocates of reform were in close contact with each other, which must have served to strengthen not only their sense of resolve but also their impact.

The contrast with England here is revealing, for England, unlike France, did have a tradition of gradual reform resulting from public pressure. So the British advocates of factory reform, unlike their French counterparts, sought to enlist a broad base of support in their campaign and to harness the power of public opinion. The advocates of child labor reform in England were in fact a large and diverse group that included representatives of business and manufacturing, ministers of various churches, political figures, writers, activist reformers, and even labor leaders. More important, the pleas for action voiced by the leaders of the child labor reform movement there were supported by widespread worker agitation and by expressions of public sympathy.[38]

The contrast between the French and British approaches to reform can be seen not only in their midcentury movements to end child labor abuse but also in their antislavery movements. According to one authority, the abolitionist movement in France was "usually confined to a very small political or cultural elite," it was "reluctant or unable to seek mass recruitment," and it was "confined to one or two localities, [including] the

38. Among the works that best illuminate the widespread support for child labor legislation in England are J. T. Ward, *The Factory Movement, 1830–1855* (London, 1962); Hutchins and Harrison, *Factory Legislation*, 1–70; Thomas, *Early Factory Legislation*; and Roberts, *Victorian Origins*, esp. 36–38. The popular support for child labor legislation is also revealed in the biographies of some of the leaders of the English campaign for reform; see J. L. Hammond and Barbara Hammond, *Lord Shaftsbury* (New York, 1923), 10ff; Cecil Driver, *Tory Radical: The Life of Richard Oastler* (New York, 1946); and S. E. Finer, *The Life and Times of Sir Edwin Chadwick* (London, 1952), 50ff. On the specific issue of entrepreneurial support for child labor legislation in England, see Elie Halévy, *England in 1815*, trans. E. I. Watkin and D. A. Barker (New York, 1961), 283–88; on the specific issue of worker support for child labor restrictions, see E. P. Thompson, *The Making of the English Working Class* (New York, 1963), 331ff. For a general discussion of the important role of public opinion in the formulation of English legislation, and its relative insignificance in the formulation of French legislation, see A. V. Dicey, *Lectures on the Relation Between Law and Public Opinion in England During the Nineteenth Century* (London, 1920), esp. 1–12.

capital." By contrast, the "Anglo-American" antislavery movement "attempted to bring public pressure to bear on reluctant or hostile economic interests and agencies of government" and at critical moments "used mass propaganda, petitions, public meetings, lawsuits and boycotts." Organizationally, this movement "tended to be decentralized." What a comparison of abolitionism and child labor reform suggests is that already very early in the industrial era two distinct models of nineteenth-century social reform were emerging, one focused on private initiative and lobbying at the centers of power, the other dependent upon marshalling the forces of public opinion, one predominant in France, the other in England and America.[39]

The other important factor working in favor of the advocates of child labor reform in France was the increasing disquiet among many of those who dominated society and government over the condition of the newly emerging industrial working class. More and more, the elite were troubled by what they perceived as the wretchedness and the dangerousness of this class, though most of those who were distressed about working-class misery saw it as an organic problem and thought about it only in general terms.[40] Thus, whereas the active advocates of factory legislation were quite few in number, those concerned with the general physical and moral condition of working-class families constituted a larger group that included many government leaders and legislators. The champions of child labor reform themselves often adopted an encyclopedic view of the social problems of industrial society. What differentiated them from most of their concerned compatriots was that they had reached, however reluctantly, the stage of proposing a specific solution to a limited aspect of the *question sociale*. They had come to focus on child labor because it impressed them as among the most striking of the new social problems born of industrialization and because they believed children were both more deserving of and more susceptible to rescue from the evil environments into which fate had placed them. It may have been true that "much of the alleged cruelty in the factories was but a reflection of the brutality of life outside them," as one English historian has said, but to these reformers, somehow the cruelty inflicted on laboring children seemed especially intolerable.[41]

39. See Seymour Drescher, "Two Variants of Anti-Slavery: Religious Organization and Social Mobilization in Britain and France, 1790–1870," in Christine Bolt and Seymour Drescher (eds.), *Anti-Slavery, Religion, and Reform* (Folkstone, Eng., 1980), 43–63.

40. See Perrot, *Enquêtes sur la condition*, and Joseph Aynard, *Justice ou charité? Le Drame sociale et ses temoins de 1825 à 1845* (Paris, 1945).

41. Pinchbeck and Hewitt, *Children*, II, 410.

Given the social and political environment of mid nineteenth-century France, what the champions of child labor reform had to do was convince a body of decision makers who were disinclined to focus on the specific matter of child labor and generally disinclined to countenance government interventionism to accept the idea of trying to remedy one aspect of working-class misery through legislation while they continued to search for a more comprehensive approach to the overall plight of the working classes. The possibility of their being reconciled to a minimal factory law existed both because many within the French elite were aware of the implications working-class conditions had for the stability of the society they dominated and because many of them were humanitarian liberals, Social Catholics, or at least notables with some vague sense of social responsibility. Here again the position of the reformers within society was crucial. Few as they were, the advocates of legislation were identified with several of the prevailing socioeconomic philosophies of the era, so they were in a good position to influence those who shared their political and ideological perspectives. Thus, the stand taken by Bourcart, Penot, and Legrand could legitimate acceptance of child labor reform among manufacturers, as could the stand of Villeneuve-Bargemont and Gérando among Social Catholics and of Villermé among liberal intellectuals.

The general indifference toward child labor reform in French society lost much of its weight in the face of the tactics adopted by the crusaders for factory legislation. They had to win not popular approval for their program but only the approval of those in power. They had been able to move their campaign along by using the political process as they understood it and by appealing to the general concern among the dominant classes with the *question sociale*. As the debate over the exact nature of child labor legislation continued throughout 1840, the strategies of concentrating on the decision makers of France while virtually ignoring public opinion and of arguing in terms of a general concern with the physical, educational, and moral development of the industrial working class would continue to inform the campaign of the champions of legislation.

FOUR

The Child Labor Law of 1841

The child labor bill introduced to the Chamber of Peers in January of
1840 by Laurent Cunin-Gridaine, then minister of commerce, was a far
cry from the kind of bill most advocates of child labor reform had been
demanding throughout the 1830s. The administration bill suggested
little more than authorizing local governments to adopt their own child
labor regulations. Cunin-Gridaine's own attitude toward child labor legislation seems to have been one of some ambivalence, and the seven-
page explanatory text appended to the bill he prepared reveals that the
government still maintained opinions militating against strong controls.[1]
The government continued to argue, for instance, that "the representations which have been made of abuses existing in France are not free
from a certain degree of exaggeration." The main point in Cunin-
Gridaine's explanatory text was that because there were great local variations in factory conditions, in the abilities of children, and even in "climate and temperature," any legislation controlling child labor simply
had to be localized. Moreover, the minister observed, while the inquiry
of 1837 had uncovered "a unanimous zeal for and interest in the well-

---

1. Horner, *Employment*, 40, provides a contemporary opinion that Cunin-Gridaine
"appeared by no means favorably inclined towards any law on the subject" of child labor,
whereas Ducpétiaux, *Condition*, II, 265, counts Cunin-Gridaine among France's benevolent
manufacturers, and Armand Audiganne, *La Nouvelle Loi sur le travail des enfants et la famille
ouvrière depuis 35 ans* (Paris, 1874), claims that he was very much in favor of a law and is
not given enough credit for his stand. Cunin-Gridaine's own pronouncements tend to confirm the view of Marcel Pournin, *L'Inspection du travail* (Paris, 1903), that the minister was
hesitant at first but became committed to the child labor law after its passage.

being of children," it had "at the same time revealed a great divergence [of opinion] over what measures to propose." Having thus assessed the situation, the administration not only declined to sponsor any forceful national legislation but even suggested that in any system of local regulation adopted, all family industries should be exempt from control and all but the gravest incidents of parental mistreatment of children overlooked.[2] Nonetheless, the introduction of a government bill in the Chamber of Peers did provide a point of departure for further legislative debate, and thus it marked a turning point for the child labor reform movement in France. The task of the movement was no longer to force a legislative consideration of child labor; its task now became to see that any child labor law enacted would truly improve the condition of laboring children.

No immediate action was taken on the proposal put before the peers by Cunin-Gridaine, but a committee was appointed to study it. The government bill might have had a better chance of being adopted without much further thought had it not been for the composition of the review committee assembled by the chamber. All of those named to the committee had previously manifested some concern over the condition of the working classes, and several had already given attention specifically to the problems faced by children. As presiding officer of the committee, for example, sat the baron Joseph-Marie de Gérando, whose early recognition of the child labor problem and whose more recent commitment to legislation have already been noted. That Gérando did not play a more active role in the ongoing movement for child labor reform, even after being named president of the peers' child labor committee, was undoubtedly due to the rapidly failing condition of his health.[3]

Acting as the secretary of the Chamber of Peers' committee was another longtime advocate of measures to aid the young, the baron Charles Dupin. Both an engineer and a teacher, Dupin had a longstanding interest in commerce, technology, and education. He had revealed his concern for the welfare of young people as early as 1824, when he appealed to the legislature for increased expenditures on schooling, and by 1840 he had published no less than eight works concerning the advantages of education and the condition of the working classes.[4] Dupin was destined

2. Cunin-Gridaine's explanatory text is in AN, F12–4705.

3. Gérando died in 1842. For background information on him, see Octavie Morel, *Essai sur la vie et les travaux de Marie-Joseph Baron de Gérando* (Paris, 1846).

4. See Charles Dupin, *Avantages sociaux d'un enseignement publique appliqué à l'industrie* (Paris, 1824). Dupin's publications are listed at the beginning of Dupin, *Travail*. See also Duvoir, *Recherche*, 158ff.

to become one of the most important champions of child labor reform France would ever see. The comte Samuel-Ferdinand de Tascher, who had introduced and supported the petition of the Société pour l'encouragement de l'instruction primaire in the Chamber of Peers in 1839, was also a member of the peers' review committee, as were Auguste Le Tellier de Souvré, marquis de Louvois, an innovative industrialist himself, the liberal economist Pellegrino Rossi, the philosopher and educator Victor Cousin, and Adrien-Etienne de Gasparin, onetime prefect of the Rhône and minister of the interior and of commerce.

Given the makeup of the peers' review committee, it is not surprising that the committee quickly rejected the administration bill presented by Cunin-Gridaine and set to work preparing a more forceful one. Of its seven members, only Rossi and Cousin supported the government bill at the outset, and Cousin later reversed his stand. Charles Dupin quickly emerged as the key figure on the committee, and it was he who composed the committee's report to the full chamber.

Dupin's report contained both the alternative to the government bill that the review committee had developed and a rather lengthy explanation of the reasoning behind the new proposal. In essence, he set out to refute some of the basic assumptions that underlay the original administration bill and to build a case for legislating specific controls over child labor rather than mere vague principles. Thus, he cited precedents for national legislation, noting with approval England's lead in the field of factory reform. Dupin observed that specific legislation had done nothing to harm English manufacturing even though it had come at the time when English commercial interests were first being challenged seriously by Continental competition. According to the report, the fact that Prussia, Austria, and Russia had all adopted measures modeled on England's and the fact that reform advocates in France were calling for similar action further bolstered the argument for national legislation.

So, too, the peers' committee report took issue with the government's assertion that the child labor problem in France was not a serious one. In attacking that assertion, Dupin, like Villermé and others before him, drew a comparison between young people raised in manufacturing areas and those reared in agricultural districts. He sought to show that the industrial employment of young people not only caused them physical harm but also adversely affected the military potential of the state, an argument that had gained great currency by 1840.[5] Although recent

5. See, for example, Gillet, *Réflexions*, and the speech by Billandel in CD, June 15, 1839.

studies have called into question the validity of statistical arguments purporting to demonstrate the ill effects of industrialization on potential recruits, Dupin considered the statistical evidence he presented in support of his position to be sound. Like many who became interested in social issues in the early nineteenth century, Dupin was enthralled by the emerging quantitative methodologies of social science research, and he was eager to sustain his arguments with "scientific" findings.[6] Of the young men examined for recruitment into the army in ten of France's more industrialized departments, 49 percent were rejected as unfit for military service, Dupin reported, and he compared this to the record in ten primarily agricultural departments, where the rejection rate was only 29 percent. Dupin's report went on to dismiss as unfounded the contention that the physical abilities of children varied locally and especially with climatic conditions, and it then passed on to a detailed description of the legislative proposal adopted by the peers' committee.

The committee's bill called for the establishment of eight years as the minimum age at which children could seek factory employment and of eight hours as the maximum workday for youngsters aged eight to twelve. Children aged twelve to sixteen would be allowed to work no more than twelve hours a day. Under the committee's plan, children would not be permitted to work at night and would also be excluded from all labor on Sundays and holidays. Children who did not have at least two years of schooling behind them when they applied for factory employment would be required to attend school while working, and the bill called for a system of educational certification to aid in the enforcement of this provision. Finally, the bill proposed that the administration be given the right to pass supplemental rulings on child labor. The peers' committee wished to see the factory act applied in specifically selected industries, as it was in England. It suggested imposing regulations in textile factories and in shops employing mechanical power or a continuous fire, but the provision for supplemental rulings would allow the government to extend the law's jurisdiction to new industries from time to time, as well as to enact specific regulations concerning the moral conduct of young workers and their physical treatment.

In order to demonstrate how important it was to regulate the moral conduct of child laborers, Dupin again offered statistical evidence. He presented figures showing that the rate of illegitimate births, as well as

6. See Perrot, *Enquêtes sur la condition,* 27ff, and Coleman, *Death is a Social Disease,* esp. Chap. 5.

the rate of crimes against persons and property, was far higher in industrialized areas than it was in those areas left relatively untouched by industrialization. To take but one example: Dupin indicated that there was one prosecution for crimes against property for every 4,792 inhabitants of nineteen departments characterized as manufacturing, while there was only one prosecution for every 8,608 inhabitants of France's other departments. The evidence he presented in an attempt to show the adverse effects of industrialization on the morality of the young, like his evidence on recruitment, was seriously flawed. For example, Dupin completely ignored the possibility of stricter law enforcement and of more accurate reporting of crimes in urbanized areas. On the surface, however, the statistical evidence he presented seemed most convincing.

The report of the Chamber of Peers committee concluded with some thoughts on the enforcement of the legislation it was proposing. It advised that both factory owners and parents should be subject to penalties if child labor regulations were violated, and it suggested that prefects, subprefects, and mayors be charged with the implementation of any factory law that was adopted. The peers' committee proposed that these officials, together with an accompanying physician, be empowered to enter and inspect manufacturing establishments at will.[7] The committee submitted the report of its deliberations to the full Chamber of Peers on February 22, 1840, and the chamber's debate on child labor legislation began on March 5. During the debate a number of the basic principles underlying factory legislation came under discussion anew, as did several less critical matters.[8]

The first major issue to be raised in floor debate was once again whether child labor legislation should be national or local. Defending the government's original concept, Pellegrino Rossi reiterated the argument that children in different areas of the country had different physical capacities. He argued that even if national legislation were eventually to be adopted, a period of strictly localized legislation would be needed first, in order to establish what compromises would have to be made in formulating a law for all of France. Anticipating the objection that local legislation implied inequality before the law, Rossi insisted that children would be treated equally everywhere in that they would not be com-

7. The peers' committee report appears in Dupin, *Travail*, xxxiii–lvi, and in translation in Horner, *Employment*, 42–61.
8. See CP, March 6–11, 1840. The peers' debate is discussed in Dupin, *Travail*, 1–17, Horner, *Employment*, 61ff, Touren, *Loi de 1841*, 74–81, and Gueneau, "Législation restrictive," 470–77.

pelled to engage in labor beyond what was considered suitable in each locality. To bolster his position, Rossi claimed that even Dupin was a partisan of less-than-uniform labor legislation, because he wished to leave enforcement under local control and to see only certain specific industries subject to a factory law.

Dupin was quick to parry Rossi's attack. To say that advocacy of local enforcement as a practical matter was the same as advocacy of local regulation was absurd, Dupin retorted. As to the law's applicability only in selected industries, the baron pointed out that there were only certain ones in which children were overworked and that the precedent for measures couched in limited terms had been set by the 1813 ban on the employment of mineworkers under ten years of age. He concluded by drawing an analogy between the fields of medicine and law. In medicine there were no panaceas, but there were certainly cures that could have their effect everywhere; such was also the case with labor legislation, he contended. Along with Dupin, other speakers also advanced arguments against locally variegated legislation. Laborers would simply migrate from areas with strict measures to those with more lenient regulations, the champions of a nationwide scheme observed. They cautioned, too, that those highly industrialized areas where legislation was most needed were also the places where manufacturers had the most power and could be expected to advocate relatively weak local regulations. Finally, they recalled, in other laws with similar import for the nation—for example, those covering military service or criminal responsibility—there was no variation from place to place.

A second matter much discussed in the March debates was the prospect of compulsory education for child laborers. The advocates of forceful legislation consistently asserted that something had to be done to guarantee the intellectual and moral well-being of working-class children, in addition to safeguarding their bodily health. Some, like Pierre Bigot, baron de Morogues, wanted schooling to be required even beyond a two-year minimum. Still, not everyone agreed with the concept of required education. Victor Cousin, newly installed as minister of public instruction, for instance, had serious reservations about this feature of the bill. He contended that there was no proof of the efficacy of compulsory education. Although that system existed in parts of Germany and Switzerland, he said, the Dutch, "the most industrious and the most moral [people] on the face of the earth," were doing quite well without it. Besides, he argued, the French did not like being ordered to do anything, and legislating compulsory education might have the effect of turning the populace against education completely. Cousin declared himself content to rely on the education law of 1833, which, with its provisions for elementary school facilities in every commune and its imposition of some control over the quality of instruction, had made schooling generally available and had increased the number of children being taught. The minister expressed his belief that the whole issue of compulsory education had been settled definitively in 1833 and that it was improper even to raise that matter again. What was needed, he said, was "a system of encouragement" and not one of compulsion. The basic problem that the minister declined to face was that though there was now a legal requirement that schooling be made available, factory children, as well as a great many others, were often unable to take advantage of the educational opportunity being offered because they were required to work from the very earliest age.

Like Pellegrino Rossi, Cousin was concerned with the problem of inequality before the law, an example of which he believed he saw in compelling only those children who worked in protected industrial shops to attend school. Abel-François Villemain, Cousin's predecessor at the Ministry of Public Instruction, tried to allay the minister's fears. He suggested that a compulsory education measure applicable to factory children would in fact establish a situation of greater equality in education, since it was the parents of factory children who most needed to be coerced into sending their offspring to school. "When a child remains under the parental roof, however humble it may be, . . . that child will naturally be sent to school," said Villemain, as he observed that once children were sent off to labor in the mills, they lost all opportunity for formal education. Joseph-Marie de Gérando concurred with Villemain's opinion and added that whereas in most trades there was at least some apprenticeship involved, in factory labor no skills whatsoever were acquired. Both Villemain and Gérando were greatly oversimplifying the truth, of course, but their statements were probably made in good faith and they reflected the belief of social reformers that the elite could look out for the interests of working-class children better than anyone else. Still not satisfied, Rossi objected to what he viewed as a legal provision that would unfairly penalize children for their parents' neglect. He constructed the theoretical example of a child who, having had no schooling and having lost his job in an industry not covered by the proposed legislation, would find it impossible to acquire a new job in a protected plant. Dupin silenced concern over this specific problem by pointing out that the youngster in Rossi's example would simply be required by the proposed law to attend school while working.

One other major issue that came under discussion, not unexpectedly, was infringement upon entrepreneurial rights (there seemed to be far less concern in the chamber about infringement upon parental rights). When the Social Catholic Charles de Montalembert emotionally attacked the tyranny of industrialists, for instance, the physician J.-L. Gay-Lussac rose to their defense. Gay-Lussac contended that factory owners should be considered complete masters of their own shops; this was a right they paid for by assuming all the risks of establishing a business. Dupin retorted that by employing large numbers of people, factories assumed something of a public character and thus could be subjected to some government regulation. In a more conciliatory tone, however, Dupin called to mind the praiseworthy efforts of some industrialists who had voluntarily acted to improve the lot of their young workers, and he added that the legislation being proposed was hardly a radical attack on entrepreneurial rights, as Gay-Lussac had charged. Although legislation was called for, Dupin concluded, the importance of a strong and free industrial system in France had also to be remembered.

Another interesting issue that received the attention of the peers in the course of their debate involved the inclusion in the child labor bill of a prohibition against work on Sunday. The objection to such a provision, raised by Victor Cousin, was based on the realization that an existing 1814 law already banned Sunday work and that the inclusion of a similar ban as part of a factory act would imply the de facto abrogation of the earlier measure. Although Cousin reported unhappily that the 1814 law was largely ignored, he thought the child labor regulation under debate should content itself to rely on the existing prohibition. The comte de Tascher had the last word on the subject, however, asserting that only a new law compelling Sunday rest would have any force.

After six days of discussion, the bill proposed by the peers' study committee finally came to a vote, and it was adopted by a majority of ninety-one to thirty-five. The only major amendment made to the bill prepared by the child labor committee was the deletion of its provision for compulsory education. The arguments of Charles Dupin and the others who spoke in favor of a relatively strong national child labor law in the Chamber of Peers had obviously had an impact. The advocates of national legislation had been able to build upon the growing concern with the condition of the working classes that had been evident among France's governing elite throughout the 1830s and to capitalize on the increasing interest in child labor that had been apparent since 1837. By the spring of 1840, the champions of reform had found that many in the Chamber of Peers were willing to accept the principle of factory legislation as long as actual restrictions did not go too far. Indeed, most of the debate had taken place over the specific provisions of a child labor law, rather than over the legitimacy of its enactment.

Both the groundwork laid in the 1830s and the rhetorical skills of the reform advocates in the Chamber of Peers had been important in generating support for a national child labor bill, but the atmosphere that led to the adoption of such a bill also owed something to the ongoing propaganda efforts the champions of legislation maintained outside the chamber. The introduction of Cunin-Gridaine's bill at the beginning of 1840 had prompted the composition of several works intended to influence the peers to take swift and decisive action on the child labor issue, for the crusaders who had devoted so much effort to pressuring the government to initiate action were not about to let down their guard when victory appeared to be in sight. As early as January 29, 1840, for example, Achille Penot of the Société industrielle de Mulhouse issued a short report attacking the initial administration factory bill for its weakness, and on February 6, 1840, Jean-Jacques Bourcart published a brochure reiterating his ideas of 1827 and defending child labor legislation against charges that it unfairly impinged upon personal freedom. Awhile later, another familiar voice was again heard in Paris, as Daniel Legrand made known some specific ideas he had about legislation to foster the well-being of factory children. He prepared a brief pamphlet, *Projet de loi sur le travail et l'instruction des enfants*, and as its title indicates, its main thrust was that legislation designed to see to the education of the young ought to go hand in hand with that designed to ensure their protection in industry.[9]

Revised and reissued also in January of 1840 was a pamphlet by an official named Gillet from Paris' eleventh *arrondissement*. Gillet's publication had appeared in its original form just after the 1837 child labor inquiry, and the catalyst for its reappearance was the introduction of Cunin-Gridaine's bill, the rationale for which Gillet characterized as "nothing but a repetition of the lame arguments directed against serious reform in the past." Gillet placed the primary responsibility for the

9. Achille Penot, *Observations sur le projet de loi* . . . (Mulhouse, 1840); Jean-Jacques Bourcart, *Du travail des jeunes ouvriers* (Paris, 1840); [Daniel Legrand], *Projet de loi sur le travail et l'instruction des enfants* . . . (Strasbourg, 1840).

abuse of working children on the misery of their parents, and he argued that a strong child labor law could legitimately encroach on parental authority because that authority was here in conflict with "the moral law of society." He complained that the "noble and holy cause" of child labor reform had before inspired only "silent sympathy" in the chambers, but he added that he was confident the reform movement would now find strong support among the eminent men of the legislature. Gillet punctuated his plea for an effective French factory act with a patriotic appeal: "France has in the past initiated great social improvements, and on that fact depends . . . her ascendancy over other nations. I do not know if we always show enough jealousy over this. England and Prussia have already surpassed us [in some things]. . . . When I see our glorious precedence thus pass into other hands, it seems to me that France is abandoning the place that is assigned to her among the peoples. What will happen if we hesitate to proceed on the path of amelioration [of the child workers' lot]?" [10]

The child labor bill adopted by the Chamber of Peers was sent along to the Chamber of Deputies on April 11, 1840, but the bill did not immediately leave the deputies' committee that was charged with submitting it to the full chamber, for the 1840 session of the lower house was nearing its end and many of its members had already left Paris. The deputies' committee decided nonetheless that during the chamber's summer recess the Ministry of Commerce should conduct a new child labor inquiry to follow up on the one conducted in 1837. On July 1, 1840, a questionnaire went out to the same bodies that were queried three years earlier.[11] At about the same time, deputy for the Seine Hippolyte-Lazare Carnot, who had already conducted some research on the child labor situation in England, was dispatched to report on developments in the German states as well. Thus, the government remained involved with the child labor issue throughout the latter months of 1840.

Nor did interest in the child labor bill wane during the summer and fall of 1840 among the champions of reform, for those who wished to influence the final disposition of the bill recognized that they still had a chance to do so through propaganda and lobbying efforts. As soon as the debate in the upper house was completed, for example, Charles Dupin published a hastily composed volume aimed at winning the Chamber of Deputies over to his position. In his book, Dupin provided an account of the peers' debate on child labor and a comparison of the original

10. Gillet, *Réflexions, passim*, esp. 12, 32, 80, and 15–16.
11. See Deputy Renouard's report in CD, December 12, 1840.

government bill with the bill eventually adopted in the upper house. And he engaged as well in some unabashed propaganda. He began by observing that the reaction of the press to the child labor bill that had emerged from the Chamber of Peers was generally favorable, and after relating how the peers had come to realize the gravity of the child labor issue during their extensive parliamentary debate, he called upon the deputies to show that they, too, "care for the children of our people." Endeavoring to again connect the specific issue of child labor reform to larger concerns about the future of France's industrial society, Dupin characterized the proposed factory act as one that would advance "the welfare of the laboring class, . . . the future of industry . . . [and] the strength of the nation." In an interesting tactical maneuver designed to assure that the Chamber of Deputies would treat the child labor issue with due consideration, Dupin defended the legislators of the lower house against an imagined charge that they would treat the subject frivolously. Dupin even went so far as to list the names of over two dozen deputies whom he expected would address themselves to the matter of factory legislation.

Dupin also took up some specific issues, beginning with the matter of mandatory schooling for factory children, in his book. Reminding his readers that "the future of our constitutional regime" depended on education, Dupin appealed to the deputies to restore the compulsory education provision that had been voted down by the peers. He then went on to defend the prohibition of Sunday labor contained in the bill that was sent to the lower house. He characterized attacks on the prohibition as atheism that "masquerades under the mantle of tolerance," maintaining that to protest, in the name of a hundred thousand Jews, against a measure that would benefit thirty-four million people (as some had apparently done) was insupportable.[12] Like most of the early crusaders for factory legislation, Dupin was essentially against government interventionism, and he felt compelled to defend himself against the accusation that as an advocate of factory legislation, he was a promoter of utopianism. Dupin not only refuted the contention that factory legislation was inherently Saint-Simonian but also reminded his critics that he had openly fought Saint-Simonian ideas in the years following the

12. In a characteristic example of how French Jews often sought to prove their loyalty to France and to protect their status of equal citizenship, the banker and deputy Achille Fould would rise before the Chamber of Deputies during its debate on child labor legislation and confirm Dupin's opinion in these words: "We live in a land where Sunday is observed [as the day of rest]. It is for us to follow the custom. We submit to it with no inconvenience." See Gueneau, "Législation restrictive," 495.

Revolution of 1830. Finally, he concluded his volume with an article-by-article analysis and defense of the factory act as he envisioned it in its final form.[13]

Like the energetic secretary of the peers' committee, its president, the baron de Gérando, also put his thoughts on child labor in writing during this period. He did so in a volume concerning the general question of avenues for the amelioration of the condition of the working classes. For this book he was awarded a prize by the Société industrielle de Mulhouse in 1840. Gérando believed, as he had indicated earlier, that it was most important to rescue the children of the poor from their destructive environments, and in his study he took up the then-immediate issue of child labor reform in the context of a more general program for the reshaping of industrial society. Gérando pointed with favor to the pending child labor law. "If the authorities have in the past overstepped their prerogatives," he wrote, "in our days, perhaps, they are too unsure of themselves and thus weaken themselves still further, for they lack confidence in their rights and in their power." He suggested that as a complement to government action must come increased efforts on the part of the working classes to gain education and provide a positive family experience. He also counseled factory owners to show more concern for their workers, and he urged laborers to nurture the growth of mutual aid associations. So too, Gérando expressed the hope that *patronage* societies for youths would proliferate. These newly-created voluntary associations were designed to allow the privileged classes to provide both practical aid (often in the form of apprenticeship training) and moral guidance to the children of the less fortunate.[14]

Evidently feeling that their pronouncements early in 1840 were not sufficient, both the Société industrielle de Mulhouse and Daniel Legrand reiterated their positions a few months later in several letters and pamphlets they prepared in anticipation of the child labor debate in the Chamber of Deputies. Both the society and Legrand dispatched new communications to the policy makers in Paris, and both apparently reissued some of their earlier writings on child labor in newly edited collections. On the heels of the peers' debate, the Société industrielle de Saint-Quentin also addressed a pamphlet, prepared by its president,

13. Dupin, *Travail*, passim.

14. Joseph Marie de Gérando, *Des progrès de l'industrie dans leurs rapports avec le bien-être physique et morale de la classe ouvrière* (Paris, 1845), 61–119. On *patronage* societies, see Lee Shai Weissbach, "*Oeuvre industrielle, oeuvre morale*: The *Sociétés de patronage* of Nineteenth-Century France," *French Historical Studies*, XV (Spring, 1987).

Mallet, to the decision makers in Paris. Mallet's work stressed the importance of inspection for effective enforcement and urged that an independent inspectorate be created to oversee the implementation of factory legislation.[15]

One of Daniel Legrand's most interesting appeals to the legislature in this period was presented in the form of a fictional tale designed to illustrate the suffering that would result if no legal provision was made to prohibit the institution of a relay system in factories. The relay system had come into use in England after the passage of the 1833 factory act because even though the act allowed children under thirteen a workday of no more than nine hours, it permitted them to do their work anytime between 5 A.M. and 9 P.M. Employers thus could schedule the work of their young laborers on a rotating basis, so that the adults with whom they worked would maintain a full workday. This practice gave rise to a number of abuses. Some manufacturers kept children at work more than nine hours in the confusion of the scheduling; others required children to be available at the factory for entire workdays yet observed the letter of the law by having them actually labor no more than nine hours. Legrand warned that a relay system could also lead to employing more rather than less youngsters in manufacturing, to the continual replacement of children over thirteen by younger ones, and to the maintenance of a grueling and uncompromised sixteen-hour workday for adults. His warning proved to be a cry in the wilderness, it seems, as the dangers of the relay system went largely ignored by both the proponents and the enemies of child labor legislation.

The initiation of a legislative debate on child labor in 1840 even elicited reactions from radical social critics for the first time, though these critics saw the child labor bill under discussion as an innocuous and meaningless measure upon which they could heap only scorn. Eugène Buret, for example, complained that "while there are laws prohibiting the landowner from gathering his grain prematurely, and from harvesting his vines in bloom, there are none prohibiting industry from abusing the nascent generations." He believed that among the faults of the child labor law under consideration was its failure to address the true educational needs of factory children. "We know what kind of moral education one receives in the factory," Buret observed sarcastically, and, arguing

15. See the manuscript letter from Dollfus of Mulhouse in AN, F12–4704; Société industrielle de Mulhouse, *Documens relatifs au travail des jeunes ouvriers* (Mulhouse, *ca.* 1841); [Legrand], *Lettre . . . à M. le Baron Charles Dupin*; Mallet, *Travail des enfans* (Saint-Quentin, 1840). See also Touren, *Loi de 1841*, 94.

that children acquired no real skills in factory labor, he asked, "What will become of these thousands of young workers, veritable orphans of industry, when they reach the age of fifteen?" Buret concluded that the "protection" offered by the proposed child labor law was "absolutely insufficient."[16]

Similarly, Louis Blanc could not see much good in the reforms being proposed, though he was extremely sympathetic to the children of the working classes, who, he said, "spend their lives in the filth of the gutter until they are able to augment the wealth of their families by a few coins through painful and brutalizing labor." Blanc observed cynically that "the philanthropy of the legislators is so great that the Chamber of Peers has fixed the age at which a child may be made a part of a machine at eight years."[17] Buret and Blanc both believed that a fundamental change in the relationship between labor and capital was necessary before such social problems as the abuse of child labor could be dealt with successfully. Their approach to remedying the plight of child laborers was a far cry from the approach that dominated the ongoing campaign for reform, and in the final analysis it was to have no perceptible effect on the debate over child labor legislation.

By the time the Chamber of Deputies convened for its 1841 session, it had available to it a wealth of data for consideration: not only the thoughts of numerous propagandists but also the results of the new Ministry of Commerce inquiry and a report on Carnot's mission to Germany. Although the child labor inquiry conducted in 1840 seems to have been taken even less seriously than the one in 1837 had been, its results probably had some effect on the deputies, and they are worth a brief consideration.

The circular that had initiated the 1840 inquiry had contained a report on the government's initial child labor bill and an account of the subsequent bill adopted by the Chamber of Peers. It had also included a third proposal for legislation, which the child labor committee of the Chamber of Deputies had conceived early in the summer under the chairmanship of Cunin-Gridaine, who was then no longer minister of commerce. The respondents to the 1840 inquiry had been asked to submit their replies with these three suggested systems of legislation in mind.

16. Eugène Buret, *De la misère des classes laborieuses en Angleterre et en France* (Paris, 1840), II, 37–38. See also Rigaudias-Weiss, *Enquêtes ouvrieres.*
17. Blanc, *Organisation du travail,* 21, 32.

With less than a dozen exceptions, the hundred or so bodies that submitted returns in 1840 all recognized the necessity of some sort of legislation to protect working children. A few even wanted to see a factory act that would speak to the problems of adult laborers as well. The small number of respondents who objected to the very concept of labor legislation still contended that the misery of the workers was not due to factory conditions, that industry was beginning to regulate itself, and that complicated regulations would only force employers to stop hiring children completely, leaving the families of those children destitute. Near unanimity was expressed over not only the necessity of a child labor law but also the desirability of its being national in scope. In answering a question about which industries should be covered by the law, a few returns indicated a desire for universal coverage, but most wanted to see at least small, family-operated firms exempted, for fear of intruding upon parental authority while also rendering the law difficult to enforce.

The majority of respondents to the 1840 inquiry indicated that they favored a minimum age of eight years for employment, though some wanted it to be as high as twelve. Almost all the returns agreed that the number of working hours permitted youngsters should be graduated with their age, and there was general agreement that the plan adopted by the Chamber of Peers, allowing children eight to twelve years old an eight-hour day and children twelve to sixteen a twelve-hour day, was satisfactory. Suggestions from those who were unhappy with the peers' scheme included some that would make the minimum age for employment relatively high and would allow children to work the same hours as adults and several variously graduated systems other than the one favored by the majority: six hours for the younger children and eight for the older, nine for the younger and thirteen for the older, eleven for the younger and twelve for the older. Most respondents agreed that children should be prohibited from working at night and on Sundays, but some proposed exceptions in cases where a fire had to be kept burning or machines had to be cleaned.

In addressing the question of compulsory education for factory children, most of the respondents in 1840, like the child labor committee of the Chamber of Deputies, suggested that a provision for schooling be reintroduced into the child labor bill. A return from the highly industrialized Eure reflected the general feeling about enforced schooling for factory children: an education provision, it said, was "the most essential point of the law." The respondents to the 1840 survey did, however, shy away from the idea of placing any authority over the enforcement of compulsory education other than the factory owners who employed the children concerned.

Unlike the 1837 inquiry, the 1840 probe asked those consulted to comment on the need to establish an inspection system to oversee the implementation of factory legislation. The government's original bill had had no specific provisions for inspection, leaving the problem to local authorities, and the bill passed by the Chamber of Peers proposed leaving inspection in the hands of existing communal and departmental officials. The committee organized in the Chamber of Deputies, by contrast, suggested the nomination of special factory inspectors. Those responding to the 1840 inquiry had still other suggestions for the organization of inspection. These included empowering prefects to designate factory inspectors from the ranks of existing functionaries or charging the inspectors of primary education with factory inspection as well. There were also those who felt strongly that the appointment of officials charged solely with factory inspection was vital, especially in heavily industrialized departments. Proponents of this view reasoned that to place the task of overseeing child labor legislation on the shoulders of officials with preexisting responsibilities was not only to depend on people lacking knowledge of factory production but to burden the overburdened still further. Even those who agreed that a separate corps of inspectors was needed, however, could not agree on how they were to be chosen or on whether or not they were to be salaried.

The child labor inquiry of 1840 revealed a considerable diversity of views among local notables concerning specific aspects of factory reform and a general reluctance on their part to countenance overly extensive government interference in industrial affairs. However, the inquiry did leave the distinct impression that there was far greater support for a national child labor law in France in 1840 than there had been just a few years earlier. So little opposition to factory legislation was voiced in 1840 in part because the primary respondents to the government survey of that year were departmental councils, *conseils généraux*, rather than bodies that represented business and manufacturing interests more directly. Only about half as many *chambres consultatives des arts et manufactures* responded to the 1840 survey as had responded to the one in 1837, for example, and returns from *conseils généraux* outnumbered responses from all other sources combined. Moreover, by the middle of 1840 there seemed to be little point in raising fundamental objections to a concept that had already been accepted by the Chamber of Peers and about which most provincial notables cared very little in any case.[18]

Like the responses to the 1840 inquiry, Carnot's mission to Germany revealed a panoply of attitudes concerning child labor legislation. Carnot's report showed that recently enacted factory legislation in Prussia— legislation based on the English model but without a provision for a paid inspectorate—had evidently been received with satisfaction by all concerned. Neither factory owners nor heads of families had serious objections to it. In Saxony, by contrast, widespread opposition to labor legislation had stalled all attempts to see it adopted in that relatively industrialized state. Carnot reported that in Bohemia there was also entrepreneurial opposition to child labor legislation, though some decrees concerning working youngsters and their education were in force there nonetheless.[19] There was clearly much background information for the deputies to digest in their consideration of child labor legislation, if they were inclined to do so.

When the full Chamber of Deputies finally undertook its discussion of the employment of children late in December of 1840, a new cabinet had been installed and Laurent Cunin-Gridaine, chairman of the deputies' child labor committee, found himself once again the minister of commerce. The debate in the lower house was quite extensive, and it allowed those manufacturing interests that were still opposed to any legislation one more chance to speak out. Deputies from the Nord and from the Seine-Inférieure who were themselves factory owners again argued that workers' misery was their own fault, that a labor law's application only to larger factories was unfair, and that, in general, the state had no authority to inhibit the right of laborers to work and the right of entrepreneurs to dominate their own shops. Abel-François Villemain, again the minister of public instruction in the new cabinet, answered this final objection of the manufacturers with the powerful statement that

18. Responses were received from 67 *conseils généraux*, 21 *chambres de commerce*, 21 *chambres consultatives des arts et manufactures*, and 20 *conseils des prud'hommes*. Only 106 of these 129 responses were complete, however, as 23 responding bodies claimed to have no industries in their region and thus to be unable to furnish facts or render opinions. Material on the 1840 inquiry is in AN, F12–4704 and F12–4706. For the results of the inquiry as summarized by Renouard, see CD, December 12, 1840. The *Moniteur* in December, 1840, published a summary of the probe, on which Touren, *Loi de 1841*, 84ff is based. The 1840 inquiry is also discussed in Gueneau, "Législation restrictive," 479–88.

19. Hippolyte-Lazare Carnot, *Lettre à Monsieur le Ministre de l'Agriculture et du Commerce sur la législation que règle, dans quelques états de l'Allemagne, les conditions du travail des jeunes ouvriers* (Paris, 1840). See also Ducpétiaux, *Condition*, 11–13, and Horner, *Employment*, 94–104.

government "not only has a right to intervene in this matter, but an obligation; it is a debt owed to society, and a debt past due."[20]

Just as the deputies opposed to reform aired their views in the chamber, so also did others who wanted a factory law far stronger than the one under consideration. The manufacturer Victor Grandin of Elbeuf, for example, argued that the purview of factory legislation should be expanded to include even small shops. He was apparently concerned lest the small competitors of large firms such as his own escape the labor law's provisions. Alban de Villeneuve-Bargemont, who now had a seat in the legislature, approached the matter of strengthening the law from a more philosophical perspective. He and a few other deputies suggested that if a factory law was to have a salutary effect on the working classes, it should be applied to the entire laboring population. In the end, however, those who wanted to make extreme alterations in the course of child labor reform had little influence on the deputies' debate.

Turning to the specifics of the child labor bill before them, the deputies resolved the initially divisive issue of compulsory education quickly. The lobbying of Dupin and others and the results of the 1840 inquiry convinced them to require that factory children have some schooling. Taking up the controversial matter of factory inspection and of the enforcement of child labor regulations in general, the deputies considered the variety of proposals that had been aired and in the end opted for a system of special child labor inspectors. The determination of its exact nature, however, was left extremely vague. The child labor bill adopted by the Chamber of Deputies was basically the same as the one passed by the peers the previous March, but with provisions for education and inspection added and its applicability slightly broadened. The deputies approved the bill by a vote of 185 to 50.

Cunin-Gridaine returned the child labor bill to the Chamber of Peers in February of 1841, announcing before its members that, despite his responsibility for the original administration proposal, the stronger bill adopted by the deputies now had his complete support. Charles Dupin tried to stimulate additional discussion of the entire child labor issue, but the peers were content to accept, with virtually no debate, the bill as it was sent to them from the lower house. On February 23, 1841, they adopted it by a vote of 104 to 2. The second vote on the bill in the

20. For the deputies' debate, see CD, December 21–24, 26, 28–29, 1840. See also Alban de Villeneuve-Bargemont, *Discours prononcé à la Chambre des députés . . . dans la discussion du projet de loi sur le travail des enfans dans les manufactures* (Metz, ca. 1841), and Gueneau, "Législation restrictive," 494–96.

Chamber of Deputies was simply *pro forma*, and this time the bill passed by a margin of 201 votes, 218 to 17.[21] The law was promulgated on March 22, 1841.

The provisions of France's new child labor law were embodied in thirteen articles. The first of its articles defined the establishments that were covered by the provisions contained in subsequent articles as all those establishments that depended on mechanical power or the continuous maintenance of a fire and all those that employed over twenty workers. The law's second article declared eight to be the minimum age for employment in factories covered by the new legislation, and it established maximum workdays. Children eight to twelve years old were allowed to labor no more than eight hours, and children twelve to sixteen were limited to twelve hours a day. This article also required that youngsters have breaks during their work and that certificates be issued by the authorities to verify the age of working children. Article three defined night work as any work performed between 9 P.M. and 5 A.M. and prohibited all children under thirteen years of age from engaging in it. Night work by older children was to be tolerated only in exceptional situations, where their presence was judged indispensable, and every two hours of their work was to be counted as three. Article four excluded all protected youngsters from work on Sundays and legal holidays, and article five contained the rather demanding compulsory education provision inserted into the factory act by the Chamber of Deputies. It required that working children under the age of twelve attend school even as they worked. Children over twelve were exempted from school attendance only if they possessed a certificate issued by the local mayor that showed they had completed their primary education. The fifth article also required that heads of subject establishments keep a record of their young employees and that they enter the dates of their employment in their *livrets*, their personal employment booklets. The sixth article charged mayors with providing a *livret* for each child, showing the child's full name, age, place of birth, and place of residence, and the child's record of school attendance.

Articles seven and eight revealed the extent to which the legislators were satisfied to rely upon the discretion and the initiative of the administration in the implementation of the child labor law they had enacted. The wide-ranging seventh article of the new law granted the administration the right to add subsequent regulations to the existing legislation.

21. CP, February 23, 1841; CD, March 11, 1841.

The administration could extend the law to establishments not initially covered; it could raise the minimum age for employment or shorten the workday of children in industries deemed to be particularly hazardous or exhausting; and it could even exclude workers under sixteen completely from certain industries or from the performance of certain tasks. By the same token, the authorities could grant a dispensation for children to work on Sundays and holidays or at night. Article eight of the child labor law placed upon the administration the responsibility for seeing that the new law be put into effect, that high moral standards be observed in protected shops, that both primary and religious instruction be made available, that child laborers not be physically abused, and that the general health and safety of young workers be protected.

The law's ninth article simply dictated that a copy of the new legislation's provisions be posted in all establishments to which they applied, and article ten concerned the naming of factory inspectors. Because factory inspection had emerged as the most controversial aspect of the reform issue, the Child Labor Law of 1841 did not delineate how factory inspectors were to be selected or organized; these matters were left to the administration. However, the law did require the creation of some system of inspection, and it did provide for certain rights inspectors would have in order to facilitate their work. An inspector would be allowed, for example, to bring with him a physician on his factory inspection tours. Article eleven directed that factory inspectors prepare reports of any violations they encountered; an inspector's report would be considered proof of a violation unless counterevidence was forthcoming. First-time violators of the child labor law were to be brought before a justice of the peace, according to the law's twelfth article. Justices were given the right to levy fines of up to two hundred francs in cases involving the employment of underage children, and fines of up to fifteen francs in other child labor cases. Those charged with a second offense within twelve months of their first were to be brought before a police court, where fines were one hundred francs in general and could reach five hundred francs if underage children were involved. The final article of the child labor law provided for its taking effect six months after its promulgation.

The lopsided final vote on the factory bill in the two chambers of the French legislature should not be taken to mean that there was overwhelming support for the Child Labor Law of 1841 where there had been at best only hesitant and lukewarm support for factory legislation a few years earlier. The truth is that there was still much indifference or even hostility toward child labor reform, even among the members of the Chamber of Peers and of the Chamber of Deputies, those people being directly lobbied by the champions of legislation. Of the peers voting on the child labor bill on its first reading, 28 percent had opposed the measure, as had 21 percent of the deputies voting on the first reading. Moreover, about half the peers and deputies of France did not take part in any balloting on the measure.[22] The members of the chambers were, after all, overwhelmingly from landed society, and many of them remained unconcerned with the child labor issue altogether, despite the best efforts of the crusaders for reform.[23]

It should also be recognized that while enough lawmakers were willing to accept the idea of a child labor law to allow for its passage, they were not willing to make that law as rigorous as many reformers would have liked. Even though the advocates of reform, led by Charles Dupin, had been able to convince the legislature to reject the initial government bill of 1840 in favor of one patterned on the stronger English Factory Act of 1833, the French law in its final form was not made applicable beyond the largest shops, nor did it require the paid factory inspectors that the English experience had shown to be critical.[24] The continuing reluctance over child labor reform in much of French society would be reflected further in the difficulty the new law would face when its implementation was attempted.

22. See Tudesq, *Notables*, II, 583.
23. See, for example, Sherman Kent, *Electoral Procedure Under Louis-Philippe* (New Haven, 1937), 57–58.
24. For comments on the expressed objections to paid inspection, primarily from within entrepreneurial circles, see Tudesq, *Notables*, II, 594; Bénet, *Capitalisme libéral*, 303; and Jean Bron, *Histoire du mouvement ouvrier français* (Paris, 1968), I, 97.

FIVE

The Initiation of
Child Labor Restrictions

The Child Labor Law of 1841 was not in itself a radical measure. Its provisions, even if they could be strictly enforced, would not cause any major industrial reorganization. Indeed, the inherent weakness of the law helps to explain how it came to be passed at all. Nonetheless, the enactment of the Child Labor Law of 1841 was significant for a number of reasons, not the least of which was that it demonstrated the power of lobbying. The adoption of the law revealed that it was possible for a program of legislation to be instituted in France through the efforts of a handful of crusaders, even if they were acting in defiance of prevailing public attitudes, as long as those crusaders had some access to the centers of power and could build a case for their program that would appeal to the instincts of the governing elite.

Moreover, the passage of the law marked the emergence of a serious state concern with the supervision and protection of childhood in France. In the early decades of the nineteenth century, those who controlled government and society were becoming increasingly interested in the nature of childhood. They were beginning to recognize childhood as a tremendously important stage of life, during which individuals are both very vulnerable and very impressionable. At the same time, they were coming to believe that they, as privileged members of society, had a certain obligation to protect and guide the children of those whom they considered ill-equipped to do so themselves. The Child Labor Law of 1841 was enacted in large part because the privileged classes were starting to see in the protection and education of working-class youths a way of improving the entire laboring population and ultimately society as a whole. As one Catholic social critic observed during this period, "it is through childhood that God renders centuries corrigible, and nations susceptible to healing."[1] In a sense, child labor reformers in the era of the July Monarchy were as much interested in shaping the future of French society as they were in protecting working class children per se, and though they had no intention of creating an elaborate apparatus of state intervention, in retrospect the Child Labor Law of 1841 can be seen as the first element in the system of governmental social control that would eventually emerge in France.[2] There was, indeed, an inadvertent hint of things to come in a comment made by Abel-François Villemain during the legislative debates on child labor. "One starts with what is possible," he had observed. "One takes the great examples of abuse and changes them; . . . one begins the work of reform, and leaves to others its perfection."[3]

The issue of child labor reform in midnineteenth-century France was so closely bound to the elite's reevaluation of the importance of childhood that it is even possible to see an association between the passage of a factory law and the development of a new precision in the use of the word *child*. In traditional society, the term *child* (*enfant*) had always been used, rather loosely, to designate anyone from an infant to an adolescent in his teens. In general, as long as an individual remained a socially dependent being, he was referred to as a child, and the distinction between infants and children in the modern sense, as well as between children and adolescents, always remained vague. Only when individuals established their independence did they cease to be children in the popular mind. It was generally marriage, and perhaps the acquisition of some property, that marked the entry into young adulthood. Individuals who remained in subservient positions, such as domestics or soldiers, were sometimes referred to as children even after they became adults in a biological sense.[4]

But for those within the elite who were developing a better understanding of the nature of childhood, such a loose definition would no longer suffice. When they began to see youth as a distinct phase of life

1. Armand de Melun, quoted in Amédée D'Andigné, *Un Apôtre de la charité: Armand de Melun* (Paris, 1961), 168.

2. On the development of state intervention for social control, see Donzelot, *Policing*.

3. Quoted in E. Levasseur, *Histoire des classes ouvrières et de l'industrie en France de 1789 à 1870* (Paris, 1903–1904), II, 128n.

4. Ariès, *Centuries*, 25–29; Gillis, *Youth and History*, 5–9; and Musgrove, *Youth and the Social Order*, 33–37.

with important ramifications for future development, and when they began to devise a system of protective legislation, they also began to construct a more precise definition of childhood. Their new definition was based on considerations of chronological age and developmental factors rather than on social status. For the purpose of writing legislation, in fact, they had to devise a strict, age-related definition of childhood. In setting the age limits that would apply in the restriction of child labor, the framers of the 1841 child labor bill had obviously relied on the English precedent, but they had also begun to confront the concept of age grading and the modern distinction between childhood and adolescence. When the French legislature enacted the Child Labor Law of 1841, it also produced one of the country's first legally precise definitions of childhood.

It is interesting, incidentally, that in all the discussions of age classifications and limitations that surrounded the formulation of France's first child labor legislation, there was little distinction made between boys and girls. Although many of those concerned with the *question sociale* were beginning to discuss the unique role of women in working-class society, the reformers who were considering the protection of laboring youths apparently viewed children as an essentially genderless category of individuals. When they talked of the adverse effects of mixing the sexes on the shop floor, for example, they seemed to consider these effects equally damaging to boys and to girls.

Just as the factory law of 1841 was tremendously important as the nation's first substantial child protection measure, so it also had great significance as the first major piece of legislation to break with the rather consistent policy of noninterventionism that had characterized the relationship between government and industry in France since the French Revolution. Even though the breach with the policy of nonintervention was premised on the idea that children are not truly free to interact with their employers in the first place, the passage of the law indicated that there was a new flexibility in French liberalism—a flexibility that recognized the need for state intervention in cases where the greater good of society was at stake. There was also now a willingness on the part of the privileged classes to challenge paternal authority, even if only on the assumption that working-class parents were incapable of properly exercising their rights over their children in certain instances. Those who were concerned with political ideology during the July Monarchy realized that the Child Labor Law of 1841 was as important for its precedent-setting theoretical implications as it was for its practical provisions, and much of the early reaction to the new law stressed its relationship to liberal theory. *Lois principales de 1841*, a contemporary annotated reference volume, praised the legislation for erecting "a system that protects youth without overlooking the sacred rights of paternal authority and the principle of the right to work."[5] The Social Catholic journal *L'Atelier* belatedly welcomed the legislation as the beginning of government intervention between the "exploiters and the exploited."[6] Speaking on the child labor law before the Académie des sciences morales et politiques in 1845, Hippolyte Passy argued that "the government may be mistaken in the protective measures it adopts, but its right to intervene is incontestable." In the same year and from the same platform, Jérôme-Adolphe Blanqui went so far as to proclaim: "The intervention of the government can have nothing but good results. . . . With us, great and lasting things have been accomplished only with the aid of the State. The State demands sacrifices from the young, it enrolls them in the army; it should look after them, protect their health and vigor, and assure them the benefits of education."[7]

Increasingly, even some of the most ardently liberal political thinkers of the 1840s were expressing a willingness to accept state intervention on behalf of minors, and it was the debate over child labor reform that had been instrumental in bringing them to this position. Gustave Dupuynode, for example, reasoned thus in 1845: "Child labor legislation . . . is without doubt a contradiction of the principle of competition, but a necessary, legitimate contradiction. Political economy, which demands that obstacles be removed, that private interests be trusted, does not alone direct the world; with it, above it, is morality and discretion. . . . The state owes children protection; it owes other persons only freedom." Similarly, Théodore Fix wrote supportively of the child labor law in 1846, though he was careful to qualify his praise for the measure with the observation that "it would be more difficult to limit the adult workday [for] that would be to restrain liberty."[8]

Just as the supporters of government intervention on behalf of minors often recognized the implications that the passage of a child labor law had for liberal doctrine, so, too, did many of it opponents. Pronouncements against factory legislation had for years been phrased in theoreti-

5. J. B. Duvergier, *Lois principales de 1841* (Paris, ca. 1842), 2.
6. Quoted in Touren, *Loi de 1841*, 107.
7. G. S., "Revue mensuelle des travaux de l'Académie des sciences morales et politiques," *JE*, XII (September, 1845), 164, 165.
8. Gustave Dupuynode, *Des lois du travail* (Paris, 1845), 116–19; Théodore Fix, *Observations sur l'état des classes ouvrières* (Paris, 1846), 275.

cal terms: as defenses of the right to work, of paternal authority, and of the sacrosanct rights of the entrepreneur. Objections to the law enacted in 1841 continued in the same vein. The most articulate critics of the new legislation attacked it not primarily for its specific provisions but for the precedent of state interference with industry that it set. In the legislature, the physician J.-L. Gay-Lussac had called the child labor law "the beginning of Saint-Simonism or of Phalansterianism," and Gustave de Beaumont had worried aloud that "today it is only a question of under-age children, but surely it will not be long before it becomes also a question . . . of regulating the work of adults." Beaumont eventually came to accept the notion that "it is necessary to guard against a proclamation of the principle of nonintervention by the State in terms that are too absolute," but he always cautioned that it was essential "to pinpoint the instances where intervention is bad and those where it can be beneficial and effective."[9]

Perhaps the chief spokesman for the opposition was the liberal philosopher Charles Dunoyer. He denounced the child labor law because of the rift with classic liberal doctrine it represented, and he continually expounded on his position in print and on the floor of the Académie des sciences morales et politiques in the years immediately after 1841. A staunch defender of entrepreneurial innocence in the maltreatment of children and a frequent critic of the child labor law's practical shortcomings, Dunoyer was, above all, an opponent of the law's theoretical basis. Despite his having hinted to the Société industrielle de Mulhouse in 1828 that child labor restrictions were perhaps permissible, by the 1840s he was apparently unwilling to allow any breach of laissez-faire. "It is not for [society] to determine, [even] in the interest of humanity or of security, the length of the workday," he wrote. He argued that where the abuse of children was concerned, it was not the economic system but "inhumanity" itself that should be attacked.[10]

Its theoretical implications aside, the child labor law was intended to produce some immediate practical results. Its stated aim, after all, was to curtail the abuse of child laborers. Many of the details concerning the

9. See Levasseur, *Histoire*, II, 126–28, and G. S., "Revue," 162.
10. Charles Dunoyer, *De la liberté du travail* (Paris, 1845), II, 367–72. See also L. V., "Revue mensuelle des travaux de l'Académie des sciences morales et politiques," *JE*, X (December, 1844), 74–75; G. S. "Revue," 161ff; and Edmond Villey, *L'Oeuvre économique de Charles Dunoyer* (Paris, 1899), esp. 111ff, 209ff. On the break with liberalism represented by child labor legislation more generally, see Albert Copin, *Les Doctrines économique et les débuts de la législation ouvrière en France* (Lille, 1943), 37ff.

implementation of the law had been left in the hands of the administration, however, so the actual institution of controls depended on government action. The most important matter left in the hands of the administration, the initiation of factory inspection, was the subject of a circular dispatched by Cunin-Gridaine at the Ministry of Commerce on March 25, 1841. The circular was addressed to the prefects of France, and it instructed them to set about the work of choosing the local factory inspectors called for by the law.

Although the job was to be nonsalaried and there were areas where it was rather hard to find people willing to fill the new positions, at least some ambitious Frenchmen believed that appointment as a factory inspector was an honor worth pursuing. Applicants seeking positions as inspectors used various approaches in their efforts to win appointment, and, in general, they argued their own cases. One man cited his long involvement with education as a qualification. Another produced advertising copy from his textile firm to uphold his claim that he had the necessary background. Yet another, describing himself as both a physician and a lawyer, expressed the hope that he would merit appointment on the basis of his competence in two relevant professions. Sometimes applications for the position of inspector were less direct. The wife of one doctor wrote on behalf of her husband; the minister of justice recommended a functionary in his office. At least one man apparently hoped sympathy would win him a post, and a salaried one at that. Charles Lehérard pleaded that money be found to hire him as a paid factory inspector, since he was not only a well-qualified applicant but also the victim of a disaster: his factory had recently burned down, and he was faced with destitution.[11]

At the outset, it seemed that at least some officials were making an effort to live up to the demands that the new child labor law had placed upon the government. Not only did the Ministry of Commerce turn its attention to the appointment of factory inspectors within days of the promulgation of the 1841 law, but it soon began to issue a series of memoranda dealing with other aspects of the law's implementation. A circular of August 14, 1841, for example, initiated a survey aimed at determining what the administration should do with the power granted it to clarify and revise the list of industries in which child labor practices

11. See the circular in AN, F12–4704, reproduced in *Documents relatifs au travail des enfants et des femmes* (Brussels, 1871), 302–304. Various letters concerning the appointment of inspectors are in AN, F12–4708.

were to be regulated. The circular asked every prefect to list and categorize the industrial establishments in his jurisdiction to which the factory law applied. It also asked each prefect to indicate those industries or factories to which he believed the child labor law should be extended, those in which the minimum age should be raised, and those from which children should be excluded entirely. Finally, each prefect was asked to suggest in which establishments the provisions forbidding night and Sunday work should be relaxed. Responses to this survey came in slowly, in part because many prefects (willing enough to identify those factories in which the new law clearly applied) were reluctant to respond to the more complicated and subjective latter questions of the survey, and also because many prefects lacked the resources to gather any of the information requested. As late as September, 1845, no responses had yet been received from either the Seine-Inférieure or the Rhône, both of which were among France's more industrialized departments.[12] Nevertheless, a circular issued on October 25, 1841, did contain preliminary definitions of twenty-two industries in which child labor restrictions were to apply broadly, twelve industries from which children were to be totally excluded, and four in which the provisions of the law could be slightly relaxed.[13]

Many other circulars issued in this period also demonstrate the involvement of the Ministry of Commerce in the implementation of the factory law. A circular of April, 1842, dealt with correspondence between prefects, subprefects, and child labor inspectors, for example; and a circular of September, 1843, concerned the documents required by the law. Nor was it the central government alone that took steps to set enforcement of the child labor law in motion. In some departments, most notably the Nord, departmental authorities initially took an active interest in making the child labor law work. Despite the fact that many local notables had opposed the institution of child labor restrictions, the prefecture of the Nord seemed intent on enforcing the law of the land. It printed its own posters advertising the law's provisions, circulated models of the *livrets* to be issued, and distributed a pamphlet explaining a departmental regulation of fifty-two articles enacted to ensure execution of the law. In the Isère, as well as in the Nord, the prefect's office printed standardized forms to be used by factory inspectors. The prefect of the Seine-Inférieure sent a set of printed instructions concerning child labor

12. Correspondence in AN, F12–4713.
13. AN, F12–4706, F12–4708. The circular of August 14 is also in *Documents*, 304–307.

to functionaries in his department, and he also placed an article in the local press announcing the initiation of controls on child labor.[14]

But despite the genuine early interest of certain key government figures in seeing the new child labor law implemented efficiently and completely, it soon became apparent that their good intentions would not be enough to overcome the serious problems inherent in the legislation and the serious opposition that the law still faced. The crusaders who were responsible for the adoption of child labor legislation in France had been able to convince many legislators, government officials, and community leaders of the necessity for such legislation. Convincing working-class parents and ordinary entrepreneurs—those most directly involved with the employment of children—proved, however, to be a much more difficult task. These groups were much less willing to grant that child labor was an evil to be eradicated.

Most factory owners had allowed the struggle for child labor legislation to get by them largely unnoticed. Forced to deal with the reality of its existence, however, many took steps to circumvent or even to defy it. Often factory owners simply did not want to go to the trouble of conforming to the new regulations, and some still believed that the new legislation would be economically damaging to industry. Others, like the crystal manufacturer Maës at Clichy, near Paris, complained that the new law interfered with the voluntary paternalism of factory owners, to the detriment of their young workers.[15] In some places, entrepreneurs complied with the law fully, until they discovered that their compliance put them at a disadvantage vis-à-vis rivals who ignored the measure in whole or in part. Even in the Nord, where the child labor law had been met initially with such enthusiasm by the departmental authorities, the prefect soon adopted the attitude of business and explained in 1843 that the hard times local industry was experiencing had convinced him "of the necessity to temporize [in implementing the law] for fear of rendering the position of the industrialists and of the workers more disastrous." The prefect of the Ardennes expressed much the same sentiment as late as 1847.[16]

Entrepreneurial noncooperation was manifested in various ways. Some manufacturers refused to keep the records required by the child labor legislation or produced falsified records. Factory owners at Roubaix in

14. AN, F12–4706; *Documents*, 307–309; AN, F12–4712, F12–4713.
15. The Maës case is described in various letters of 1846 in AN, F12–4713.
16. Letter from the Nord, July 6, 1843, in AN, F12–4712; letter from the Ardennes, November 10, 1847, in AN, F12–4709.

the Nord and at Duclair, Maromme, and Pavilly in the Seine-Inférieure refused to allow members of the local child labor commissions to inspect their plants. It was not uncommon for entrepreneurs unhappy with the new measure to obey the letter of the law but ignore its spirit. They would, for example, reduce the size of their work force or adopt a putting-out system, in which laborers did their work outside the shop, in order to avoid having to comply with the legislation, or they would adopt a relay system with all its faults. At times entrepreneurs simply fired all their young workers. Such was the case in the Loire, where a report of April, 1846, complained that the number of children employed in protected factories had dropped from nine hundred to only two or three hundred because of mass firings and further that most of the children dismissed simply went to work in unprotected shops. Even Jean-Jacques Bourcart fired all his workers under the age of twelve.[17] This unintended result of the law was especially hard on the working families whose children were turned out of their jobs, for the income the children had earned was critical to the families' survival. Although manufacturers, such as Bourcart, who dismissed their youngest employees probably believed they were acting in the youngsters' best interests, their behavior reveals a surprising lack of sensitivity to the nature of working-class family economies. The problem of summary firings had, in fact, been forseen by both enemies and supporters of factory legislation. Some opponents of child labor legislation had cited this problem in their responses to the Ministry of Commerce inquiry of 1840. On the other side, the *Populaire*, a journal which generally praised the passage of the child labor law, asked rhetorically, "When the manufacturers expell their young workers, who will give them bread?"[18] No precautions against wholesale firings had been taken, however.

In general, parents and children were only too eager to cooperate with factory owners in circumventing the child labor law. Thinking in terms of their own precarious family economies, parents would not voluntarily cut off what they saw as a vital source of income. Moreover, traditional work patterns still had a strong hold on many working-class families, and children were naturally expected to go to work as early as possible. Working-class children themselves often wished to enter factory employment at an early age in order to show, as the English factory inspector

17. Letter concerning Roubaix, February 20, 1844, in AN, F12–4712; letter concerning Duclair, Maromme and Pavilly, March 27, 1843, in AN, F12–4713; Report of April 10, 1846, in AN, F12–4711; Report of October, 1843, in AN, F12–4712.

18. Quoted in Touren, *Loi de 1841*, 106.

Leonard Horner observed in reference to France, that they were "no longer in a state of pupilage."[19]

A reminiscence of Louis Wolowski reveals the attitude of many mothers and fathers toward their working children. In 1868, lecturing to a class in political economy and industrial legislation, he told of an incident that had taken place just after the promulgation of the 1841 factory law. Wolowski had accepted a position as a volunteer factory inspector and was visiting a spinning mill in Paris' faubourg Saint-Antoine when he encountered "a pale, sickly child" of seven and the child's mother. Both labored full workdays in the mill. "What are you doing?" Wolowski demanded of the mother. "You are killing your child! This cannot go on; the law prohibits it, and even without the provisions of the law, your motherly instinct ought to deter you." The mother's response was sharp and to the point: "I was raised this way, and now it is my child's turn to do what I did; I suffered this pain, now it is his turn to suffer. Why do you interfere?"[20]

The problem of enforcing the child labor law in the face of widespread entrepreneurial and parental opposition was compounded by the fact that, despite the initial eagerness of some of them for appointment, the factory inspectors of the 1840s proved, for the most part, to be lax and irresolute. Members of local child labor commissions were drawn almost exclusively from the more comfortable classes, and they were generally biased in favor of entrepreneurs. For example, the first child labor commission organized by the prefect of the Haut-Rhin included two mayors, three physicians, three manufacturers, a notary, and a minister; and the nine members of the child labor commission of the *arrondissement* of Saint-Etienne in the Loire around 1845 were a local baron, a captain of artillery, two public office holders, the director of a bank, one active and one retired manufacturer, one physician, and one man who was both a physician and a manufacturer. Those commissioners best equipped for their posts—those most knowledgeable about the workings of the factory and best able to evaluate the situations they observed—were industrialists themselves. Thus, from the outset, most of the local commissions tended to make judgments prejudiced in favor of factory owners' interests. One journal observed that when it came to inspection visits, "everything is arranged in advance and after the tour of the plant, the inspectors dine with the industrialists."[21] In Lille, even

19. Horner, *Employment*, 33n.
20. Louis Wolowski, *Le Travail des enfants dans les manufactures* (Paris, 1868), 19.
21. *L'Atelier*, quoted in Pournin, *Inspection*, 41.

a member of the Barrois family became a factory inspector, and he was apparently charged with the surveillance of his own mill. Having none of the independence that would have come with a salary, inspectors, even fair-minded ones, feared offending the factory owners with whom they had to deal. More generally, the voluntary nature of the commissioners' positions discouraged their expending much time or energy on their jobs.[22] Appointing the inspectors of weights and measures, who regularly visited factories, to local child labor commissions was one attempt the government made to improve the commissions' functioning, but it proved rather unsatisfactory.[23]

The national government never did encourage a truly forceful inspection system. On the contrary, the administration made it clear that it wished to discourage an overzealous inspectorate. Even Laurent Cunin-Gridaine's first message to the prefects, while it urged the appointment of well-qualified, serious commissioners and while it conceded that "without a good system of inspection, the law will be a dead letter, without importance and without effect," nonetheless counseled the use of friendly persuasion before any legal sanctions were imposed. Cunin-Gridaine stressed that the inspectors appointed at the local level should be men with respect for the entrepreneur and for the principle of private property.[24] A Ministry of Commerce circular of October 13, 1843, reaffirmed the official preference for informal pressure on factory owners in lieu of legal action, even though it reiterated the idea that "the execution of the law of March 22, 1841 should be everywhere the same, and everywhere complete."[25] Echoing the administration position, the prefect of the Nord reminded newly installed factory inspectors around 1844 that they were to proceed slowly, that they were "to prepare the parties involved, by their benevolent intervention, to submit themselves gradually, and to accustom themselves to a regime that would change working conditions and the habits of the working population quite profoundly."[26] At about the same time, the prefect of the Seine-Inférieure

---

22. On Barrois, see Pierrard, "Patronat," 60. For descriptions of the problems of inspectors and inspection in two local histories, see André Colomès, *Les Ouvriers du textile dans la champagne troyenne* (Paris, 1943), 144–57, and Kahan-Rabecq, *Classe ouvrière*, 192ff. See also Thouvenin, "Influence," 101.

23. There is evidence in AN, F12–4773, that the inspectors of weights and measures received a small bonus for serving on local child labor commissions.

24. Circular in AN, F12–4704.

25. The text of the circular of October 13, 1843, appears in *Documents*, 309–10.

26. From a printed pamphlet in AN, F12–4713.

claimed that the announced policy of the central government had made his department's factory inspectors hesitant to embark upon serious enforcement of the child labor law.[27] Moreover, when child labor cases were brought to trial, judges were reluctant to find factory owners guilty of violations, in part because some of the fines stipulated in the law were relatively heavy.[28]

Clearly, much of the distaste for government interference with the conduct of business that had been apparent in the pre-1841 period, and a general lack of enthusiasm for child labor legislation, still lingered. The courts, the administration, and the local child labor commissions all held back their full commitment to factory reform. Those factory inspectors with a seriousness of purpose met with constant frustration, and there never seemed to be enough individuals willing to serve as local commissioners. From the Nord, the Haut-Rhin, the Allier, and the Tarn, there were reports of an inability to organize local child labor commissions in the first place. Even at Mulhouse a child labor commission was established only with great difficulty, and it fell apart within a few years. By 1845, the only commissioners functioning in the Ardennes were the inspectors of weights and measures.[29] In the same year, the *Quotidienne* reported that only half of the eighteen hundred inspectors appointed under the 1841 legislation were still functioning and that those who remained were not even able to supply the government with enough data for the Ministry of Commerce to prepare a report on the child labor situation. The journal compared the state of affairs in France to the situation in England, where the existence of only four paid inspectors made it possible for the government to publish semiannual reports.[30] Of forty-eight child labor inspectors initially appointed for Paris, twenty resigned in frustration. So did several in Lille.[31] Even Louis Villermé, who had accepted a post as a factory inspector under the law he had done so much to promote, threatened in 1843 to resign over what was, on the surface, a minor disagreement with the Prefecture of Police in Paris.

27. Letter from the prefect of the Seine-Inférieure, December 5, 1843, in AN, F12–4713.
28. See, for example, the report on the court case that established the precedent that factory owners were not personally responsible to see that their young employees attended school: "Cour de Cassation (14 mai, 1846): Travail des enfants. . . . ," *Mémorial du commerce et de l'industrie*, X (1846), jurisprudence sec., 516.
29. Various correspondence in AN, F12–4709, F12–4712, and F12–4714.
30. A copy of this *Quotidienne* article is in AN, F12–4706.
31. Touren, *Loi de 1841*, 125–26; Pierrard, "Patronat," 63.

The argument concerned a technical point of procedure, but it was an indication of what could happen when inspectors faced noncooperation and frustration.[32]

As the 1840s progressed, evidence of some of the faults inherent in the child labor law itself began to emerge as well. One source of the law's defects was the arbitrary nature of some of its provisions. The definition of a factory with more than twenty workers as an establishment subject to the new legislation fostered unfair competition between firms of only slightly different size. The minimum age of eight for employment was certainly too low to be ideal; the eight-hour workday for children eight to twelve years old did not lend itself to a half-time system that could complement a twelve-hour workday for adults. Another fault of the law was that it did not protect certain children that it probably should have protected: apprentices remained beyond the scope of the law, and children in small shops, where their work load was not shared with machines and where public scrutiny did not help to protect them, also could not seek shelter in the new legislation. The government's commercial census of the mid-1840s revealed that there were over seventy thousand workshops in France. Unfortunately, how many of these workshops employed child laborers is not certain, but a Ministry of Commerce report in 1845 indicated that only about five thousand of them were subject to child labor regulations.[33]

One of the greatest faults of the 1841 law related to its requirement that factory children acquire some schooling. Although the law stipulated that working youngsters must receive an education, it did nothing either to define how extensive that education was to be or to see that adequate facilities for schooling were provided. Some evening classes were established to accommodate new students, some factories opened their own schools, and there were places where existing educational establishments were expanded or augmented, but there were simply not enough new facilities to cope with the needs of the new pupils. Steps

32. Extensive correspondence on this matter is in AN, F12–4706.

33. If the figures in the Ministry of Commerce report are accurate, it appears that whereas only about 7 percent of French workshops were covered by the law, 49 percent of young workers were protected. The report indicates that about 70,000 children were protected by the law, and the commercial census completed in 1845 reveals that there were approximately 144,000 working children in France. The *Populaire,* quoted in Touren, *Loi de 1841,* 106, reported at about this time that less than 1 percent of France's shops were subject to the law, contending that only three hundred of fifty thousand establishments fell under its jurisdiction.

were rarely taken to hold classes for factory children during the times they were free.[34] The framers of the legislation, on top of everything else, failed to foresee the problem of an illiterate twelve-year-old who, according to the law, could put in a full workday but was required to attend school in addition. One report on the department of the Seine that intended to reflect a favorable impression of the child labor law showed that in 1843 only 548 laboring children in a sample of 1,904 (28 percent) either were attending or had attended school. By 1847, the report stated, 1,847 of 3,879 children (48 percent) had gotten or were getting an education. The situation had perhaps improved, but even in 1847 less than half the working children in the Seine were being educated.[35]

Even with all the inadequacies of the law and all the problems of its enforcement becoming apparent, most of the government officials charged with overseeing its implementation preferred to think that only its infancy was responsible for its shortcomings. Preparing a message for the king on the progress made in fighting the abuse of child labor, the minister of commerce in September of 1844 asked the prefects of France to report in the strictest confidence on what degree of success they had met with in implementing the child labor law.[36] The report presented to the king on July 18, 1845, reflected the responses of the prefects and glowed with optimism. It claimed that factory surveillance was regular and effective and that those monitoring the condition of child laborers had witnessed a real improvement in their situation. The report noted with pleasure that the improvement had been achieved with the use of gentle persuasion only; the minister of commerce declared himself "happy to inform Your Majesty that the honorable men who have accepted the position of Inspector have justified the confidence of the government." Only as an afterthought (if one can judge from the manuscript copy of the report) did the minister add to this statement the words "almost everywhere."

The message to the king minimized the fact that certain provisions of the child labor law were still very far from being universally observed.

34. See Touren, *Loi de 1841*, 122, and Stearns, *Paths*, 93–94. For the area around Mulhouse, where the educational situation was better than average, see Véron, *Institutions*, 358ff. See also a letter from Emile Dollfus in AN, F12–4712.

35. From a printed report prepared for a Chamber of Peers' debate in 1847, preserved in AN, F12–4707. See also letters of July 17, September 24, 1844, and November 20, 1846, concerning the situation in the Seine, all in AN, F12–4713.

36. Circular in AN, F12–4706.

Although the report informed the monarch that some children under twelve still worked more than eight hours a day, that some children who were supposed to attend school did not, and that not all children had the required *livrets*, it stressed the fact that progress was being made. It noted, for example, that whereas only 300 of 777 working children surveyed in Paris (39 percent) had *livrets* in August, 1843, by January of 1844, 750 of 1,140 children (66 percent) had them. The report indicated, as might have been expected, that those provisions of the law most in conflict with existing industrial practice were the ones least often observed.[37]

While many of those confronted with the provisions of the child labor law either ignored or defied them, and while most of those charged with making the child labor law work complacently enforced what was easily enforceable and made excuses for what was not, there were some people dissatisfied enough with the status quo to set about inducing change. As in the 1830s, these were, for the most part, people who could remove themselves from the direct impact of any changes that complete implementation of the law might have brought about; they generally saw the child labor problem as one aspect of the larger *question sociale*. They were comfortable manufacturers, academic economists, legislators, journalists, novelists. The basic concerns expressed by these reformers were the same ones that had been aired in the 1830s. Children had to be protected, educated, and given proper guidance not only for their own sakes but for the sake of society as a whole. France had to ensure itself successive generations of able defenders and productive workers. As Théodore Fix wrote in 1846, "One sees not only individual victims; it is the entire body of society that is being protected from certain harm."[38]

Much of what was said after 1841 about the need for further reform involved the resolution of the practical problems arising from the legislation as it was written, and many of the champions of reform who had come forward before 1841 again voiced their concerns. As early as 1843, the leaders of the Société industrielle de Mulhouse realized that the new child labor law was being implemented only incompletely, and having learned that the situation in Saint-Quentin, Reims, and Lille was no better than it was in their own town, they addressed an appeal to the two houses of the legislature, asking that paid factory inspectors be ap-

37. The manuscript copy of this report is in AN, F12–4706, and the report is reproduced in *Documents*, 324–29.
38. Fix, *Observations*, 275.

pointed in an effort to make the law effective.[39] The baron de Gérando had also come to believe before his death that a regularized inspectorate was required, and his opinion came to light publicly in 1845 when the baron's son prepared a second edition of *Des progrès de l'industrie*, Gérando's work on the relationship between industrial progress and the well-being of the laborer.[40]

The liberal economist and journalist Léon Faucher also launched a scathing attack in the 1840s on the weaknesses of the child labor law. He expressed his views before the Académie des sciences morales et politiques and also published his ideas in the *Revue des deux mondes* in 1844. Concentrating on an analysis of the situation in Paris, Faucher pointed out that enforcing the 1841 law in the capital was even more difficult than enforcing it in provincial industrial towns. In places like Rouen, Lille, Sedan, Mulhouse, or Reims, the existence of only one major type of industry made it simpler to keep track of the child labor situation. Attacking almost every aspect of the condition of young workers as he perceived it, he asked rhetorically, "Must we depend so much on the zeal of amateur functionaries who have a defective law in their hands, obstacles without number before them, and a nearly indifferent government behind them?" Observing that "the way things are now, nothing is easier than evading the law," Faucher called for reforms in France's child labor legislation that would ensure its effectiveness and that would, above all, guarantee working children an education.[41] Frédéric Bastiat, writing in the *Journal des économistes* in 1845, concurred in Faucher's analysis of the problems inherent in depending on nonprofessional notables to enforce the child labor law, but he suggested that society's basic concern should be not simply to prevent children from laboring in factories but to eliminate the need for children to work.[42]

39. See Achille Penot, "Rapport fait au nom d'une commission, . . . dans le séance du 25 janvier 1843, sur la loi du 22 mars 1841 . . . ," *BSIM*, XVI (1842–43), and the letter from Mulhouse, in AN, F12–4704. See also the 1846 correspondence between Penot and the Belgian government in *Documents*, 329–33.

40. Gérando, *Progrès*, 62ff.

41. Léon Faucher, "Le Travail des enfans à Paris," *RDM*, n.s., VIII (1844), 643–65; L. V., "Revue," 70ff. See also Duvoir, *Recherche*, 14off. When Faucher attacked the child labor law in the Académie, both Dupin and Villermé felt called upon to defend it, perhaps because they had played such a dominant role in the struggle for its passage.

42. Frédéric Bastiat, "Sur les questions soumises aux conseils généraux de l'agriculture, des manufactures et du commerce," *JE*, XIII (December, 1845), 12–14. There were, concurrent with the appeals for an improved system of factory inspection, arguments raised specifically against a paid inspectorate. Pierre Clément in *JE* defended the charity of industrialists as a sufficient guarantee of the child labor law's implementation, and an article

As the lack of adequate provision for inspection came under attack in the 1840s, so did other features of the law. For example, in a wide-ranging article published in 1846, the Lille physician Jean-Pierre Thouvenin criticized the low minimum age authorized by the law, as well as several other aspects of the legislation.[43] The denial of protection to young industrial workers in small shops also came in for criticism. As early as June of 1842, one Paris journal reported the arrest of a man who had beaten an apprentice into a state of "complete idiocy," and it editorialized that society had to protect young workers from such "atrocious cruelties" even if these actions took place within the "sheltered life of the family." The paper continued, "We are not demanding . . . that people live their lives in public or that all walls be made of glass, but . . . children can not be allowed to be the victims of such cruelty."[44]

It is interesting that the 1840s was also the time when the French literary world first turned its attention to the plight of the working-class child. Increasingly, literary works reflecting a social concern were being published, and it was not uncommon for children to figure significantly in these writings. In Romantic literature in general, children were beginning to emerge as inherently interesting characters rather than as the peripheral figures they had been in the past.[45] Although there is no evidence that the new literary concern with working children was tied in any direct way to the campaign for child labor reform, there can be no doubt that French writers were influenced by the ongoing debate over child labor (and other aspects of the *question sociale*) and that they in turn influenced attitudes among the literate elite.

Eugène Sue's 1843 novel, *Les Mystères de Paris*, for example, contains several passages intended to arouse concern for the laboring child and indignation over the effects of too short a childhood. There is, for instance, this remembrance of childhood by one of Sue's characters:

I have a dim recollection of having strolled about in my childhood with an old rag and bone picker, who almost knocked the life out of me. . . . My first employment was to help the knackers cut horses' throats at Montfaucon. I was

---

in *Le Commerce* protested the prospect of further burdening the government bureaucracy with personnel and expenses. See Mataja, "Origines," IX, 749n.

43. Thouvenin, "Influence," 96–101.

44. Quoted in Ducpétiaux, *Condition*, I, 40. On the defects of the 1841 law as they were perceived in Belgium, see *Documents*, 99–103.

45. See David Owen Evans, *Social Romanticism in France, 1830–1848* (Oxford, 1951), 7–29; Louis Cazamian, *A History of French Literature* (Oxford, 1955), 297–300; Jean Calvet, *L'Enfant dans la littérature française* (Paris, 1930), I, ix–xi, 57ff; and Clifford Stetson Parker, *The Defense of the Child by French Novelists* (Menasha, Wisc., 1925), 11–12.

about ten or twelve. When first I began to slash these poor old beasts it had quite an effect on me. At the end of the month I thought no more about it; on the contrary, I began to like my trade. . . . When I had cut the animals' throats, they gave me for my trouble a piece of the thigh of some animal that had died of disease. . . . I went with it to the kiln like a wolf to his den, and then with the leave of the plaster-burners, I made a splendid broil on the ashes.[46]

The lament of another character in *Les Mystères de Paris*, an artisan living in one room and eking out a living for his family of eight, reveals Sue's understanding of the dilemma of working-class parents and his attempt to build sympathy for their children:

Happy are those who can have their children with them, and guard them from dangers; but who will protect the working girl?—no one. As soon as she is old enough to earn anything, she goes in the morning to her employment and comes back in the evening. During the day the mother and father are forced to work too; so they have no opportunity to watch over the conduct of their children: and then folks exclaim at the misconduct of these poor girls, as though their parents had the means of keeping them at home, or looking after their morals when they are out. . . . It is, above all, to us poor people that the affections of a family are salutary and consoling; and yet, as soon as our children can use their faculties, we are compelled to part with them.[47]

Like the novelist Sue, the great historian of the Romantic era, Jules Michelet, also turned his attention to children in his writings. Michelet thought of the children of France as embodying the national spirit, and he was understandably concerned about their well-being. He wrote about his own childhood in the preface to *Le Peuple*, published in 1846, and wondered aloud what would have become of him if he had been sent out to work at an early age: "if my parents, in obedience to mere reason, had made me a workman and had saved themselves, should I have been lost?" In discussing the life of French workers, Michelet again spoke of the plight of the children. He compared the lot of the factory child to that of the apprentice, and, aware of the relatively neglected problem of children in small shops, he concluded that factory children, miserable as they were, were nonetheless better off than apprentices. The unskilled labor of the factory, he observed, "left . . . the child free at a fixed hour: night, at least, allowed him repose." The apprentice, on the other hand, belonged "day and night to his master."[48]

---

46. Eugène Sue, *The Mysteries of Paris* (London, n.d.), Pt. 1, p. 15.
47. *Ibid.*, Pt. 1, p. 180. See also John Moody, *Les Idées sociales d'Eugène Sue* (Paris, 1938), and Cazamian, *History of French Literature*, 329–30.
48. Jules Michelet, *The People* (London, 1846), v, 13, 40–42. See also Cazamian, *History of French Literature*, 333–53.

There were poets, too, in the 1840s who revealed a social conscious-ness in their works and who wrote about the plight of the laboring young. In "Physique de l'espèce," for instance, Victor-Louis-Amédée Pommier painted this picture:

> Industry, seizing the poor creature
> Shuts it up forever in some mill,
> A sickening penal colony, a poisoned blister.
> Where from his early years the imprisoned child
> Grows old over work that he incessantly repeats,
> And in this stultifying job he becomes brutalized and dazed. . . .
> Industrial arts have this side to them
> They burden the state of a base, frightful people.[49]

Similarly, in his 1847 song about the Lyon silk industry, "La Soie," Pierre Dupont tempered his enthusiasm for industrial progress with these words:

> In this enchanted labyrinth
> The spirit filled with wonder is lost
> Why how many suffocated souls there are
> At this work, like the worm!
> I heard a young girl
> Say, crying over her spindle:
> "I am like the lowly silkworm
> And I too spin my tomb."[50]

Even Victor Hugo, perhaps the greatest French literary figure of the Romantic period, penned a lament for the factory child. In his 1846 *Melancholia* appear these lines:

> Where are all these children going, not one of them laughing?
> These sweet pensive beings wasted by fever?
> These eight-year-old girls you see walking alone?
> They are going to do, from dawn to dusk, eternally
> The same motion in the same prison.[51]

Although the literature of the 1840s must have sensitized the literate public to the suffering of working children, those actually campaigning for further child labor reform were, as in the period before 1841, rela-tively few in number. However, again as in the previous decade, they

49. On the social consciousness of French Romantic poets, see Elliott Mansfield Grant, *French Poetry and Modern Industry, 1830–1870* (Cambridge, Mass., 1927), 1–65. The Pom-mier poem is quoted on p. 30 of this work.

50. Quoted in Grant, *French Poetry*, 54.

51. Quoted in Grant, *French Poetry*, 45; Evans, *Romanticism*, 7; and Parker, *Defense of the Child*, 12.

were, for the most part, highly prominent, and the government could not easily ignore their persistent demands that the work of reform begun in 1841 be completed. Moreover, the most vocal advocates of reform increasingly found that they had more muted support in many quarters. The minority of manufacturers who accepted reform were distressed that their good intentions were being thwarted by their neighbors' and their competitors' noncompliance with the law. So, too, some factory inspectors were upset that even their limited activity was often frustrated, and local officials expressed concern that they often found themselves in an untenable position with respect to the law.[52] Ultimately, the fact that most working-class parents and most employers of children were disinclined to cooperate in the implementation of the 1841 law seems to have made far less of an impression on the government than the fact that the lobbying against the exploitation of child labor was continuing. In light of all this, in 1846 the minister of commerce asked his General Council of Commerce to study again the child labor situation in the country and to recommend appropriate action.

The General Council of Commerce appointed a committee to undertake the task with which it had been charged, and the committee concluded that several changes in the 1841 law were necessary. The report presented to the full council by the committee's secretary, Joseph-Eugène Schneider, recommended that the minimum age for factory employment be raised to ten and that all children be allowed to work a twelve-hour day. It recommended further that children be required either to produce a certificate verifying their completion of a primary education or to attend school, while working, until the age of sixteen, not twelve, as required in the 1841 law. What is more significant, the committee advised an extention of the labor law's protection to working children in all French shops, the institution of a salaried inspectorate to complement local child labor commissions, and a limitation of twelve hours on the workday of adults whose labor was tied to that of children. The committee was very bold in suggesting that the factory act be extended to cover adult workers, given the tremendous philosophical controversy that had raged over the issue of child labor legislation in the very recent past. But the suggestion for such an extension was rooted in practical concerns: the framers of this proposal realized that the temptation to overwork young children would remain strong as long as the

52. For examples of local officials' calls for some remedial actions, see letters from the Nord in AN, F12–4712, from the Allier in AN, F12–4709, and from the Seine-Inférieure in AN, F12–4713.

adult operatives who depended on the aid of youngsters continued to work longer than twelve hours a day.[53]

The administration considered the suggestions that had come out of the General Council of Commerce, and in February of 1847 it introduced to the Chamber of Peers a bill intended to rectify some of the problems of the 1841 child labor law. Adopting some of the ideas of the council, the government proposed to make child labor regulations applicable in all establishments where youngsters were employed and to raise the minimum age for employment to ten but allow all children to work a twelve-hour day. The new government bill, however, made mention neither of a limitation on the workday of adults nor of a salaried inspectorate. These measures would have been significant attacks on liberal doctrine, and the administration was not yet prepared to suggest such a strong policy.

As in 1840, Charles Dupin was appointed secretary of the committee created by the Chamber of Peers to study the government's child labor bill, and as he had done seven years earlier, he oversaw a significant alteration and strengthening of the administration's proposal. The results of his efforts were revealed in the report Dupin submitted to the Chamber of Peers in June of 1847. His committee agreed in principle that all working children should be protected by the law, but it feared that measures already extremely difficult to enforce when they applied in only a relatively small number of factories would certainly be unenforceable if applied universally. It suggested instead that factory legislation be extended only to those shops employing ten or more workers or at least five workers who could be protected by the law's provisions. Rejecting the assumption that children forced to wait two extra years before entering the work force would naturally spend those years in school, the peers' committee opted for maintaining the existing minimum age of eight and the eight-hour workday for children under twelve. The members of the committee did, however, want to do something to encourage the education of factory children, so they proposed that three times a week the workday of adolescents be shortened to eleven hours in order to make time for a required one hour of schooling. Although the administration bill had said nothing about a paid inspectorate, a provision for establishing a corps of inspectors was embodied in the bill that emerged from committee. The committee proposed a system involving four inspectors-general and sixteen divisional inspectors.

53. Material on this report is in AN, F12–4707.

Finally, the peers' child labor committee, like the General Council of Commerce, also made a suggestion concerning adult workers. It recommended that all labor regulations applied to children aged twelve to sixteen be imposed as well upon all female workers, regardless of age. Like the suggestion of the council of commerce regarding adult operatives who worked with children—a suggestion never pursued further—the idea of restricting the labor of adult women was a daring expansion of the kind of interventionism that the 1841 law had initiated. Like the council's suggestion, too, the peers' proposal was justified solely in terms of child welfare. Nothing was more important in child rearing, Dupin's committee reasoned, than a mother's attention, and the legislation proposed concerning women was intended simply to allow mothers to devote more time to their offspring.[54] In the minds of most middle-class reformers in the 1840s, only such a justification could make interference with the "right to work" palatable.

Before the discussion of a new child labor law was undertaken in the full Chamber of Peers, the government decided to poll interested parties, as it had done in the past, for their reaction to the proposed measure. The vehicle for this survey of opinions was a circular of October 21, 1847, from the minister of commerce.[55] Unfortunately, a complete accounting of the results of this inquiry is unavailable, but judging from the fragmentary evidence that is available and from what would transpire shortly in the Chamber of Peers, one would be safe in assuming that there was general support for improvements in France's child labor legislation. The major battle over the concept of factory legislation had been fought in the 1830s and early 1840s, and now that a child labor law was on the books, there seemed to be a general consensus that if new legislation was needed to make the law effective, it should be adopted. Several opinions on factory reform published at the time of the 1847 survey confirm the impression that the prospect of new legislation was greeted with general approval among French notables.

The Société industrielle de Mulhouse, which preserved its response to the ministerial survey, as well as an earlier consideration of the original administration bill, in its *Bulletin*, generally favored the action proposed

54. See Dupin's report, preserved in AN, F12–4704, and reproduced in *Documents*, 340–67.
55. Some material on this inquiry is in AN, F12-4707. A list of the questions posed in the October 21 circular is included in Achille Penot, "Rapport sur un projet de loi réglant le travail des enfants dans les ateliers; lu à la séance du 29 décembre 1847 . . . ," *BSIM*, XXI (1848).

by Dupin's committee. The Société industrielle did suggest, however, that the maximum workday for the youngest workers be reduced to six hours. This shortened workday, modeled on the one adopted in England in 1844, not only would be more bearable for the youngsters, the society explained, but would also lend itself to the introduction of a half-time schedule.[56]

The published ideas of Léonce Curnier, who prepared a response to the ministerial inquiry on behalf of the chamber of commerce of Nîmes, also supported the legislation proposed in the report Dupin authored. Curnier believed that the Chamber of Peers' bill remained faithful to the principle established in 1841 of carefully restraining liberty so as to prevent its abuse.[57] Count Armand de Melun also expressed his approval of the bill prepared under Dupin's guidance. During the mid-1840s, Melun had emerged as one of the most influential leaders of Social Catholicism. He had organized a national society and a journal to promote charitable endeavors, and he had initiated a number of projects aimed at ameliorating social conditions. Despite his devotion to voluntary philanthropy, however, he was prepared to support the intrusion of government controls where the welfare of factory children was concerned.[58] It comes as no surprise that the writings of Daniel Legrand during this period also concerned themselves in part with improvements in France's child labor situation. Legrand went so far as to suggest an international agreement regulating the employment of the young.[59]

As the year 1848 began, the bill contained in Dupin's report to the Chamber of Peers seemed well on its way to becoming law. Despite continuing opposition to reform at the grassroots level, the champions of new legislation seemed on the verge of strengthening France's system of child labor restrictions. In mid-February, the Chamber of Peers formally

56. Achille Penot, "Rapport présenté . . . dans la séance du 29 avril 1847 . . . sur diverses modifications à apporter à la loi du 22 mars 1841 . . .," *BSIM*, XX (1847); Penot, "Rapport . . . 29 décembre 1847." See also Véron, *Institutions*, 277ff.

57. Léonce Curnier, *Rapport sur la nouveau projet de loi relatif au travail des enfants* (Nîmes, 1848), esp. 28.

58. Armand de Melun, *Rapport à la Société d'économie charitable sur le projet relatif au travail des enfants* ([Paris?], 1847). See also D'Andigné, *Apôtre*, 159ff; Duroselle, *Débuts*, 183; and Vidler, *Century*, 27–28.

59. [Daniel Legrand], *Lettre d'un industriel des montagnes des Vosges à Monsieur Legentil . . . suivi de deux lettres adressées a Monsieur Guizot* ([Strasbourg?], 1847); [Daniel Legrand], *Appel respectueux d'un industriel de la vallée des Vosges . . . adressé aux gouvernements de la France, de l'Angleterre, de la Prusse, des autres états de l'Allemagne, et de la Suisse dans le but de provoquer des lois particulières et une loi internationale . . .* (Strasbourg, 1848). Compare the ideas of Ducpétiaux, *Condition*, ix–xii.

adopted Dupin's child labor proposal, with only two significant modifications. The new factory law was to apply in all industrial establishments, and the workday of France's youngest laborers was to be limited to no more than six hours.[60] Within days of the final peers' debates on child labor, however, revolution truncated the orderly process by which the new legislation was moving toward adoption. Of course, a concern with the condition of the working classes, and with it a concern for the laboring young, remained very much alive after the February Revolution, but under the new republic established in 1848, this concern would be manifested in rather different forms. The kind of program embodied in the 1847 child labor bill, which had come so near to adoption, would not be enacted for another quarter of a century.

60. See *Documents*, 108–10.

SIX

The Second Republic
and the
Issue of Apprenticeship

Although the outbreak of revolution in February of 1848 had brought discussion of a revised child labor law to an abrupt halt, there was reason to believe that the plight of factory children would not be overlooked by the new republican government of France. The provisional government of 1848 conceded the need to consider the problems of the working classes when it established the Luxembourg Commission under the chairmanship of Louis Blanc, and it demonstrated that it was not fundamentally opposed to interventionism when it established a maximum workday for adults. Moreover, such important advocates of child labor reform as Charles Dupin and Charles de Montalembert were elected to seats in the Constituent Assembly in April of 1848, and in May that body initiated its own extensive inquiry into working conditions.[1] Neither the Constituent Assembly nor the Legislative Assembly that succeeded it in 1849 was to take any action on the specific issue of industrial child labor, however. In its early months the provisional government was concerned above all else with political reform, and after the bloody June Days, when workers rose up against the bourgeois-dominated government, the legislature was disinclined to consider any welfare measures touching on the working classes. The Luxembourg Commission, which had received some petitions from worker organizations asking that it consider at least the condition of apprentices, was dissolved by mid-May.[2]

---

1. See Rigaudias-Weiss, *Enquêtes ouvrières*, 184ff.
2. Roger Price, *The French Second Republic: A Social History* (Ithaca, 1972), 109.

Similarly, the results of the assembly's inquiry into working conditions were largely disregarded (it had virtually ignored the issue of industrial child labor in any case). When in August of 1848 Louis Wolowski presented the Constituent Assembly with a proposal to reactivate a program for child labor reform, his appeal fell on deaf ears.[3] Nor was Louis-Napoléon Bonaparte himself inclined to pursue a policy of reform after he was elected to the presidency of the republic. "Perhaps the greatest danger of modern times," President Bonaparte said in 1849, "results from that false belief inculcated in many minds that a government can do everything and that it is the essence of every type of governmental system to respond to every exigency, to respond to every evil."[4]

Under the circumstances, some of those concerned with the cause of child labor reform thought it best to look directly to the Ministry of Commerce for support. They hoped that if the new legislative and executive powers of the republic would not act on child labor, the bureaucracy might be persuaded to take the initiative. As early as March, 1848, for example, a school inspector from Versailles named Huré wrote to the minister of commerce about the child labor problem. Adopting the agricultural imagery that had become familiar by then, Huré contended that strengthened factory legislation would "preserve for the Republic the precious seed of hope" that was being endangered by "familial avarice or misery." His "disinterested prayer" was for immediate attention to the child labor problem, and he expressed the hope that "a million innocent victims, oppressed and brutalized, will find prompt salvation in the pity of *Monsieur* the Minister of . . . Commerce."[5] A year later, a letter from one Lesage of Paris expressed a similar hope and appealed to the commerce minister's political instincts. Noting that a "stable and regular government" had by then emerged from the turmoil of 1848, Lesage suggested that a new child labor law based on the prerevolutionary legislative deliberations could certainly now be adopted. "You, *Monsieur le Ministre*, have the advantage of attaching your name to it," counseled Lesage.[6]

There is evidence that the Ministry of Commerce did maintain an ongoing interest in the child labor issue throughout the period of the Second Republic. As correspondence between the minister of commerce

3. See Levasseur, *Histoire*, II, 425.
4. Quoted in Copin, *Doctrines économiques*, 87.
5. Huré to the minister of commerce, March 9, 1848, in AN, F12–4773.
6. Lesage to the minister of commerce, March 6, 1849, in AN, F12–4708. Similar letters from the period of the Second Republic are in AN, F12–4773.

and the child labor commission of Rouen indicates, the ministry maintained an active file on factory reform in the expectation that deliberations over the law proposed in 1847 would resume.[7] Moreover, some specific programs for extending child labor legislation were prepared within the ministry itself. Less than a year after the February Revolution, a plan for revised legislation was formulated by Armand Audiganne, the new head of the ministry's Bureau of Industry (formerly the Bureau of Manufactures). Audiganne, then a young man in his midthirties, had gone to work for the Ministry of Commerce about 1841 and had begun at about the same time to publish his ideas on social reform. Audiganne had read Louis Blanc, and though he rejected most of Blanc's proposals as too radical, he praised Blanc for raising a variety of extremely important social issues. Audiganne's interest in child labor reform stemmed from his general concern with the condition of the working classes, and his attitude was colored by the increasingly common faith of the middle classes in their ability to ameliorate social conditions.

Audiganne's proposal for reform was addressed to Delambre, the former head of the commerce ministry's Bureau of Manufactures and now the director of the entire Division of Domestic Commerce for the ministry. The proposal reflected the discussions of reform that had taken place before 1848: it included provisions for extending application of the factory law to all shops of six or more workers, for raising the minimum age for employment from eight to nine, and for amending the maximum workday of young operatives. In conformity with the legislation adopted in the early weeks of the republic to govern adult labor, Audiganne proposed allowing children under twelve to work no more than six hours a day throughout France and children twelve to sixteen no more than ten hours a day in Paris and eleven hours a day in the provinces. In addition, he proposed the creation of a paid inspectorate to supplement the existing voluntary child labor commissions. He recommended the appointment of three inspectors-general and as many as six divisional inspectors who would be salaried by the state and whose only function would be overseeing compliance with child labor regulations.[8]

On April 30, 1850, yet another set of proposals emerged from within the Ministry of Commerce. This time the newly merged general councils of agriculture, manufacturing and commerce suggested the form that

7. Correspondence in AN, F12-4713, esp. letter of June 21, 1848.
8. Document in AN, F12-4707.

the needed changes in the child labor law should take. Following extensive deliberation, the merged councils declared themselves in favor of extending the factory law's applicability and reducing the workday of the youngest workers to six hours. They also proposed to give the inspectors of primary education a greater role in overseeing the schooling of factory children and to attach a salaried factory inspector to the local child labor commission in every *arrondissement* or, where extensive industrialization warranted, in every canton. Finally, the council members called for the nomination of inspectors-general, who would tour the country in an effort to assure the uniform application of factory legislation and who would issue annual reports.[9]

The ongoing discussion of new measures within the Ministry of Commerce notwithstanding, the ministry's primary focus in dealing with industrial child labor continued to be on the enforcement of existing legislation. Repeatedly, the minister of commerce urged government officials in the provinces to see to it that the demands of the 1841 law were met.[10] In addition, Armand Audiganne conceived the novel idea of appealing directly to the workers for cooperation in the implementation of the law. He was aware that worker resistance was one reason many provisions of the factory law were still widely ignored, and in a slim volume he published in 1850, *Les Ouvriers en famille*, he urged workers to take a hand in improving their own circumstances by demanding the protection of those laws that were on the books. *Les Ouvriers en famille* was essentially a transcription of talks addressed by a worker of the Seine-Inférieure named Nogaret to his fellow workers, and it appeared soon after Nogaret's death in an industrial accident. Audiganne saw in the publication of Nogaret's addresses a way of familiarizing workers with their rights and responsibilities without appearing to preach to them from a position of superiority. *Les Ouvriers en famille* was praised by many of those who had supported labor legislation under the July Monarchy—Melun, Buret, Bères, Dupin—and was honored by the Académie francaise.[11] It does not appear to have had much impact on the actions of working-class families, however.

9. See E. Délerot, "Avant-propos," *BSPA*, I (1867), 15–16; Bec, *Législation de l'inspection*, 36ff; and Emile Durand, *Inspection*, 21. The report of the council is also in *Documents*, 111.

10. See, for example, the letters from the minister of commerce to the prefect of the Nord in AN, F12–4712, and to an official in the Ardennes in AN, F12–4709.

11. See Armand Audiganne, *Les Ouvriers en famille* (Paris, 1866). The first edition of this work appeared in 1850.

Despite the apparently genuine concern over child labor expressed by Audiganne and others within the Ministry of Commerce and despite the republic's professed concern with social conditions, in the final analysis the mundane enforcement of the Child Labor Law of 1841 was no more complete under the Second Republic than it had been under the July Monarchy. A communication from the Rhône in 1849 indicated that there were no child labor inspectors in that department, that there was serious resistance to the provisions of the child labor law, and that industry had reverted to a reliance on local custom in its child labor practices.[12] An 1850 report from Lille complained that factory owners there, too, were still being uncooperative. The report cited the provision for schooling as the hardest to enforce and cried out for paid inspectors. In neighboring Roubaix, there was no longer even a child labor commission in existence.[13] According to a letter from the prefect of the Seine-Inférieure, the child labor provisions concerning the minimum age and the education of children were "rarely observed" in that jurisdiction.[14]

If there was no increased enforcement of the child labor law, neither was there a general breakdown of factory law enforcement attributable to the revolutionary upheavals of 1848. In Paris, for example, records show that despite complaints from some officials that enforcement left much to be desired, 276 establishments employing 2,845 children were visited by volunteer child labor inspectors between March, 1847, and November, 1848. In the same period, 4,406 of the *livrets* required by the child labor law were delivered by the authorities. A comparison of these figures with those for the months between February, 1846, and March, 1847, shows that the decrease in inspection activity in the revolutionary period was not a dramatic one. In the period between early 1846 and early 1847, 318 establishments employing 3,870 children had been visited, and 4,129 *livrets* had been delivered.[15]

Given the disappointment that advocates of child labor reform must have experienced when the enactment of new factory legislation was aborted in 1848, and given the chagrin they must have felt over the stagnation of the child labor situation under the republic, it is not surprising that some of the champions of reform active before 1848 spoke out again in the postrevolutionary period. The Société industrielle de

12. Report from the Rhône, September 12, 1849, in AN, F12–4712.
13. Report in AN, F12–4712. See also A.-M. Gossez, *Le Département du Nord sous la deuxième République* (Lille, 1904), 280–82, and Pierrard, "Patronat."
14. Prefect of the Seine-Inférieure to the minister of commerce, February 14, 1851, in AN, F12–4713.
15. Reports in AN, F12–4713.

Mulhouse, for example, petitioned the new administration to continue with the revision of France's child labor legislation where the Orleanist regime had left off. Among others who advocated reform with renewed zeal in the era of the republic were Jérôme-Adolphe Blanqui and Armand de Melun. During the 1840s, support for child labor legislation had become a more philosophically acceptable position than it had been before 1841, and so some new voices were heard in support of reform as well. Michel Chevalier, the one-time disciple of Saint-Simon who would become France's most important advocate of international free trade, joined the ranks of the child labor reformers, and the editors of *L'Ere nouvelle*, an important organ of Social Catholicism, also urged the government to redouble its efforts to "protect childhood from the excesses of premature labor."[16]

The conception formed earlier in the nineteenth century of what was needed to protect working children and to provide for their proper development had not changed in any fundamental way by the 1850s, so the demands of the child labor reformers of the republican era had a familiar ring to them. Reformers from the privileged classes still saw children as the most unfortunate and guiltless victims of working-class misery, and their plans for legislative action were still couched in terms of limited government intervention that would not alter the basic socioeconomic structure of France. The specific complaints expressed by reformers had all been heard before. For example, when Jérôme-Adolphe Blanqui published *Des classes ouvrières en France pendant l'année 1848*, a study he undertook at the behest of the Académie des sciences morales et politiques, he demanded that the education afforded to working-class children be made "more effective and morally uplifting."[17] Michel Chevalier lamented in familiar terms the inadequacies of the 1841 factory law and called for the appointment of competent, well-paid factory inspectors.[18] Armand de Melun went so far in expressing his frustration over the shortcomings of existing factory legislation that he termed the law of 1841 "a dead letter, a semblance of protection."[19]

16. Véron, *Institutions*, 280–81; *L'Ere nouvelle*, March 30, 1849, quoted in Ross William Collins, *Catholicism and the Second French Republic* (New York, 1923), 96.
17. Jérôme-Adolphe Blanqui, *Des classes ouvrières en France pendant l'année 1848* (Paris, 1849), 197–253, and esp. 253–55. See also Rigaudias-Weiss, *Enquêtes ouvrières*, 114–18; Mataja, "Origines," IX, 764–67; and Duvoir, *Recherche*, 79ff.
18. Michel Chevalier, *Lettres sur l'organisation du travail* (Brussels, 1850), esp. 168–69. See also Pierre Labracherie, *Michel Chevalier et ses idées économiques* (Paris, 1929), 108–19.
19. Armand de Melun, *De l'intervention de la société pour prévenir et soulager la misère* (Paris, 1849), 35. See also Pierrard, "Patronat," 61.

Although the reformers of this era believed meaningful factory legislation to be essential, they did not suggest that it was a panacea. Many were still cautious about extreme programs of government intervention (especially where the condition of adult workers was concerned), and they tended to agree that improvements even in the condition of working-class children could not be achieved by legislative action alone. They stressed the importance of inculcating in the working classes a new sense of morality through education and through the influence of the privileged classes. No one articulated this attitude at midcentury better than Armand de Melun.

As his 1847 support for a revision of the 1841 factory law revealed, already under the July Monarchy Melun had come to accept the need for government intervention in industrial affairs. Under the Second Republic he became the primary Catholic spokesman for social legislation. Melun was the person most responsible for the Legislative Assembly's appointment of a committee to study the alleviation of misery through public assistance. Still, as a leading Social Catholic, he was wary of extremism, and he always viewed voluntary activities undertaken by the privileged classes as a necessary complement to social legislation. Misery in France "should and can be combatted successfully not with one of the radical systems . . . which makes progress only through upheaval and revolution," Melun wrote in his pamphlet *De l'intervention de la société pour prévenir et soulager la misère*. Rather, misery should be fought "with enlightened and perserverant efforts, with a diligence maintained by intelligence and public good will, with a series of regulations, laws and institutions."[20]

Melun had long been concerned especially with the fate of working-class children. He was, for instance, a major force behind the *patronage* movement, whose purpose it was to organize programs of fellowship and support for working-class youngsters. In his approach to improving the condition of these youths, as in his approach to other social problems, Melun was devoted to the concept of government regulation and private philanthropy working in tandem. Thus, in 1849 he wrote to the foremost advocate of clerical education in France, the comte Frédéric de Falloux, insisting that "the success of legislation concerning young workers absolutely depends upon the introduction into our social structure of [the *patronage* system], whose good results we have already reaped in our [existing] poor, small projects."[21]

20. Melun, *Intervention*, 64–65.
21. Quoted in D'Andigné, *Apôtre*, 242–43. On Melun during the period of the Second

The one element that was perhaps different in the child labor reform literature of this period was its increasing emphasis on the problems of apprentices laboring in small shops. As midcentury approached, social reformers were becoming more and more aware of the abuse of apprenticeship; they were coming to realize that since the last decade of the eighteenth century there had been little to protect apprentices from the whims of their masters. In the first decade of the nineteenth century, a few limited regulations defining the mutual obligations of apprentices and masters had been enacted, and the Code Napoléon had mentioned apprenticeship several times in passing.[22] But apprentices still remained very much at the mercy of those under whose care they were placed. Blanqui had these young workers in mind when in 1849 he urged society to "take hold of [its] children and not abandon them before they have escaped the premature, criminal workshop labor that demoralizes and kills them." Similarly, Armand de Melun argued that new factory legislation must extend its protection to apprentices, "who have no less need of it than [do] young factory workers."[23]

Although the abuse of apprenticeship had existed for at least as long as the abuse of child labor in factories, this apprenticeship problem had gone largely unnoticed throughout the early part of the nineteenth century. Young workers in small craft shops had always been less conspicuous than those in factories, and their situation was perceived as less shockingly novel. By the 1840s, however, the impact of apprenticeship abuse was becoming more obvious. Made more widespread by the pressure of capitalist competition, the abuse was beginning to have implications for the quality of French industrial production by this time as well. Observers of developments in those trades that had always guaranteed France her position of supremacy in the market for finely crafted manufactured goods (including commentators on the periodic industrial expositions held in France) were becoming alarmed at the deterioration of artistry and craftsmanship that accompanied the disintegration of traditional apprenticeship, and their outcry helped to call attention to the condition of young workers in small shops. Workers in the artisanal

Republic generally, see also Moon, *Labor Problem*, 42–51; Collins, *Catholicism*; H. Daniel-Rops, *The Church in an Age of Revolution, 1789–1870*, trans. John Warrington (London, 1965), 335–36.

22. See material in AN, F12–4830; Julien Hayem and Jules Périn, *Traité du contrat d'apprentissage* (Paris, 1878), 1–8; Merlet, *Lois*, 14–29; Dolfus-Francoz, *Essai historique*, 34–42; and Mataja, "Origines," IX, 755n.

23. Blanqui, *Classes ouvrières*, 253; Melun, *Intervention*, 35.

trades were themselves also beginning to appreciate the problems of apprenticeship in an industrializing economy and to propose remedies.[24] Moreover, the very passage of child labor legislation in 1841 helped to expose the condition of apprentices, for factory children could now find at least nominal protection in the law, but youngsters in small shops still could not.

Some had seen legislation controlling apprenticeship as a necessary corollary to the child labor law of 1841 ever since the passage of that first factory act. The need to grant apprentices at least as much protection as factory children enjoyed began to be noticed in the press soon after the 1841 law was promulgated, and as early as January of 1842, the general councils of manufacturing and of commerce began discussing the possibility of regulating apprenticeship.[25] The source of the problem was articulated accurately and succinctly for the general councils by officials of the Ministry of Commerce: "Under the regime of masters and guild wardens, apprenticeship occupied a rather large place in [its] system of laws. All eventualities were forseen, every minute condition was defined. When corporations disappeared, for a long time nothing replaced the old regulations covering apprenticeship. For fear of seeming to attack the freedom of industry and of labor, regulation of even the most basic points was avoided."[26] It is significant that arguments about "the freedom of industry and of labor" were no longer seen by the government as sufficient cause to deter its acting to control the abuse of apprenticeship. The struggle over child labor reform that had culminated in 1841 had apparently discredited absolutist appeals to noninterventionism once and for all.

The discussions of apprenticeship abuse in the General Council of Commerce and in the General Council of Manufacturing led these bodies to conclude that it would be wise both to codify the various apprenticeship regulations adopted since the time of the French Revolution and to augment the existing regulations where necessary. Thus, by 1845, the administration had ready a specific proposal for apprenticeship legislation. Presenting this proposal to the general councils of his ministry for further consideration, the minister of commerce observed that the ap-

24. See Georges Duveau, *La Pensée ouvrière sur l'education pendant la Second Republic et le Second Empire* (Paris, 1948); César Fichet, *Mémoire sur l'apprentissage et sur l'education industrielle* (Paris, 1847); Weissbach, "Artisanal Responses," 67–81; and Johnson, "Economic Change," 87–114.
25. See, for example, Faucher, "Travail des enfans," 662ff.
26. Report in AN, F12–4830.

prenticeship measure was intended to fill "some regretable gaps in our industrial legislation" and that it was seen within the ministry as the "indispensable complement of the law of March 22, 1841."[27]

In 1846 and 1847, while it was also involved in preparing the ill-fated revision of the 1841 factory act, the Ministry of Commerce prepared several new versions of its original apprenticeship bill. At the same time, appeals for action on apprenticeship could be heard within the legislature itself. In 1847, for example, the deputy Jean-Marie Boissel exhorted his colleagues: "It is time to remedy those vices of apprenticeship that debase the population of our great cities and that are among the leprosies of our industry. It is time that the apprentice ceases to be sold body and soul to a master who exploits him and exerts himself only in order to make him produce as much as possible for the present, without worrying about what might become of him later."[28] Nevertheless, not one of the government's apprenticeship bills formulated in the mid-1840s had yet been brought forward for legislative debate when the July Monarchy came to an abrupt end.

By 1848, as the child labor reform literature of the republican era reveals, the concern over apprenticeship legislation and the concern over extended factory reform had become intertwined to a large extent. Still, the legislators of the republic apparently saw the issue of young workers in small shops as the more urgent. Even as they declined to revise the factory law of 1841, they saw fit to take action on apprenticeship. In August of 1848, the worker deputy Henri-Alexandre Peupin proposed the enactment of an apprenticeship bill based on the concepts under discussion within the Ministry of Commerce since 1845, and his initiative was pursued.

Peupin's proposal for legislation was referred to a committee of the legislature, where it was amended and reported out on February 12, 1849, by F. E. Parieu (who would shortly become minister of public instruction). In its report, the committee recommended specific measures for the control of apprenticeship and emphasized its belief that legislation was imperative. "The condition of children employed in factories has been regulated by protective measures for eight years already," the committee observed, but the condition of "the more numerous apprentices employed in shops with less than twenty workers . . . remains aban-

27. Report in AN, F12–4830.
28. Quoted in Louis Moreau-Christophe, *Du problème de la misère* (Paris, 1851), III, 494n.

doned to the often incomplete control of those [traditional] conventions that tie [apprentices] to their masters."[29] The time to regularize the control of apprenticeship had arrived.

Before any definitive action could be taken on an apprenticeship bill, however, the Constituent Assembly elected in 1848 was replaced by a Legislative Assembly. The new body decided that before it would act on the apprenticeship measure prepared in February, it would conduct the same kind of survey of interested parties that had been conducted in connection with previous measures for child labor reform. Thus, on June 30, 1849, a circular was dispatched by the Ministry of Commerce to chambers of commerce, *chambres consultatives*, and *conseils des prud'hommes*, soliciting their criticism of the pending apprenticeship law.

The basic concept of apprenticeship legislation elicited virtually no negative reaction from those who responded to the government's inquiry. The need to regulate apprenticeship seems to have been widely recognized, and it appears that French notables in the provinces, like officials within the government, no longer questioned the basic right of the state to regulate employer-employee relations, at least where minors were concerned. Indeed, those manufacturing interests that had complained that the nonregulation of small shops left them at a competitive disadvantage may well have been pleased to see steps taken to control the employment of young workers in places other than factories. That the apprenticeship measure before the assembly was relatively conservative must also have made it generally acceptable to those polled by the government. Contention arose only over relatively minor points of the proposed law: Should the minimum age for apprenticeship be twelve, as most agreed, or eleven? Should masters release their charges to attend school or see to their charges' elementary education themselves? Should the fines imposed on offenders be relatively large or (at the five or ten francs proposed) relatively small?

The committee charged with drafting a final version of the apprenticeship bill took into account the results of the 1849 survey and some of the ideas that emerged from the 1850 session of the new General Council of Manufacturing, Commerce, and Agriculture. It must also have been aware of the ongoing discussion of apprenticeship within the group organized by Armand de Melun to study public assistance.[30] Of course, the committee members, especially Auguste Callet, who pre-

29. Document in AN, F12–4830.
30. See Moon, *Labor Problem*, 48–49.

pared the final report, also injected their own ideas into the formulation of the apprenticeship bill on which the assembly would ultimately vote. The committee proceeded on the assumption that relations between masters and apprentices were of a more private nature than those between entrepreneurs and workers and that though master-apprentice relations were unquestionably liable to regulation, they had to be more carefully protected than other employment relationships against undue intrusion. The major change the committee made in the apprenticeship bill reported by Parieu in February, 1849, was to abandon altogether its provision for a minimum age. The committee reasoned that no such provision was necessary if the proper treatment of young apprentices was guaranteed by law, and it hesitated to deprive poor parents of the opportunity to place their children in a situation where they would get good care and training from an early age. The committee further weakened the bill by eliminating the maximum limit imposed on the number of apprentices any one master could take on, obviously ignoring the impact of such a move on the continuity of French craftsmanship.[31]

France's first comprehensive apprenticeship law was finally enacted on February 22, 1851. The first two articles of the law defined the nature of apprenticeship contracts and indicated how they were to be formalized. Although the prevailing practice of making contracts verbally was allowed to continue, the new apprenticeship law made it clear that written contracts drawn up and formally registered were preferable. The third article of the law described the specific information that was to be provided when an apprenticeship agreement was concluded. Articles four through seven defined certain conditions that would disqualify individuals from taking on apprentices. These articles forbade craftsmen with a criminal past and those under the age of twenty-one from supervising apprentices in most cases; they also prohibited unmarried male masters from providing lodging for any young female apprentices who might be in their care. This last clause is one of the few instances in which the specific issue of gender surfaced in France's early legislation regarding the labor of children. The motive behind this provision is easy to discern: because one of the prime concerns of middle-class reformers in the nineteenth century was improving the moral condition of the laboring classes, the reformers were naturally interested in prohibiting an arrangement by which young working girls could be compromised. This

31. The Callet report was submitted December 26, 1850. See Hayem and Périn, *Traité*, 5–10.

provision of the apprenticeship law would have had very little practical impact, however, even if the law had been strictly enforced. Most master craftsmen were married men, and most of their apprentices were boys. A tradition of male dominance was well established in most skilled trades, and the apprenticeship system had always perpetuated that dominance. In the few crafts dominated by women, such as high-quality artificial flower production, both masters and apprentices were usually females.[32]

Several articles of the 1851 law described the mutual obligations of apprentices and masters. Article eight of the measure charged masters with general responsibility for the behavior and the welfare of their apprentices. "The master must conduct himself toward his apprentice as a good father," the law advised. Masters were to oversee the conduct and morals of their wards "both at home and outside." Imposing limits on the work apprentices could do, article nine of the law decreed a ten-hour workday for youngsters under fourteen and a twelve-hour day for those between fourteen and sixteen. Most labor at night and on Sundays and holidays was also prohibited for apprentices under sixteen. By the terms of article ten, the masters of apprentices with insufficient education were obliged to allow them the opportunity to complete their schooling. Apprentices were expected to be able to read, write, and calculate and also to have had at least some "religious education" by the time they were sixteen. Article eleven of the 1851 law required that apprentices be faithful, obedient and respectful to their masters and that they work to assist their mentors to the best of their ability. Article twelve stipulated that masters had to train their apprentices properly in their trade.

Articles thirteen through seventeen of the apprenticeship law dealt with various matters pertaining to the duration of apprenticeship agreements and detailed the conditions under which apprenticeship contracts could be legally revised or terminated. Among other things, this section of the law designated the first two months of an apprenticeship as a probationary period. The final five articles of the apprenticeship measure gave *conseils des prud'hommes* primary jurisdiction in disputes concerning apprenticeship contracts and considered other matters of legal procedure. Article twenty set the punishments that could be imposed for violations of the apprenticeship law. The penalties for first offenses were rather light: fines of five to fifteen francs. The penalties for repeat offenses were more rigorous. Masters found guilty of having entered

32. See Marilyn J. Boxer, "Women in Industrial Homework: The Flowermakers of Paris in the Belle Epoque," *French Historical Studies*, XII (Spring, 1982), 401–23.

into apprenticeship arrangements despite their having been convicted of a crime or a breach of morals, for example, could be fined up to three hundred francs and sentenced to as many as three months in prison.[33]

The Apprenticeship Law of 1851 was another step in the direction of guaranteeing the welfare of France's laboring children. But as the apprenticeship law extended the state's protection to a new group of working youngsters, it tended also to create new complications in the overall picture of France's child labor legislation. Even though the apprenticeship law was something of a complement to the more fundamental Child Labor Law of 1841, the two measures were not totally compatible, thus giving rise to some contradiction and confusion. Children under the age of eight, for example, could not be taken on as laborers, but they could be employed as apprentices; factory children under twelve could work only eight hours a day as laborers, but they could work ten hours a day if they were called apprentices. In many cases youngsters in similar situations who obviously deserved the same protection were subject to two different standards.

Further, the 1851 law shared a major fault with the law of 1841: it lacked an effective system of enforcement. Neither strict penalties nor adequate provisions for inspection were attached to the apprenticeship law. Indeed, the legislature had specifically rejected an amendment intended to promote compliance with the new measure. The deputies Joseph Benoit and Esprit Doutre, one a silk worker and the other a printer, had proposed that *conseils des prud'hommes* be charged with the actual surveillance of small shops. The majority in the assembly, however, had shunned such an arrangement as excessively interventionist.[34] The intrusion of outsiders to monitor the condition of young workers had been accepted by France's legislators in the context of factory legislation, but the craftshop and the home workshop were still seen as essentially private domains to be supervised in a more circumspect manner.

With the passage of an apprenticeship law in 1851, more of the groundwork was laid for installing the French state as the ultimate protector of the nation's youth and the ultimate arbiter of working conditions. However, the discussions surrounding the enactment of the 1851 law and especially the reluctance of France's legislators to sanction the inspection of small shops reveal that the leaders of French society under

33. Material on the passage of the apprenticeship law, including material on the 1849 inquiry, is in AN, F12–4830. See also Mataja, "Origines," X, 252–55. Complete legal analyses of the law are in Hayem and Périn, *Traité*, 13ff, and in Merlet, *Lois*, 27–85.

34. Merlet, *Lois*, 62–64.

the Second Republic were still uncomfortable with the notion that the government could involve itself deeply in family affairs. Here again is a reminder that though policing various aspects of working-class life would eventually become a significant function of the French bureaucracy, at midcentury there was still a great reluctance to promote that function. Indeed, children were so often targeted by legislative programs and voluntary efforts for reform not only because they were seen as more malleable than their elders but also because intruding into their lives did not demand a complete abandonment of noninterventionist doctrine. It could be argued that children were not independent beings in the first place and that the leaders of society were acting (either directly or through the state) *in loco parentis*. The privileged classes still wanted to avoid blatant intervention into the lives of working-class adults, for in their minds there was still a serious conflict between their roles as the guarantors of freedom on the one hand and the guardians of public welfare on the other.

SEVEN

The Dilemma of Enforcement
Under the Second Empire

The coup d'etat of Louis-Napoléon Bonaparte in 1851 and the establishment of the Second Empire a year later were momentous events in the history of France, but these developments had no immediate impact on the status of France's laboring young. Throughout most of the period of Napoleon III's rule, neither the Child Labor Law of 1841 nor the Apprenticeship Law of 1851 had a decisive impact on the conduct of business in the nation's factories and shops. How to enforce existing regulations remained the great child labor dilemma of the imperial era. The Ministry of Commerce continually received reports about the problems of regulating schooling and moral standards, about the difficulty of finding people to serve on child labor commissions, and about the reluctance of factory owners and working families to cooperate in the implementation of the factory law. The situation during the 1850s was so bad in some places that the administration could not even get responses to its requests for information. After 1860, when the Ministry of Commerce issued a directive requiring that departmental authorities prepare annual statements concerning the enforcement of child labor regulations, reports from the provinces were still irregular at best. Those annual reports that did reach Paris in the 1860s, as well as other correspondence from that period, indicate that well into the empire's second decade many child labor regulations were being given mere lip service.[1]

---

1. See for example reports from the Ardennes, the Calvados, and the Allier in AN, F12–4709; from the Indre and the Loire in AN, F12–4711; from the Haut-Rhin in AN, F12–4712; from the Seine-Inférieure in AN, F12–4713; and from the Gironde in

The most often ignored provisions of the Child Labor Law of 1841 appear to have been those concerning schooling and *livrets*, no doubt because these were the provisions most burdensome to the parents and the employers of young laborers.[2] Working-class parents in the 1850s and 1860s still considered formal schooling of little practical benefit to their children (especially to their girls), and few were inclined to go through the seemingly senseless procedure of securing *livrets* for their children from the local authorities. The employers of factory children, who were supposed to verify school attendance and the possession of *livrets*, very often closed their eyes to parental noncompliance.

Other provisions of the child labor law were frequently violated as well. An 1864 report from the Calvados revealed that children there were still made to work on Sundays, and as late as 1867 a report from the Aveyron told of children under twelve working more than eight hours a day in the local glassworks and forges. At about the same time, one child labor inspector reported encountering children as young as four working thirteen hours a day in a match factory. An 1862 report from the prefect of the Indre, though perhaps an extreme example, nonetheless reflects the variety of child labor violations under the empire. About five hundred children were employed in industry in the Indre, and the prefect reported that they were generally admitted to factory labor only at age twelve or thirteen, after their First Communion. He observed further, however, that "their admission is allowed without anyone inquiring if they have received a primary education, or if they are attending school." Many of the most basic provisions of the 1841 law "have never been implemented," the prefect continued. "None of the children has a *livret*. Heads of establishments do not have the [required] register books. . . . There are neither internal regulations nor posted laws in the workshops. Morals and conditions of hygiene leave much to be desired."[3]

Noncompliance seemed to pervade the entire country. Throughout the 1850s and the 1860s, some of France's less industrialized departments still found comfort in claiming simply that the national child labor

---

AN, F12–4718 and F12–4720. See also the incomplete responses to a circular of September 25, 1854, in AN, F12–4720; and Audiganne, *Nouvelle Loi*, 11.

   2. See, for example, correspondence from the Allier in AN, F12–4709 and F12–4717; from the Ardennes in AN, F12–4709; from the Calvados in AN, F12–4709; and from the Loire in AN, F12–4711.

   3. Reports in AN, F12–4717 and F12–4718; Eugène d'Eichthal, "Les Lois sur le travail des enfans," *RDM*, 2nd per., C (1872), 427–28; Report in AN, F12–4717.

legislation did not apply to them, while some of her more industrialized departments continued to report major failures in enforcing the law.[4] In 1865, the prefect of the Seine-Inférieure related that in his region "application [of the child labor law] is not general," and the prefect of the Rhône confessed that, though the child labor situation was satisfactory in the city of Lyon, he was helpless to control it elsewhere. No one cared to enforce factory regulations in most of the department, he said, and parents often connived in evasion of the law. From the Haut-Rhin the prefect wrote that in Mulhouse, where there had previously been problems organizing factory inspection, the local child labor commission had now virtually ceased to function. Most of its members had died, and they had not been replaced.[5]

Even when the Ministry of Commerce received more positive reports concerning local compliance with child labor regulations, these seem to have been indications of temporary success rather than of a pattern of serious and consistent respect for the law. An 1854 report from the Department of the Tarn, for example, indicated that local inspection there had recently been rejuvenated, but a communication of 1856 revealed that the reorganization effort had failed and that local control of child labor was again a shambles. Yet another push for effective enforcement was undertaken after 1857, and a letter of 1859 explained that the factory law was being obeyed "thanks to the zeal of the subprefects, the activity of a few [volunteer] factory inspectors, the severity employed in the small number of circumstances [where it was necessary], and the [scholarship] prizes awarded to children."[6]

Similarly, a letter of March, 1853, from the Var indicated that the child labor law was fully observed in those few local establishments where it was applicable, but a report of September, 1855, showed that the child labor situation in the department's chief urban center, Toulon, was "disorganized." Many members of the local child labor commission had left town, and the mayor wanted nothing to do with the problem. Less than a year later, the situation had apparently changed again, with officials claiming that industry in the Var was in full compliance with the law. (The minister of commerce, however, expressed the fear that they

4. See, for example, correspondence of the 1860s from the Pyrénées-Orientales in AN, F12–4712, and from the Var in AN, F12–4719.
5. Correspondence in AN, F12–4713, F12–4719, and F12–4727. A situation similar to that in Mulhouse was reported in the Haute-Vienne: see the letter of September 18, 1865, in AN, F12–4727.
6. Correspondence in AN, F12–4714.

could make this claim only because the law was being interpreted too loosely.) By 1864, all pretense of enforcing the factory law had been abandoned, and the prefect was arguing that it was "not applicable whatsoever in the Department of the Var, which cannot be considered an industrial department."[7]

The Apprenticeship Law of 1851 fared no better under the Second Empire than did the child labor law. Despite the 1851 legislation, masters still only rarely introduced their apprentices to all aspects of their craft. More often, they set their charges to work at routinized tasks that could be performed quickly, without much attention to quality, detail, or instruction. The law's clearly stated preference for written contracts was also consistently ignored. An 1853 inquiry into the implementation of the apprenticeship law revealed that dealings between masters and their apprentices were virtually unaffected by the new legislation. "The specific terms of the law have brought about no perceptible modification of the existing state of affairs," wrote the prefect of the Nord, and the prefect of the Finistère pointed out that the illiteracy of many masters hampered the introduction of written apprenticeship contracts. "Even those who know how to write," he continued, "do not yet seem to appreciate the advantages offered by written contracts in cases where controversies arise."[8] An observer of the textile industry found in 1860 that though "custom had established an eight hour workday" for apprentices, that workday was very often prolonged "by two or even four hours, despite the prescriptions of the law concerning apprenticeship contracts."[9] In 1864, a study of apprenticeship in Paris confirmed the persistence of several grave problems. The study showed, for example, that of the city's 19,752 apprentices, only 4,523 (22.9 percent) had written contracts governing their service.[10]

In the first decade of the empire, about the only place where the child labor situation seemed to be under control was the Department of the Nord. Only there did anything approaching a regular and consistent enforcement of the 1841 child labor law exist. The Nord was successful

7. Correspondence in AN, F12–4714. A letter of 1869 similar to the one written in 1864 is in AN, F12–4717.

8. Material on the 1853 inquiry is in AN, F12–4830. For the particularly bad situation of children apprenticed to chimney sweeps during the Second Empire, see the Ministry of Interior circular of December 23, 1862, in AN, F12–4830, and C.-F. Bugniot, *Les Petits Savoyards* (Châlon-sur-Saône, 1863).

9. Jules Simon, *L'Ouvrière* (Paris, 1867), 49–50.

10. See Dolfus-Francoz, *Essai historique*, 51–52, and Mataja, "Origines," X, 367n.

because late in 1851 its *conseil général*, despairing of any action by the central government to deal with the problem of factory inspection, had voted an annual budget of fifteen hundred francs to pay the salary of a departmental factory inspector. The Nord's first factory inspector, a former notary, mayor, and volunteer child labor commissioner named Dupont, assumed his office in April of 1852.[11]

Throughout the early years of the empire, Inspector Dupont seems to have functioned enthusiastically and effectively. During 1853 (if Dupont's reports are to be believed), all work by children on Sundays and at night was eliminated in the Nord, and the number of factory children in Lille complying with the education provision of the law rose from 2,537 to 6,925. By 1854, nearly every child subject to the education provision of the child labor law was in compliance. In each year between 1854 and 1859, Dupont visited about seven hundred establishments employing some 1,200 children, and in each of those years the inspector compiled an impressive record in his prosecution of offenses. In 1854, Dupont brought charges against violators of the child labor law twenty-seven times and won twenty-seven convictions. In 1855, he brought charges eighty-four times and won eighty-four convictions, and in 1856 he won all but two of the twenty-three cases he prosecuted. The inspector's record was again perfect in 1857 and in 1858. Basic compliance with the law was so dramatically improved through the efforts of the factory inspector that the departmental authorities of the Nord were able to turn their attention to the finer points of child labor policy. During the 1850s they updated the form of the *livret* required by the factory law and attempted to replace all night schooling with day classes. The situation in the Nord was clearly exceptional.[12]

The great disparity between the ideal child labor situation as it was envisaged in the laws of 1841 and 1851 and the actual situation throughout most of France can be explained largely in terms of the distinction between those who promoted reform, on the one hand, and those who were expected to abide by reform legislation, on the other. Those who had fought for factory reform and apprenticeship controls during the quarter-century between 1827 and 1851 were, for the most part, individ-

11. See the report of September 22, 1851, in AN, F12–4712, and various other documents in F12–4712 and F12–4773. By 1854, the departmental inspector was receiving thirty-two hundred francs a year as salary and expense money. In 1855, four thousand francs were allocated, and by 1859 the figure was up to forty-seven hundred francs.
12. On child labor inspection in the Nord during the 1850s, see the correspondence in AN, F12–4712, and Reddy, *Market Culture*, 236–39.

uals who approached the matter of child labor from an ideological or humanitarian perspective. They were social critics of one sort or another, concerned about the well-being of those raised in a working-class culture and about the impact of the working classes on society as a whole. In general, the promoters of laws to protect factory children and apprentices were individuals not directly affected by the changes they advocated. They were professionals, journalists, intellectuals, and government officials. Those reformers who were involved in commerce or industry represented the industrial economy's more progressive sectors, which were less labor-intensive and less susceptible to small changes in labor costs. For the vast majority of the advocates of child labor reform, there were no intervening structural considerations to deter them from promoting changes in the way children functioned in the nation's factories and workshops.

Whereas the elite that speculated on social problems and formulated government policy could allow itself to view working children as victims of abuse who needed to be nurtured and guided both for their own sakes and for the sake of society, most of the employers and working-class parents who confronted the reality of child labor at the local level every day had more traditional and straightforward perceptions of laboring children. They viewed the children not as malleable beings who might someday be the salvation of society but rather as young wage earners who kept shops and factories running and whose earnings supplemented family incomes. Those for whom the employment of children was, above all else, a practical matter were quite willing to comply with the features of the new employment laws that were not too disruptive of established industrial practices, but they often chose to ignore or evade those provisions that were too intrusive. Working-class parents saw no viable alternative to employment for their children, and there was still a strong feeling among manufacturers that their relationship with their employees was their own affair. This feeling was perhaps even stronger among the masters of small craft shops, who saw their workplaces as extensions of their homes.

Local notables and government officials, for their part, were caught in the middle. They had child labor and apprenticeship laws to enforce— and they may well have agreed with the sentiments that underlay those laws—but (except in the Nord) they did not have the machinery necessary for serious enforcement. Neither the Child Labor Law of 1841 nor the Apprenticeship Law of 1851 provided for a rigorous, systematic inspection of factories and shops. The hesitancy of the French elite to make a clean break with the concepts of laissez-faire and of absolute paternal prerogative had left local authorities in an untenable position. They had to contend with the fact that adherence to the nation's child labor regulations depended on the economic circumstances and the personal inclinations of individual factory owners, craft shop masters, and parents more than it depended on any other factors.

Faced with the realization that child labor remained uncontrolled in many factories and workshops, local officials in a growing number of departments appealed to the imperial authorities for more central direction and for a greater national effort to guarantee complete and uniform enforcement of the factory law. As the following year-by-year listing indicates, the *conseils généraux* of no less than seventeen separate departments petitioned the government between 1852 and 1865; a dozen of these councils represented departments that were among France's twenty-five or so most industrialized:

1852   Eure, Seine-Inférieure
1853   Eure, Nord, Orne, Seine-Inférieure
1854   Pas-de-Calais
1856   Pas-de-Calais, Somme
1857   Pas-de-Calais, Nord, Somme
1858   Ardèche, Aube, Calvados, Pas-de-Calais
1859   Calvados, Haut-Rhin, Nord, Pas-de-Calais
1860   Ardèche, Haut-Rhin, Nord, Pas-de-Calais
1861   Haut-Rhin, Nord, Pas-de-Calais, Seine, Somme
1862   Haut-Rhin, Pas-de-Calais, Seine
1863   Haut-Rhin, Nord, Oise, Pas-de-Calais, Seine, Vosges
1864   Ardennes, Haut-Rhin, Nord, Oise, Somme, Seine, Tarn, Vosges
1865   Loire-et-Cher, Marne[13]

The *conseil général* of the Nord was in an especially good position to turn its attention to the national child labor problem, and among the suggestions it put forth in the 1850s were extending child labor regulations to mines and to factories with as few as ten workers and raising the minimum age for employment. The council also called attention to the need for action to prevent industrial accidents and for efforts to eliminate the problem of cheating on working hours. By employing complex relay systems, by shortening rest periods, and by juggling the times at which work commenced and ceased, factory owners could and did cir-

13. This listing appears in both Délerot, "Avant-propos," 24, and *Documents*, 112.

cumvent the maximum workday stipulated in the 1841 law. Above all, the *conseil général* of the Nord was concerned about the uniformity of factory law enforcement throughout the country, and as early as 1852 it urged the central government to encourage other departments to follow the example it had set and to select their own salaried factory inspectors.[14]

The desire of local notables and government officials for a more rigorous enforcement of child labor regulations was, no doubt, altruistic to some extent, and the individuals who sat on departmental advisory councils (especially in more industrialized areas) were precisely the kind of people who would have been interested in the regeneration of the working classes in general. However, there was also a practical motive behind the demands of the councils. Since at least a marginal economic advantage accrued to factories that employed child laborers, the councils were concerned about limiting unfair competition between areas of lax enforcement and areas where regulations were observed with somewhat greater regularity. In the Nord, of course, this motivation for urging uniform enforcement was extremely relevant.

While the notables of several industrial departments were petitioning the administration directly in the fifties and early sixties, propagandists who favored improvements in the child labor situation were disseminating their thoughts more widely. Some of the child labor reform literature of this period concentrated on the immediate question of how to enforce the provisions that were already law; some went further to call for new and more restrictive measures to control the employment of children. The great concern over enforcement was reflected, for example, in the writings of several reform advocates who had been active under previous regimes. The bulletin of the Société industrielle de Mulhouse came out with a two-page notice in 1857 on the poor state of factory law enforcement in the Haut-Rhin, and at about the same time, Daniel Legrand issued a new appeal for international cooperation on child labor. Armand Audiganne, who had become interested in child labor under the republic, was still doing whatever he could to enforce compliance with existing child labor regulations and to publicize the need for improving the enforcement of the factory law. In *Les Populations ouvrières et les industries de la France*, first published in 1854 and reissued in 1860, Audiganne wrote:

14. Correspondence in AN, F12–4712.

If, in evaluating the present state of compliance with the 1841 law, some traces of its positive influence are discovered, in truth it must be said that those traces are only partial and shallow. Many gaps remain to be filled; the benefit [of the law] must be generalized, the application of the measure must become uniform. The level of compliance with the law . . . is not rising; it even seems at times to fall. One need only consider the demands of competition to realize that evil must engender evil. As long as compliance is not general, the law is condemned to fall into disuse.[15]

As writers had done for several decades, the reform advocates of this period also linked a consideration of child labor to the middle-class concern for the moral and physical reconstitution of working-class life. The connection between child labor reform and the larger *question sociale* was nowhere more clearly drawn than in the writings of Jules Simon. Under the empire, Simon was gradually emerging as an important spokesman for liberal Catholicism and moderate republicanism, and in his attitude toward the working classes, he was typical of bourgeois liberals. He considered the inequalities that existed in industrial society to be inevitable, and he objected to the idea that the state should try to eliminate poverty or control industrial affairs. At the same time, Simon was sensitive to the plight of those who were defenseless victims of industrial society, and he thought that they deserved some support in their formative years. Perhaps if they were given a good start in life, he reasoned, they could escape the deprivation and depravity of their parents. Thus, he supported efforts to improve education, to provide vocational training, and to restrict industrial child labor. Simon's views are reflected in his book *L'Ouvrière*, published in 1861. Although the book focuses on the plight of working women, it often speaks in general terms about the condition of the working classes, and it describes the hardships of apprentices and factory children. As other reformers of the time did, Simon decried the shortcomings of France's child labor legislation. The law of 1841, he observed, was far less demanding than the factory laws of other industrialized states, and even its rather weak provisions were not uniformly enforced. "Despite our destructive and debilitating mania for creating functionaries for every purpose," wrote Simon, "we do not have a genuine inspection of child labor, and this renders the law feeble and nearly useless." He argued that meaningful child labor legislation had to be

15. [Emile Dollfus], "Lettre . . . sur l'inobservance de la loi sur le travail des enfants . . . ," *BSIM*, XXVIII (May, 1857), 126–27; Material in AN, F12–4720; Armand Audiganne, *Les Populations ouvrières et les industries de la France* (Paris, 1860), II, 293.

introduced, along with public housing, old age and accident insurance, and improved education, if the working classes were to be reformed and uplifted.[16]

Demands for attention to the condition of child laborers and apprentices came also from Armand de Melun and his followers. The Société d'économie charitable and its journal, *Annales de la charité*, both of which Melun had founded in the 1840s, concentrated a tremendous amount of interest in the period of the Second Empire on the child labor issue. The pages of the *Annales* were filled with articles that stressed the importance of rescuing the children of the poor. The journal also carried reports on the work of voluntary *sociétés de patronage* and appeals for the improvement of France's labor legislation.[17] In 1858, a committee of the Société d'économie charitable conducted an extensive study of compliance with the Child Labor Law of 1841 and the Apprenticeship Law of 1851 and concluded that new legislation was a critical necessity. The committee's report, which was published in the *Annales*, urged the enactment of a new law to impose child labor regulations in more shops, reduce the workday of children under twelve to six hours a day, and introduce a system of salaried factory inspection. The promotion of equitable competition was cited as one of the chief rationales for salaried inspection. "Uniformity in the execution of the law will keep some localities from finding themselves at a disadvantage in relation to others, and will render the conditions of competition freer and fairer," the committee observed.[18]

Turning to a consideration of the apprenticeship law, the study committee of the Société d'économie charitable suggested that neglect of the provision for Sunday rest was the matter most in need of attention. This provision, it argued, was "the most important from the point of view of a child's physical development, as well as from the point of view of his

16. See Simon, *L'Ouvrière*, 49–59, esp. 52. See also Philip A. Bertocci, *Jules Simon: Republican Anticlericalism and Cultural Politics in France, 1848–1886* (Columbia, Mo., 1978), 124–26.

17. See, for example, Paul de Caux, "Patronage des apprentis et jeunes ouvriers," *Annales de la charité*, XIV (1858), 473–85; "Execution de la loi sur le travail des enfants dans les manufactures," *Annales de la charité*, XV (1859), 159–65; and Armand de Melun, "Courrier des oeuvres: Oeuvre des apprenties et des jeunes ouvrières," *Revue d'économie chrétienne: Annales de la charité*, n.s., IV (1863), 532–53. For a more complete discussion of Melun and the work of *patronage*, see Weissbach, *"Oeuvre industrielle."*

18. Ludovic Delamarre, "Exécution de la loi du 22 mars 1841 sur le travail des enfants dans les manufactures et de la loi du 4 mars 1851 sur le contrat d'apprentissage," *Annales de la charité*, XIV (1858), 193–210.

moral and religious interest." In order to promote compliance with the requirement that apprentices be released from work on Sundays, the committee recommended new legislation requiring apprentices to report in person to the municipal authorities each Sunday to verify their absence from the workshop. This scheme would probably not have been a very practical one (the committee itself admitted that it was imperfect), but that it was proposed at all indicates the frustration middle-class reformers felt when they saw the laws they considered so important being ignored.

One of the most dramatic appeals for further child labor reform to appear in print during the first decade of the empire was contained in a pamphlet published in 1855 by L. de Waziers van der Crusse, a volunteer child labor commissioner from the Nord who also happened to be the father-in-law of Armand de Melun's twin brother. This pamphlet insisted that France had to better the lot of its child laborers, if only to save face in the eyes of civilized Europe. It proposed enacting a new child labor law that would guarantee quality education for all children and uniform factory inspection by salaried agents. The appeals for reform in the pamphlet were punctuated by references to sensational instances of abuse, such as those perpetrated by an artificial flower manufacturer who had systematically mistreated his twenty young workers until he was arrested: "He beat them with instruments of torture, with a rubber whip, with a cat-o'-nine tails. Two young girls died in the hospital of maltreatment soon after leaving his shop. He made these children work from six in the morning to eleven at night; sometimes all night long. He kept one boy of fourteen in bonds for eleven weeks for daring to resist him."[19]

Despite the persistence of the child labor problem under the empire and despite appeals for action from several quarters, the imperial government did not appear to be alarmed. The policy of the Napoleonic state, like that of the republican administration before it, was characterized by a sense of ongoing concern, but no sense of urgency. In practice, this meant the imperial bureaucracy was willing to attempt to improve compliance with the existing law but it was disinclined to consider any child labor policies that would depart significantly from those of previous regimes. The Ministry of Commerce was especially eager to clarify

19. L. de Waziers van der Crusse, *Projet de règlement d'administration publique* (Paris, 1855), esp. 3. On the relationship of Waziers van der Crusse to Melun, see D'Andigné, *Apôtre*, 22.

the provisions of the 1841 child labor law in an effort to make it easier to enforce. In a circular of June, 1854, the ministry reiterated the inapplicability of the factory law to mines; in a dispatch of September, it detailed the organization of factory surveillance; in an exchange of letters in 1855 with a child labor inspector in the Nord, it explained the government's policy concerning travel expenses incurred by volunteer factory inspectors.[20]

At times, the ministry even sought new ways to improve the policing of factories without altering the fundamentally local character of factory law enforcement. In this regard, the situation in the Nord proved to be of special interest to the commerce ministry, for the presence there of a salaried factory inspector was having the effect of tightening compliance with the factory law without violating the concept of local inspection. In 1853, reacting to the recent suggestion of the *conseil général* of the Nord, the Ministry of Commerce contacted the prefects and *conseils généraux* of eleven industrialized departments and urged them to consider the selection of salaried factory inspectors to serve locally. All the *conseils généraux* rejected this proposal, however. The council of the Aube decided that it did not have enough industry to warrant the naming of an inspector, and the council of the Pas-de-Calais said that it still hoped local voluntary commissions could be made effective. The councils of the Eure and of the Seine-et-Oise claimed that it was too late to revise their budgets, and the council of the Haut-Rhin refused to name a departmental inspector on the grounds that what was really needed was a national corps of inspectors. Late in 1854, when the idea of appointing a paid inspector was raised before the *conseil général* of the Seine-Inférieure, that body also voted to leave enforcement of the factory law to the existing authorities.[21]

While encouraging the appointment of paid inspectors in some departments, the ministry also communicated with the authorities in several others where factory law enforcement seems to have been especially lax, urging them to strengthen their voluntary child labor commissions. The ministry suggested, for example, that clergymen and government functionaries might be coopted by these boards.[22] In 1854 and 1855, obviously disappointed with the response evoked by its attempt to build

20. See various documents in AN, F12–4720 and F12–4733.
21. Correspondence in AN, F12–4713 and F12–4773.
22. See documents in AN, F12–4709; material on a circular of September 30, 1854, in AN, F12–4720; and a letter of June 10, 1853, from the prefect of the Marne in AN, F12–4773. See also Mataja, "Origines," X, 361.

on the experience of the Nord, the government considered asking local councils of hygiene or local overseers of abandoned children to take responsibility for enforcing the child labor law. At one point the Ministry of Commerce even toyed with the idea of officially placing enforcement in the hands of the police, but all these schemes were soon abandoned. They all would have meant further burdening the already overburdened, and the plan involving the police authorities was judged to conform "neither to the spirit nor to the letter of the law of 1841."[23]

In effect, a kind of vicious circle had been created in the discussion of child labor reform. Whereas departmental authorities (and reform advocates in general) confronted with noncompliance were looking to Paris for more determined administrative actions and for an improved system of factory inspection, the imperial administration continued to view enforcement as an essentially local matter. Still, the administration did have an interest in seeing that the 1841 factory law was enforced. The government had no philosophical problem with child labor legislation, for the existing factory law fit well with the Bonapartist view that the French economic system needed not a major overhaul but only some fine-tuning to make it more efficient and humane. The factory law was compatible as well with the somewhat paternalistic attitude of the bureaucracy of the empire.[24] Moreover, the empire had consistently stressed its concern with French industry and with the welfare of industrial society, and it always promoted itself as the guarantor of efficient government and social stability. "Order is heaven's first law," declared Eugène Rouher, one of Napoleon III's closest collaborators and the minister of commerce from 1855 to 1863.[25] If a law was on the books—and especially if that law concerned the organization of production and the well-being of the laboring classes—the empire was inclined to try to enforce it. Thus, as the Ministry of Commerce became more fully aware of the state of factory law enforcement in the early years of the empire, it was forced to begin questioning the efficacy of local factory inspection, and a decade after the discussion of the 1847 child labor bill had been interrupted, the ministry finally revived the idea of creating a paid central inspectorate. By that time, of course, central inspection was being

---

23. A. Colmart, *De l'inspection du travail en France* (Paris, 1899), 51–52; document in AN, F12–4773.
24. See Stuart L. Campbell, *The Second Empire Revisited* (New Brunswick, N.J., 1978), 7ff, and Pierre-Léon Fournier, *Le Second Empire et la législation ouvrière* (Paris, 1911), 89ff.
25. See G. P. Gooch, *The Second Empire* (1960; rpr. Westport, Conn., 1975), 154–60, and R. D. Anderson, *Education in France, 1848–1870* (Oxford, 1975), 195.

advocated by many propagandists, several *conseils généraux*, and even the Senate of France.

In 1857, the secretary general of the commerce ministry (the official who acted as liaison with the Conseil d'état, where all new legislation was initiated) began preparing a dossier on the feasibility of implementing centralized factory inspection. The ministry outlined a system involving an inspector-general at Paris and seven divisional inspectors to act in conjunction with the local child labor commissions in France's thirty-three most industrialized departments. On February 10, 1858, the ministry dispatched a circular to the prefects of the departments involved, asking them to appraise the likelihood that their respective *conseils généraux* would both accept the proposed plan for factory inspection and be willing to fund it at least in part. The replies to the circular were encouraging: nineteen prefects said they believed their departmental councils would favor the plan, six found they had no basis on which to reply, and only two responded negatively. On July 23, the prefects contacted in February were instructed to present to their departmental councils the idea of a national inspectorate funded jointly by the departments and the state. The reaction in the councils to the commerce ministry's scheme, though essentially positive, was qualified. A summary of the councils' replies, prepared in September, 1858, shows that they all acknowledged the need for an improved method of factory inspection but that only fourteen of the *conseils généraux* contacted were willing to vote the money necessary to fund the ministry's program, whereas eighteen were not. As in many other instances where the issue of child labor was concerned, philosophical agreement gave way to practical considerations. Support for reform in theory was one thing; a financial commitment was another. The councils of the very highly industrialized departments of the Nord, the Rhône, the Seine-Inférieure, the Bouches-du-Rhône, the Loire, and the Haut-Rhin all approved funding the scheme proposed to them in 1858, but this was perhaps because they realized that some form of salaried inspection would soon have to be implemented (the Nord already had such a plan), and they therefore welcomed the prospect of having the state provide at least a part of the necessary financing.

On May 6, 1859, the dossier prepared in the Ministry of Commerce was presented to the Conseil d'état. At that point the dossier contained not only the responses to the inquiries of February and July, 1858, but also other correspondence concerning factory legislation and some material on the child labor situation in England, where new legislation enacted in 1856 had increased the number of factory inspectors significantly.[26] The discussions that took place in the Conseil d'état revealed that despite the initiative of the commerce ministry, the top policy makers of France were not yet prepared to abandon the idea of locally supported inspection. Any new system of factory inspection, they decided, "ought not to have but a local character and thus its cost can under no circumstances be charged to the public treasury." They did concede, however, that "in light of the costs that already burden the departments," it would be very difficult to have the departments bear the cost of paid inspection "in whole or in part." Thus, even though the Conseil d'état agreed that the existing system of inspection was totally inadequate, and even though it approved the ministry's proposed scheme of inspection in principle, it could see no way of funding the plan other than having the establishments that were subject to the law pay for factory surveillance themselves. The council ordered that a circular be dispatched to solicit the reaction of France's prefects, and of other interested parties, to this new and rather unique idea.

Responses to the inquiry initiated by the Conseil d'état came in slowly during the latter part of 1859, and at the end of February, 1860, a summary of the communications received in Paris was prepared by the director of the Division of Domestic Commerce, Julien. According to this summary, the existing system of child labor law enforcement was judged inadequate in fifty-six departments and was considered sufficient in only ten. In nineteen departments, no opinion was rendered. Obviously a proponent of reform himself, Julien reported, on the basis of these results, that judgments about the sufficiency of the existing system of enforcement were, "one could say, unanimously in the negative." When it came to the question of charging factory owners for the surveillance of their own shops, Julien's summary showed opinion to be much more divided. The authorities in thirty-one departments favored having factory owners bear the financial burden of inspection, but the authorities in forty other departments opposed such an idea. Not surprisingly, those who supported the plan were almost exclusively representatives of nonindustrial departments. Julien himself tended to agree with the respondents from France's more industrialized regions that the cost of inspection should not be borne by entrepreneurs. He pointed out to the secretary-

26. See material in AN, F12–4707; and Overbergh, *Inspecteurs*, 83ff. On English factory legislation during this period, see Hutchins and Harrison, *Factory Legislation*, 43ff, 96ff.

general of the commerce ministry that the amount of money involved would not justify setting up the machinery necessary to collect it from factory owners.[27]

Those who received the government questionnaire of 1859 were also asked what they thought of a proposal to appoint an inspector-general of factories. Respondents from twelve departments favored the idea, but respondents from twenty-nine other departments contended that the appointment of an inspector-general was not necessary. Julien was apparently disappointed with these responses, for instead of including them in his report, he simply observed that departmental officials were not in a position to pass judgment on the need for central direction.

The responses to the 1859 government inquiry revealed that there was latent support for the implementation of centralized factory inspection, even if there was no great enthusiasm for it, and no agreement on exactly how it should be funded. No immediate action was taken, however. Confronted with this inertia at the highest levels of government, Julien continued to press for centralized inspection, and over the next few years various *conseils généraux* urged that the plan developed in 1857 be revived.[28] There is fragmentary evidence of a government study in 1860 of labor conditions that also confirmed the need for a system of centralized inspection.[29] In 1862, in 1864, and again in 1866, the problem of factory surveillance was brought before the Conseil d'état for consideration, but the council continued to keep the idea of centralized inspection in limbo.[30] Although the file on the inspection plan of 1857 remained open, there was still no sense of urgency in the top echelons of the administration about its implementation.

In some ways the political situation in the early 1860s resembled that of the middle 1830s. An increasing number of people in influential positions were becoming advocates of a new program of child labor reform, the government was conceding the need at least to study the possibility of new legislation, and the impression that the opinion leaders of

27. Material on the 1857–60 attempt to establish a paid central inspectorate is primarily in AN, F12–4773. Some material on the responses to the circular of June 25, 1859, is in AN, F12–4720.

28. See, for example, Julien's letter of December 8, 1860, to the secretary-general of the commerce ministry in AN, F12–4773. For the ideas of the *consiels généraux*, see, for example, correspondence of 1860 from the Nord and the Aube, and correspondence of 1862 from the Haut-Rhin and from the Meuse, all in AN, F12–4773.

29. See AN, F12–4709, F12–4720.

30. Material in AN, F12–4773; Mataja, "Origines," X, 362; and Levasseur, *Histoire*, II, 732.

French society were willing to accept new reform measures was growing. But the power of the reform movement in the early sixties, like that of the movement in the midthirties, was not yet sufficient to overcome the expressed objections to reform or to counteract the bureaucratic inertia that was probably the most substantial stumbling block in the way of a new program to curtail the abuse of child labor. In the middle and late years of the decade, however, the reform movement would gain tremendous strength.

EIGHT

The Reform Movement Quickens

The middle and late 1860s witnessed a dramatic intensification of concern over child labor. The outcry for action to alleviate the abuse of working children did not become universal, by any means, but the increase in calls for reform was marked. The basic reasons for concern over child labor were still the same in the 1860s; bourgeois advocates of reform still spoke of the need to protect vulnerable children from the foul environments of factories, of the need to educate and discipline the children of the working classes, of the need to strengthen the family, and of the need to preserve the nation's youth for the defense of the motherland. Perhaps among reformers from the privileged classes there was even something of a sense of guilt that motivated them to confront the problems of disadvantaged working-class youth.[1] But never before was there such a pronounced outpouring of support for child labor reform. Mention of the child labor problem cropped up in an increasing variety of contexts, and public appeals for reform multiplied. Specific attempts to ameliorate the condition of young workers proliferated as well in these last years of the empire. For the first time, it could be said that public opinion in the broad sense was awakening to the child labor issue, and reform was no longer the concern of only a limited number of crusaders in and out of government.

Several factors account for the tremendous new interest during the

1. On guilt in this context, see Peter Gay, "On the Bourgeoisie: A Psychological Interpretation," in John M. Merriman (ed.), *Consciousness and Class Experience in Nineteenth-Century Europe* (New York, 1979), 195–96.

middle and late 1860s in the child labor problem. One of these is the substantial advance of French industrialization under the empire. The period of the Second Empire was a time of considerable industrial growth and maturation for France. A rapidly developing credit network and infrastructure, a new generation of entrepreneurs, and an expanding consumer market all stimulated increased production. Industrial output doubled between 1852 and 1870, coal consumption tripled, and the use of steam power increased fivefold.[2] The economic ferment and the industrial expansion of the era could not help but focus national attention on the industrial sector and, by extension, on child labor as one of its more problematic aspects. Moreover, much of France's industrial strength still depended on her traditional luxury industries, and because fine handcrafted goods could compete effectively with mass-produced goods only if they retained their high quality, concern over the proper training of young workers for the future grew.[3] Attention was thus increasingly focused on apprentices in small shops as well as on factory children.

Interest in child labor reform was stimulated, too, by the fact that the fate of working children was more than ever perceived as central to the larger issue of the future of the working classes. Advancing industrialization brought with it an expanding working population and this intensified middle-class concern with the *question sociale*. By the 1860s the effort to instill middle-class values in the working classes was in full swing (the word *moralisation* had acquired a new meaning to describe this effort), and much of the bourgeoisie had come to accept the importance of influencing working-class youths if the laboring population was to be transformed.[4]

The special concern with the children of the working classes must also be explained in terms of the new attitude toward childhood in general that was being adopted by the bourgeoisie in nineteenth-century French society. This new attitude, based on the recognition of childhood as a period of nurturing and education, was a more sentimental and protective one than had held sway in times past, and it focused attention on children as unique beings with special needs. The new view of childhood

2. See Guy P. Palmade, *French Capitalism in the Nineteenth Century*, trans. Graeme Holmes (New York, 1972), 116ff; David S. Landes, *The Unbound Prometheus* (Cambridge, Eng., 1969), 193–95; and Charles P. Kindleberger, *Economic Growth in France and Britain: 1851–1950* (New York, 1964), 6–7.

3. See François Caron, *An Economic History of Modern France*, trans. Barbara Bray (New York, 1979), 135–38, and Patrick O'Brien and Caglar Keyder, *Economic Growth in Britain and France, 1780–1914* (London, 1978), 192.

4. Bezucha, "Moralization," 175–77.

implied that whereas middle-class children might need a certain liberation from traditional restrictions so that their personalities could develop naturally, working-class children needed a greater subjection to control and guidance so that they could be kept clear of antisocial influences.[5]

The sentimental and protective view of childhood was not a new one at the time of the empire; it had been developing since at least the end of the eighteenth century. Indeed, the more modern view of childhood had informed the home life of certain of the elite (including the court of Louis-Philippe) from early in the nineteenth century, and it had been one of the factors motivating the champions of France's first child labor law in the late thirties and early forties. But what is important for an understanding of the history of child labor reform in the long run is that in the decade of the sixties the more modern view of childhood finally became generally accepted within the French bourgeoisie. It became normative rather than exceptional. Almost as if it had finally reached a sort of critical mass then, the acceptance of the modern view of childhood began generating manifestations that could be seen everywhere.

It was in the 1860s that modern child-rearing literature began to make its mark; Gustave Droz's "wildly successful" manual *Monsieur, madame et bébé* first appeared in 1866.[6] It was in the 1860s that children made their appearance in French literature as completely developed central characters, with distinct personalities and full importance to plot development; this was the decade of Victor Hugo's Cosette and Gavroche.[7] It was in the 1860s that the first children's literature designed to entertain as well as to educate appeared; Pierre-Jules Hetzel's popular and influential *Magasin d'éducation et de récréation* was founded in 1864.[8] It was in the 1860s that a state system of free and compulsory education first came under serious consideration, with Victor Duruy, minister of public in-

5. See Donzelot, *Policing*; Philippe Ariès, "Le XIXe Siècle et la révolution des moeurs familiales," in Robert Prigent (ed.), *Renouveau des idées sur la famille* (Paris, 1954), 111ff; and André Armengaud, "L'Attitude de la société à l'égard de l'enfant au XIXe siècle," *Annales de démographie historique* (1973), 303–306. A good summary of the development of the modern notion of childhood is in Neil Postman, *The Disappearance of Childhood* (New York, 1982), 3–64.

6. Theodore Zeldin, *France 1848–1945* (Oxford, 1973–77), I, 295, 328; Shorter, *Making of the Modern Family*, 191.

7. Calvet, *Enfant*, I, 193ff; Aimé Dupuy, *Un Personnage nouveau du roman français, l'enfant* (Tunis, 1931), 9–17; Parker, *Defense of the Child*, passim. See also Victor Hugo, *Les Misérables*, trans. Charles E. Wilbour (New York, 1964).

8. Calvet, *Enfant*, 206ff. See also Isabelle Jan, "Children's Literature and Bourgeois Society in France since 1860," Esther S. Kanipe, "Hetzel and the Bibliothèque d'education et de récréation," and Marion Durand, "One Hundred Years of Illustrations in French Children's Books," all in *Yale French Studies*, XLIII (1969).

struction from 1863 to 1869, among its strongest advocates.[9] The blossoming middle-class concern with the protection of working children was thus a part both of the bourgeois concern with *moralisation* and of the more general discovery of childhood. Those embryonic concerns about the future of industrial society and about the nature of childhood that had been reflected in the passage of the Child Labor Law of 1841 had, by the sixties, emerged as major considerations in many middle-class circles.

By the mid-1860s it appeared that attention was being called to the child labor problem from every quarter. The issue was raised in studies of primary instruction published in 1861 and 1864, in an 1865 report on technical education, in an 1867 investigation of crime.[10] As children became increasingly important characters in poetry and fiction, depictions of them at work proliferated in popular literature. In the 1863 poem "La Fille aux bobines," for example, Eugène Manuel conjured up the image of a pregnant factory girl:

> Under the bobbins that turned,
> Reattaching each wisp of silk
> Her little fingers came and went,
> Tightened or loosened the belt.[11]

The sixties also saw factory children make their appearance for the first time in French novels. Mme. Bourdon's *Marthe Blondel*, set in Lille, and Emile Bosquet's *Roman des ouvrières*, set in Rouen, both told stories of girls in their teens thrown into factory labor during the 1840s.[12] Perhaps the most influential novelist in this area to write about laboring children was Alphonse Daudet. In his largely autobiographical first novel, *Le Petit Chose*, which appeared in 1868, Daudet revealed his interest in the experiences of childhood, and in *Jack*, published a few years later, he wrote in some detail of factory labor.

The novelists writing in this era about factory children wanted to evoke the sympathy of their readers. "The task we set for ourselves will be fullfilled," wrote Bosquet in the introduction to her novel, "if we can convey to our readers that anguished yet deep and tender sympathy

9. Anderson, *Education in France*, 135ff.
10. Délerot, "Avant-propos," 25–27; Mataja, "Origines," X, 362, 364; Anderson, *Education in France*, 164ff, 202; Jules Simon, *L'Ouvrier de huit ans* (Paris, 1867), 273ff.
11. Quoted in Grant, *French Poetry*, 190.
12. Mathilde Froment [Mme. Bourdon], *Marthe Blondel ou l'ouvrière de fabrique* (Paris, 1863); Amélie [Emile] Bosquet, *Le Roman des ouvrières* (Paris, 1868). See also Lynch, "Problem of Child Labor Reform," 232.

inspired in us by the unfortunates whose lives we trace." These novelists painted a frightening picture of the factory as seen through the eyes of a child. For Bourdon, the factory was a place "where, all too often, blasphemy, bad example, [and] scandal appear to corrupt even the air one breathes."[13] And Daudet described his title character, Jack, at work in these words:

> Little Jack is working the screw! And I might for ten years search unsuccessfully for any other words that could express more exactly the feeling of terror, suffocation, and horrible anguish which his surroundings caused him.
> First of all, there was that frightful deafening noise, three hundred hammers falling simultaneously upon the anvil, the whistling of leather bands, the working of pulleys, and all the uproar of a hive of busy workers, three hundred chests, bare and panting, strained to the utmost, and cries that bore no longer the least resemblance to anything human.

The experience of the factory, Daudet related, placed Jack in danger of becoming "the typical factory boy: that wretched, overworked, stifled, stunted being whose face ages more and more as his body wastes away."[14] Daudet's writings have been compared to the novels of Charles Dickens, and Daudet himself allowed the similarities: "In my heart I sense the love Dickens felt for the unfortunate and poor, for children entangled in urban miseries; I had, like him, a harrowing entry into this life, the obligation to earn a living before the age of sixteen; I imagine it is in this that our greatest resemblance lies."[15]

The clearest manifestation of intensified interest in child labor reform in the middle and late sixties was the proliferation of specific appeals for new government initiatives to protect and educate factory children and apprentices. The most important of these appeals were penned by middle-class opinion leaders whose interest in child labor reform had been molded in previous years. Armand Audiganne, for example, included an important section on child labor in his study *Les Ouvriers d'à present*, which appeared in 1865. The essence of what Audiganne had written in *Les Populations ouvrières et les industries de la France* was repeated in his new book, but *Les Ouvriers d'à present* contained some specific new suggestions for reform as well. Although Audiganne was basically satisfied with the provisions of the 1841 factory law, and though he cau-

---

13. Bosquet, *Roman*, ix; Froment [Bourdon], *Blondel*, vii.
14. Alphonse Daudet, *Jack*, trans. Marian McIntyre (Boston, 1900), II, 1–3. Compare the similar description in Froment [Bourdon], *Blondel*, 29ff.
15. Quoted in Dupuy, *Personnage nouveau*, 13. See also Parker, *Defense of the Child*, 13–16.

tioned against the expectation of an overnight amelioration of factory conditions, he was concerned that there was no effective system of inspection to foster compliance with the law. Thus he advocated a new enforcement scheme. He suggested retaining local child labor commissions as the principal organs of enforcement but supplementing them with salaried inspectors. Audiganne also wanted to see the influence of the local commissions enhanced by their augmentation with retired laborers and their efficiency improved through more forceful central direction. He suggested placing enforcement of the 1851 apprenticeship law in the hands of the invigorated local boards as well.[16]

Jules Simon was also at work on the child labor issue again, publishing articles in the *Revue des deux mondes* in 1864 and 1865 and an important book, *L'Ouvrier de huit ans*, in 1867. Looking across France's border at a Germany newly reorganized under Prussian leadership, Simon began his 1867 discourse with a reminder that France had to remain militarily strong; the entire population had to be a sort of reserve army, "incapable of attacking, [but] invincible if attacked." This vigilance meant that France's youth had to be protected from the horrors of industrial life. Simon underlined his point with descriptions of the travails of the working young. He characterized the eight-year-old youngster sent into a factory as an "untamed, lively vagabond, [a] rambling unrestrained child," and he described what awaited the child on the shop floor: "All of a sudden he is shut up within four walls and is shown that there is no longer time to laugh and that henceforth it is only a matter of paying attention to the work. He remains there silent, deafened by the din of machines, surrounded by big people who are often neither sensitive nor exemplary [in their behavior]; if there are other children there, he sees them from afar, without being able to exchange one word with them." Simon, like Audiganne, proposed a specific program of reform. He called for instituting a half-time system for children under twelve, for extending the application of factory regulations to all shops, and for harmonizing the law covering child labor with the one covering apprenticeship. He also demanded that more attention be paid to professional education. Carrying his arguments for protecting the young even further, Simon contended that it was harmful for children to be deprived of their mothers' attention; he attributed high infant mortality rates among worker families—33 percent of children under the age of one at Mulhouse, 35 percent at Lyon—primarily to the absence of the mother.

16. Armand Audiganne, *Les Ouvriers d'à present* (Paris, 1865), 207–22, 229.

Thus, he suggested that female labor, like child labor, should be strictly limited.[17]

The Polish emigré Louis Wolowski, one of the most consistent advocates of child labor reform in France, was active in the sixties as well. Wolowski had spoken in favor of child labor legislation in his first lecture at the Conservatoire des arts et métiers in 1840, he had become a volunteer inspector after the passage of the 1841 law, and he had proposed revision of the factory law under the Second Republic.[18] But never was his call for child labor reform stronger or more widely heard than in 1868. In that year, he expounded his ideas in two lectures as part of his course in political economy and industrial legislation at the Conservatoire, and these two lectures were subsequently published and reprinted for wider distribution. Returning to the popular agricultural imagery so frequently employed in reference to child labor reform, Wolowski prefaced his discussion of factory legislation with the observation that such legislation "has as its goal preventing the sapping of childhood strength, [preventing] a premature harvest." He applauded the factory law of 1841 as "an effective protest against the idolatry of profits," but he complained that the absence of a vigorous system of factory inspection was a very grave fault. Because he saw rigorous inspection as the "very sinew of serious legislation," he called for its introduction without further delay. Like Simon, Wolowski, too, called for the extension of factory legislation to cover all female laborers, regardless of age. He defended his suggestion by contending that females, like children, are not totally free in their dealings with their employers to begin with. "Whatever might be said to the contrary in England," he assured his audience, "women do not have liberty as complete as that of men."[19]

As middle-class spokesmen for factory legislation, Audiganne, Simon, and Wolowski all expressed the dominant bourgeois attitude toward child labor reform. They all recognized that child labor reform touches on some of the most basic philosophical concerns of bourgeois society; child labor legislation raises questions "of industrial freedom, of parental authority, and of [free] competition," wrote Wolowski.[20] And they all worried about the economic disadvantages that would result from child

17. Jules Simon, "L'Ouvrier de huit ans," *RDM*, 2nd per., LIV (1864), 715–35; Jules Simon, "L'Apprentissage des jeunes ouvriers dans la petite industrie," *RDM*, 2nd per., LV (1865), 717–42; Simon, *Huit ans*, 3–67, 307–308, 69–285.
18. See Wolowski, *Le Travail des enfants*, 19, 28–29.
19. *Ibid.*, esp. 5, 24, 30.
20. *Ibid.*, 5–6.

labor restrictions; many at that time favored international agreements on child labor to counteract inequalities in legislation from country to country.[21] Still, all three conceded that the adoption of new legislation to control child labor would have to entail some further compromises with absolute liberty.

Although the numerous bourgeois reformers of the 1860s tended to favor increased efforts to perfect France's child labor legislation, they also believed that state action was not sufficient to ensure the well-being of working youngsters or, for that matter, the future of workers in general. Like reform advocates in previous decades, they insisted that hand in hand with new factory legislation had to come persistent efforts to alter the moral character of the working classes. Jules Simon dubbed "the progress of morality" as the "king of remedies" for the "cruel evil" of child labor abuse, and he argued that improvements in the status of France's working youth had to be the result of "good institutions and well directed [philanthropic] endeavors" as well as "good laws." Likewise, Senator J. B. Dumas declared in 1867 that while "laws concern themselves with the child in the workshop or the factory, . . . they leave it to the family and to public morality to concern themselves with him outside of working hours." The appeals of the middle-class reformers during the later years of the empire were often reasoned and calm, but they could also be impassioned. Louis Wolowski avowed that child labor reform was "not an isolated and individual question, but a question of society itself," and Simon expressed the sense of urgency of many reformers in the sixties when he wrote this call to action: "Alas! . . . It is life itself that is in danger. . . . What father, what patriot, who that has a heart can console himself over these dissipated, atrophied generations, over these children condemned from the cradle to fatigue, to instruction rendered impossible or ridiculous, to devastated families, and precocious deprivation. Still, what is needed to cure this evil? No sacrifice is necessary. The will is enough."[22]

Although the French Church had traditionally been silent on the issue of state intervention to help the laboring young, in the increasingly reformist atmosphere of the sixties, a number of clergymen broke with the Church's tradition of silence, just as a handful of religious leaders had

---

21. See, for example, Audiganne, *Populations ouvrières*, 297–99, and Wolowski, *Le Travail des enfants*, 35ff.

22. Simon, *Huit ans*, 311; [J. B. Dumas], "Séance d'inauguration: Exposé de M. le Président," *BSPA* (1867), 52; Wolowski, *Le Travail des enfants*, 20; Simon, *Huit ans*, 212.

done immediately before 1841. In 1864, the abbé Hubaine addressed a petition to the Senate calling for improved factory law enforcement, and his concern attracted the attention especially of senators Charles Dupin and J. B. Dumas. When the child labor issue was raised for discussion in the Senate early in 1867, Cardinal Henri Bonnechose spoke in favor of new legislation. And a sermon by the père Hyacinthe on the subject of factory reform was given wide circulation. One of those who heard Hyacinthe speak observed that the priest had combined "the science of economics" with "evangelical charity" to such an extent that he "forgot he was listening to a sermon" and "believed he was hearing a lecture."[23]

But it was not only the rhetoric of the sixties that reflected the increasing concern with the laboring young. More than ever before, various groups and individuals took the initiative to aid factory children and apprentices in a variety of practical ways. Numerous programs to ameliorate the condition of young workers were initiated by Christian philanthropists in the sixties, despite the Church's lack of interest in legislative action. Beginning in 1863, for instance, a sister of the order of Saint Vincent de Paul began providing an educational opportunity to the youngsters in the Paris wallpaper trade. In the first year of her program, the sister taught 28 children to read; in the following year, her program served 406 children, and their number continued to grow in subsequent years. Similarly, in the midsixties, Catholic, Protestant, and Jewish groups all established dormitories for working children in Paris.[24]

The *patronage* movement also flourished in this period. From its modest beginnings under the aegis of Armand de Melun in the 1840s, the campaign to establish voluntary societies that would provide material aid, educational support, good fellowship, and moral guidance to working-class youngsters grew and diversified. Not only did *patronage* societies organized along sectarian lines proliferate, but in the midsixties the first *sociétés de patronage* organized within specific trades appeared. The patronage work of entrepreneurs in the cabinetmaking trade is a case in point. The Patronage industriel des enfants de l'ébénisterie was established in 1866 to "assist, moralize, and instruct" youngsters employed in the furniture industry, and by the 1870s it was supervising the placement of some 300 children each year in carefully selected apprenticeship positions. Within its first decade of operation, the Patronage

23. Délerot, "Avant-propos," 27–28; *Documents*, 114–115; "Conférence du Révérend Père Hyacinthe," *BSPA* (1867), 180.

24. Barreswil, *Rapport sur la situation des enfants employés dans les manufactures du département de la Seine* (Paris, 1865), 12; Barreswil, *Deuxième Rapport sur la situation des enfants employés dans les manufactures du département de la Seine* (Paris, 1866), 50ff.

industriel also established a school of design and organized an annual competition in cabinetmaking.[25] One report indicated that there were some three hundred *patronage* societies serving about 80,000 youngsters throughout France by 1873, and other partial statistical evidence from the same period suggests that these estimates were probably low.[26]

Moreover, the most important and influential of all philanthropic societies concerned with the laboring young was established in the middle 1860s. This was the Société de protection des apprentis et des enfants des manufactures, founded in 1866 through the efforts of such men as Charles Dupin, Michel Chevalier, and J. B. Dumas. The society aspired to centralize the work of all preexisting *sociétés de patronage* and other voluntary organizations concerned with child labor and, at the same time, to become the major lobbying body for child labor reform. In a sense, it was the embodiment of the prevalent bourgeois attitude toward child labor reform in this period, for it stressed the importance of combining efforts to promote legislated protection for working children with voluntary charitable work aimed at inculcating new moral values in working-class youngsters and their families. Essentially a product of bourgeois concern with the still-unresolved *question sociale*, the society felt constrained to temper its enthusiasm for reform with due respect for business interests and for the traditional structure of the family. As the society declared in its statutes at the time of its founding, "The aim of the Society is to ameliorate the condition of apprentices and of children employed in factories by all means which, with due respect for the freedom of the industrialist and the authority of the father, will produce results in conformity with the ideas behind the laws concerning apprenticeship and child labor."[27] By the end of its first year, the society had established a journal and enlisted some 1,300 members, among them the Empress Eugénie.

The creation of the Société de protection des apprentis et des enfants des manufactures represents a logical progression from the elitist lobbying efforts that had stimulated the passage of France's first child labor law in 1841, for much of the society's activity was based on the assump-

25. See Lee Shai Weissbach, "Entrepreneurial Traditionalism in Nineteenth-Century France: A Study of the Patronage industriel des enfants de l'ébénisterie," *Business History Review*, LVII (1983), 548ff.
26. See NA, February 3, 1873. See also Weissbach, "*Oeuvre industrielle*"; Simon, *Huit ans*, appendix; Barreswil, *Deuxième Rapport*, 50; Christian de Coulonge, "Etudes sur les oeuvres de patronage," *BSPA* (1867), 208ff; and Mataja, "Origines," X, 368.
27. "Statutes provisoires," *BSPA* (1867), 33. For more on the society, see early issues of the *BSPA* and Mataja, "Origines," X, 363–65.

tion that reform legislation in France could best be promoted through direct contact with government officials and legislators. The champions of child labor reform in the 1830s had been among the first to realize the importance of direct lobbying at the highest levels of government, and now, banding together in a formal organization, the advocates of child labor reform in the 1860s were adopting the same tactic. Other reform groups that appeared during the Second Empire also found that the overriding importance of the central government in decision making dictated a resort to direct lobbying. In this sense, the Société de protection des apprentis et des enfants des manufactures was similar to such organizations as the Société contre l'abus du tabac (which sought to curb the use of tobacco), the Société protectrice de l'enfance (which sought to protect infants put out to nurse), and the Société protectrice des animaux (which sought to prevent cruelty to animals). All of these organizations were concerned with the moral development of the working classes.[28]

Given the new concern with child labor in bourgeois circles generally, it is not surprising that new support for child labor reform emerged at the local government level in the 1860s. At the time the empire was established, only the *conseil général* of the Nord had as yet seen fit to appoint a salaried factory inspector at the departmental level. When in 1853 the Ministry of Commerce had suggested this course of action to other relatively industrialized departments, all the *conseils généraux* approached had rejected the idea. In the 1860s, however, several departmental councils undertook the sponsorship of local salaried inspection. Developments in the Department of the Seine are illustrative of the general course taken by departments all over France.

As early as 1860, the *conseil général* of the Seine had begun importuning the departmental prefect of police, Boitelle, to do something to improve the enforcement of the 1841 child labor law. Senator J. B. Dumas was the president of the *conseil général* at the time, and he was especially concerned with the child labor issue. Boitelle temporized for several years, holding out the hope that some national effort at child labor reform would take the pressure off local enforcement, but in 1864, finally despairing of any help from the central government, he and the council agreed on the appointment of two factory inspectors salaried by the department.[29]

28. See Bezucha, "Moralization."
29. See the letter of January 23, 1865 (misdated 1864), from Boitelle to the minister of commerce, in AN, F12–4773.

A chemist named Barreswil was selected to occupy the post of chief factory inspector for the Seine, and a mining engineer named Maurice was appointed as his deputy. The first annual report on the work of the two inspectors was issued by Barreswil at the end of 1865, and it revealed that he and Maurice had spent most of the time during their first year familiarizing themselves with the child labor situation in the Seine, especially in four industries in which the use of children was particularly significant. Maurice had concentrated on the match-making industry because of the dangers it presented and on glass and crystal works because they demanded so much nighttime labor. Barreswil had focused on the wallpaper industry because it provided work for a large number of children and on the printing trade because it employed both apprentices and unskilled aids. The first annual report on inspection in the Seine is worth considering in some detail, both because it reveals a great deal about the child labor situation in the French capital and because it provides an insight into the achievements that were possible with serious and efficient factory surveillance.[30]

The investigations undertaken by Inspector Maurice revealed that there were twenty-three match factories in Paris, employing a total work force of 845 persons, of whom 289 were children. Of the twenty-three factories, the ten where conditions were found to be most dangerous escaped the scrutiny of the child labor law completely, for they each employed less than 20 workers and used no mechanical power. Maurice discovered not only that many children under twelve were working more than eight hours a day in match making but also that some children as young as six and seven were still being employed in the industry. He found, too, that employers in match making consistently ignored the legal requirements concerning educational certification and the possession of *livrets*. Maurice attributed the wholesale violations of the 1841 factory law in match making to the fact that many of the shops involved entered production only after 1848, when the initial zeal for the law had waned, and to the fact that many of those employed in match making were destitute recent immigrants to Paris.

The problems Maurice encountered in glass and crystal making were similar to those he found in match making. He discovered that about a third of all the shops he investigated did not come under the purview of the 1841 law, and he observed many instances of employers overworking children under twelve and virtually ignoring provisions for schooling.

30. The discussion that follows is based on Barreswil, *Rapport sur la situation, passim.*

Although Maurice believed that glass manufacturers were generally well disposed toward their young employees, he concluded that stricter inspection of their shops and a suppression of the night work prevalent in the industry would be very beneficial.

In wallpaper manufacturing, Inspector Barreswil found that the main violations of the 1841 factory law were familiar ones: overworking youngsters under twelve and ignoring the legal provisions regarding schooling. The inspector attributed these violations primarily to a manpower shortage in the section of the city where wallpaper manufacturing was concentrated. He pointed out that in the wallpaper industry (and in match and glass making as well), it was common practice for adult operatives to recruit their own young helpers without the intervention of either factory owners on the one side or parents on the other. Finally, among the printers of Paris, Barreswil found rather complete compliance with at least the letter of the child labor and apprenticeship laws. Only about 7 percent of the 529 children involved in printing were under twelve, and only about 6 percent were found to be illiterate. Moreover, one of the capital's model apprenticeship programs was the program run by the printer Napoléon Chaix.

On the basis of their extensive investigation of four industries and their cursory observation of several others, Barreswil and Maurice concluded that the most widespread child labor offenses concerned schooling and *livrets*, though they attested to the existence of other problems as well. The inspectors praised the concept of the *patronage* and commended the establishment of dormitories for working children where their schooling was supervised. They reiterated the importance of inspection and, in fact, called for the appointment of three additional child labor inspectors for the Seine. Finally, Barreswil and Maurice suggested that France's factory legislation be extended to cover all shops employing children, and in at least one case they advocated the erection of a new school building to serve an area with many working children. The second annual report prepared by Barreswil made it clear that he and Maurice, after their initial year of gathering information, had then turned their attention primarily to enforcing the law. The major recommendation of the child labor inspectors in their second report was that a half-time work schedule be introduced for youngsters under twelve. They thought this would ensure that young workers would receive a half-day of schooling on a regular basis.[31]

31. Barreswil, *Deuxième Rapport, passim.*

In the mid-1860s, the number of *conseils généraux* that voted money for paid factory inspection mounted. Salaried inspectors are known to have been appointed by the end of the decade in the Indre, the Oise, the Pas-de-Calais, the Seine-Inférieure, and the Somme.[32] Some departmental governments voted small sums to be paid as bonuses to functionaries who were asked to conduct factory inspections in addition to their other duties; such was the case, for example, in the Eure and the Allier.[33] The intervention of local government was not generally seen as obviating the need for a national system of factory inspection, however. In appointing their departmental inspectors, the authorities in the Seine declared that the job of these inspectors was "to assure a temporary surveillance of the child labor situation" until the national government acted.[34] Similarly, the chamber of commerce of Rouen welcomed the appointment in 1867 of a local factory inspector salaried by the department, but at the same time it expressed the view that only a national inspectorate could ensure that departments without local inspection would not gain an economic advantage over those with their own systems.[35]

By word and by deed, then, various middle-class individuals and sundry institutions dominated by the bourgeoisie revealed their intensified concern with the laboring young in the middle and late 1860s. But it was not middle-class opinion alone that turned new attention to the problems of child labor in this period. Elements within the working classes were also registering concern with the problem of laboring children for the first time, in part, perhaps, because the new, more nurturing attitude toward childhood that had already been widely accepted by the middle classes was beginning to take hold among some workers as well.[36] Working-class concern with child labor stemmed even more directly, however, from the fact that French artisans and skilled laborers were decidedly feeling the pressure of proletarianization by the 1860s. Skilled

32. *Renseignements et avis recueillis en 1867 sur le travail des enfants dans les établissements industriels* (Paris, 1867), 9, 17, 20; Mataja, "Origines," X, 363; and Colmart, *De l'inspection du travail*, 50. There is some evidence in AN, F12–4773, that the Pas-de-Calais and the Somme had already voted money for a departmental inspector in the late 1850s.
33. See AN, F12–4773. There was apparently some precedent set in the 1850s for paying bonuses to inspectors of weights and measures; see documents in AN, F12–4709 and F12–4773.
34. Quoted in Mataja, "Origines," X, 363.
35. Letter from chamber of commerce of Rouen, January 31, 1867, in AN, F12–4719.
36. This is the contention, for example, in Shorter, *Making of the Modern Family*, 193–95.

workers were convinced that the future of their crafts depended on the maintenance of high-level technical training for the young, and they certainly wanted to protect their own children from sinking to the level of unskilled factory hands. Hence, they were becoming intensely concerned with the status of young workers in an industrializing economy.

One vehicle through which French workers expressed their concern over child labor was the International Working Men's Association. In 1866, this body called for international limitations on the work of children; among other things, the International wanted a two-hour day for children nine to thirteen and a workday of no more than six hours for children as old as seventeen.[37] At about the same time, Martin Nadaud, a worker elected to the legislature under the Second Republic and exiled after 1851, propagandized French workers to follow the lead of the English trade unions in agitating for further child labor reform and factory legislation. The working conditions of child laborers even figured as an issue in an 1866 strike of wallpaper workers in Paris. As a result of the strike, wallpaper entrepreneurs ceased hiring workers under the age of twelve and agreed to afford their young laborers the opportunity to attend evening classes.[38]

In the French workers' reports issued following the Universal Exposition at London in 1862 and the one at Paris in 1867, there were quite forceful expressions of concern over the abuse and exploitation of children in large and small industrial shops. The workers who prepared these reports were aware of the child labor and apprenticeship laws that had been passed, and they used the occasions of the expositions to express their frustration over the ineffectiveness of those laws. The colored and patterned paper workers, for example, complained over the lack of progress on the child labor front: "Not a single step has been taken in the direction of amelioration for thirty years. We have living proof of this before our eyes every day; it is incontestable in the children that work with us. They begin work at as young an age as we did; they are no better educated than we, and they know only the unpleasant side of life." The paper workers spoke more specifically of the inadequacy of the education provisions of the child labor law: "You tell us that there are evening schools that [working] children can attend. But what can a

37. See Simone Béziers, *La Protection de l'enfance ouvrière* (Montpellier, 1935), 130, and Georges Weill, *Histoire du mouvement social en France, 1852–1924* (Paris, 1924), 97ff.

38. Martin Nadaud, *Discours de Martin Nadaud* (Paris, 1884), 289ff; Barreswil, *Deuxième Rapport*, 8ff.

child gain from evening classes after having spent eleven or twelve hours at grueling labor without respite, leaving his home before daybreak and not returning until night? . . . What can be required of the mind when the body is tired?" On the provisions for inspection embodied in the law of 1841, the paper workers said, "We have never seen even the shadow of an inspector in the shop."

It is interesting that the workers' arguments for reform of the child labor situation in some ways echoed those of middle-class activists who were bent on the moral improvement of the laboring classes. "Can a more monstrous coupling be imagined . . . than ignorance and liberty?" the paper workers of 1867 asked rhetorically. Their appeal for improving the working conditions of youngsters concluded with the observation that "there are no two ways about it: if one wants to produce good citizens, if one wants to prepare men for the future, the doors of the factory must be closed to every child who does not have the strength to work or who has not received a primary education."[39] The complaints of the workers' juries were underscored by the public row raised when it was discovered that some of the fine needlework on display at the Universal Exposition of 1867 was the work of girls as young as three and four years old.[40]

All this is not to say that by the 1860s everyone who considered the matter of children in industry saw a need for increased government involvement in labor law enforcement or for new factory legislation. In the less skilled segments of the industrial working class, for example, many parents did not yet see how they could abandon traditional child labor practices. In an 1867 report issued by the Lille Chamber of Commerce, the spinning-mill operator Henri Loyer was still explaining: "The worker burdened with a family has no alternatives other than work or alms as a means of keeping the family alive. He prefers work; no one would dare blame him for that." Loyer continued, "If he has 8 children, of which 4 have reached the age of 8 to 12, he places them at work in the factories."[41] Literary works such as Claude Michu's 1862 poem

39. See Arnould Desvernay (ed.), *Rapports des délégations ouvrières* (Paris, 1869), I–III. The paper workers' words are in III, p. 8 of their report. On the similarity of the demands issued by various workers' delegations in 1867, see Edgar Saveney, "Les Délégations ouvrières à l'exposition universelle de 1867," *RDM*, 2nd per., LXXVII (1868), 611–21; a portion of this article is excerpted in *BSPA* (1868), 290–91. See also Fournier, *Second Empire*, 267–89, and Weill, *Mouvement social*, 89–96.
40. Colmart, *De l'inspection du travail*, 52; Mataja, "Origines," X, 363–64n.
41. Quoted in Pierrard, "Patronat," 54. See also Weber, *Peasants*, 321–23.

"Travail et gloire" suggest that in the late imperial period, some in the privileged classes not only still accepted child factory labor but actually glorified it:

> The clock, at daybreak, calls us to the loom.
> But the work is not a shameful slavery,
> And the child of the factory is, though young, a worker,
> As a military cadet is a soldier before his time.
> We don't have the appearance of martial battalions,
> No flag to signal the slaughter!
> Risking our lives in the teeth of a gearwork,
> Our uniform—for us? it's the glory of rags!!
> > We wage battle with you,
> > Peoples of the universe!
> > Without crossing seas,
>
> And the child who works
> Practices at the loom, as one practices on the firing range;
> We have our conscripts, our heroes, our martyrs!![42]

So, too, in the early sixties was Gustave Dupuynode again raising some of the classic arguments against child labor legislation in a new book, *Des lois du travail et de la population*. Withdrawing the concessions he made in the 1840s about the need for child labor restrictions, he here argued that limitations on the use of children were philosophically objectionable, because they inevitably led to de facto limitations on adult labor as well. "How can a spinner, for example, not leave the shop when it is abandoned by his *rattacheur?*" he asked. Moreover, he had come to see the legislation enacted in 1841 as impractical to implement, and he urged that other approaches to improving the lot of factory children be adopted. He wanted, for instance, to impress upon parents their moral rather than their legal obligation to educate their children. Dupuynode alleged, too, that there were some positive aspects to factory labor for children. He warned that if children "are left free for many years, they inevitably acquire the habits of idleness and vagrancy," and he suggested that this was bad both for the children and for society as a whole. Dupuynode observed that in the factory, by contrast, children "acquire the very valuable habits of orderliness, discipline and work."[43]

There was enough opposition to new child labor legislation abroad in the 1860s that even Jules Simon felt compelled to go on the defensive in the pages of *L'Ouvrier de huit ans*. In this book, he defended his concept

42. Quoted in Grant, *French Poetry*, 145.
43. Gustave Dupuynode, *Des lois du travail et de la population* (Paris, 1860), I, 272–74.

of revised factory legislation against the attacks of "communists" and other "sectarians" by arguing that it was impossible to solve all the problems of labor at once; he also defended his ideas against the objections of those he termed "the friends of liberty" by pointing out that no new system of limitations was being proposed, only an improvement of the existing scheme.[44]

Perhaps the most important opposition to extended factory legislation in the 1860s was to be found in the Social Catholic movement. Under the July Monarchy, a number of individual Social Catholics had been among the most ardent supporters of child labor reform, and under the Second Republic, Social Catholicism had become enamored of social legislation through the influence of Armand de Melun. By the sixties, however, the tone of the movement had changed significantly. Most of its early leaders—men such as Alban de Villeneuve-Bargemont, Charles de Montalembert, and Melun himself—were either dead or no longer involved in the struggle for reform legislation, and Social Catholicism was coming to equate social legislation more and more with socialism, to which it was hostile because of socialism's increasingly anticlerical and antireligious ideology. Under the Second Empire, the mainstream of the Social Catholic movement, dominated by Frédéric LePlay, thus abandoned the concept of interventionist legislation as the solution to the nation's social problems. Unlike those who did wish to see further controls on child labor, LePlay was not prepared to abandon the hope that working-class parents could learn to wield their authority over their children properly. He was not prepared to admit that the state had to step in to replace the father in dealing with the matter of industrial child labor. Instead, he and his followers stressed the importance of religion, custom, and traditional paternal authority as guiding influences in society; they urged the upper classes to help foster a new moral tone in society by setting proper examples in their own lives and by giving of themselves in charitable and educational work among the lower classes. Social Catholics were certainly not the only ones promoting moral regeneration and voluntary action in the sixties; these ideas now had a place in all but the most radical reform philosophies. But within Social Catholicism, there seems to have been a concerted effort to deny government any role as an agent of social change. Although LePlay recognized that some good had come from early factory legislation, his philosophi-

44. Simon, *Huit ans*, 311ff.

cal objections to it were pronounced, and he categorically rejected any idea of its extension in the sixties.[45]

It was only a minority that glorified child labor and expressed opposition to extended factory legislation in the sixties, but the existence of this minority serves as an additional indication of the vitality of the debate over child labor during that decade. By the late sixties, the issue was becoming so widely discussed that the imperial government was forced to abandon the relative passivity it had maintained throughout most of the reign of Napoleon III and to regard the child labor problem with a greater sense of urgency.

45. See Moon, *Labor Problem*, 52–62; Zeldin, *France*, II, 953–59; Dorothy Herbertson, *The Life of Frédéric LePlay* (Ledbury, Eng., 1950), 74–100. For LePlay's general philosophy, see Frédéric LePlay, *La Reforme sociale en France* (Paris, 1867), I–III.

NINE

Government Policy in the Final Years of the Empire

The government of Napoleon III could not help but become caught up in the new sense of urgency about child labor in the late 1860s. The imperial government's fundamental concern with the development of a properly functioning industrial society and its overriding interest in order and efficiency had guaranteed that it would take some interest in the child labor situation from the outset. But the atmosphere engendered by the increased concern over the laboring young now motivated the government to adopt a much more active policy vis-à-vis child labor reform. The intensified lobbying efforts of the middle and late 1860s provided the background against which the administration grappled with the child labor issue in the final years of the empire.

In January of 1867, Napoleon III appointed as the new minister of commerce Adolphe de Forcade la Roquette, a man who had risen through the ranks of the imperial administration and who had recently served as vice-president of the Conseil d'état. Within a few months of Forcade la Roquette's appointment, the Ministry of Commerce embarked on a major new campaign to promote the enforcement of France's child labor legislation. The availability of a plethora of evidence on the child labor situation notwithstanding, the campaign was initiated with a new round of information gathering. In a letter of April 27, 1867, Forcade la Roquette requested that each of France's prefects evaluate the status of the 1841 law in his region and, in consultation with other interested parties, suggest ways in which the shortcomings of the law could be corrected.

Although the survey conducted in 1867 was the most comprehensive study of child labor conditions undertaken by the government since the passage of the 1841 factory law, it did little more than verify what had been learned through less systematic compilations of information in previous years and confirm many of the allegations made by the advocates of reform. For instance, the prefects reported that children under eight were very seldom employed in factories and that children over twelve rarely worked more than twelve hours a day, but they also observed that the workday of those under twelve often did exceed eight hours. The prefects confirmed that the regulations regarding night and Sunday work were generally honored, but many of them complained that education and inspection continued to present major problems. A number of prefects called attention to the ill will of parents and the connivance of entrepreneurs as factors that made enforcement difficult; they suggested that the noncooperation of parents and employers could be counteracted only by close surveillance of individual factories. Indeed, the need for an improved system of factory inspection was recognized almost universally by the prefects: some called for a corps of inspectors organized by the national government, some suggested empowering existing functionaries to visit factories, and some advocated a strengthening of local child labor commissions. Many prefects had suggestions to make as well on matters other than factory inspection. Among the ideas they proposed were the institution of half-time schedules for the youngest workers, the extension of the factory law to smaller establishments, the introduction of a requirement for schooling beyond the age of twelve, and the elevation of the minimum age for employment.[1]

Perhaps even more important than the general picture of child labor in France sketched by the reports of the prefects in 1867 was the numerical accounting they provided. Now, for the first time, the government had available to it the results of a demographic study focusing specifically on the laboring young. This study, especially when its findings were combined with those of the industrial census completed in 1865, produced an extremely detailed account of the extent of child labor in France. The figures supplied by the prefects indicated that there were 125,715 children under sixteen working in French industry, excluding apprentices and youngsters employed by their parents.[2] Of all

1. Material on the 1867 survey of prefects is in AN, F12–4722 and F12–4723.
2. The industrial survey of 1865 had reported 117,201 children in French industry, excluding child laborers in Paris, in Lyon, and in government-operated establishments. See Statistique de la France, *Industrie: Résultats généraux de l'enquête effectuée dans les années*

the young industrial workers in France in 1867, 5.1 percent were under ten, and an additional 18.1 percent were between the ages of ten and twelve. The reports of the prefects also indicated that of the 17,897 industrial establishments employing young workers other than apprentices or offspring, only 7,959 (44.8 percent) were subject to the factory law of 1841. These establishments, however, employed a full 78.9 percent of all young industrial workers.

Even though the child labor data collected in 1865 and 1867 are not strictly comparable with those collected for the 1845 industrial census and even though the accuracy of the data is open to question, a review of all this material does suggest that there had been a real decline in the use of young workers in industry since the passage of the 1841 factory law. The proportion of children in the work force, for example, had dropped from 11.7 percent in 1845 to only 7.0 percent in 1865. The decline in the use of child laborers was due partially, no doubt, to the fact that there was a factory law on the books, but the law was certainly not the only reason for the decline. Another important factor was the changing nature of industrial production in France. The tremendous economic growth of France under the Second Empire was based in part on technological modernization and the rationalization of factory production. In the textile industry, which employed the majority of factory children, self-acting spinning machinery and power looms were rapidly displacing older equipment. In the Vosges, for example, only 10 percent of the spindles in cotton textile production were self-acting in 1856, but by 1868, 73 percent were self-acting.[3] All this technological improvement meant less demand for child laborers. Children simply could not cope with the larger and more complex new machinery being introduced, and many of the jobs they had performed in early factories were well on the way to being eliminated completely.[4] Neither was there a labor shortage under the empire that might have maintained the demand for children at its previous levels. In most regions, migration from the countryside to the industrial centers meant that French factory owners were able to hire all the adult laborers they needed.[5]

Yet despite the declining use of children in industry, the number of

---

1861–1865 (Nancy, 1873), 850, 852. The numerical accounting provided by the prefects is reported in *Renseignements et avis*, 3–4.

3. Landes, *Prometheus*, 211–13; R. B. Forrester, *The Cotton Industry in France* (Manchester, 1921), 1.

4. Compare Heywood, "Market," 45–46, and Stearns, *Paths*, 69–70.

5. Kindleberger, *Economic Growth*, 236–37; Gordon Wright, *France in Modern Times* (New York, 1981), 162; and Simon, "Ouvrier de huit ans," 733.

children employed was still significant, and much that was true of the child labor situation in the midforties was still true in the midsixties. In both periods, for example, virtually every department in France employed some children in industry. The 1867 data supplied by the prefects indicated that in only fourteen of France's eighty-nine departments were less than 100 children employed, and the 1865 industrial census had identified only six departments with less than 100 child laborers. Nonetheless, France's young workers were still concentrated in a relatively small number of highly industrialized areas. As Table 3 indicates, the Nord and the Seine-Inférieure were still the two individual departments with the most child laborers, and over half of France's child laborers (53.8 percent) were still employed in her sixteen most highly industrialized departments.[6] In general, the statistical correlation between the level of industrialization of a department and the number of children employed there was very high in the midsixties (r = .91), though the correlation between industrialization and the percentage of children in the work force remained only slight (r = .29).[7]

The various textile industries were by far the largest employers of factory children in the 1860s, as they had been in the 1840s. Apparently, many children in these industries were still working alongside their parents.[8] As Table 4 shows, textiles in 1865 provided work for 59.7 percent of all French child laborers, and children accounted for 10.2 percent of all textile workers in French factories. There were six departments where the annual value of textiles produced exceeded 100 million francs, and over 40,000 of France's child laborers were employed in those six departments alone. In the sixties, relatively large numbers of children were also found in metalworking, mining, food production, construction, and ceramics, each of which provided employment for somewhere between 5.0 and 6.5 percent of the juvenile work force. Thus, even though the use of child labor appeared to be declining as the nineteenth century progressed, the employment of the young remained a significant element in several industries and in several regions of France in the

6. In 1845, 57.2 percent of French child laborers had been employed in the sixteen most highly industrialized departments. In all these calculations, child laborers in Paris have been excluded.

7. The level of industrialization here is measured by the annual value of industrial goods produced. For 1845, r = .79 for the correlation between the level of industrialization and the number of children employed, and r = .08 for the correlation between the level of industrialization and the percentage of children in the work force.

8. Reddy, "Family and Factory," 102–103.

Table 3
Industrial Child Labor by Department, ca. 1865

Department	Children Employed	Children as Percentage of Work Force	Industrial Ranking of Department*
Nord	16,146	10.7	1
Seine-Inférieure	10,064	13.4	2
Haut-Rhin	6,043	9.3	6
Orne	5,385	11.0	27
Ardèche	4,663	17.2	14
Aisne	3,462	7.2	7
Vosges	3,259	10.2	23
Pas-de-Calais	3,207	9.2	11
Loire	3,062	4.9	4
Oise	2,971	8.5	16
Eure	2,504	8.5	5
Somme	2,418	6.8	8
Ardennes	2,241	8.3	10
Gard	2,192	5.8	19
Seine, without Paris	2,105	11.0	13
Isère	2,059	5.7	18
Doubs	1,931	8.6	35
Bas-Rhin	1,699	7.5	28
Tarn	1,660	9.9	37
Bouches-du-Rhône	1,618	6.3	3
Vaucluse	1,596	13.0	22
Rhône, without Lyon	1,518	5.8	33
Saône-et-Loire	1,487	7.0	30
Drôme	1,484	10.4	36
Marne	1,362	8.6	9
Hérault	1,288	6.5	25
Calvados	1,249	5.6	24
Moselle	1,237	4.8	17
Haute-Vienne	1,186	8.8	50
Seine-et-Oise	1,161	8.1	20
Maine-et-Loire	1,153	6.8	31
Ille-et-Vilaine	1,082	7.9	15
Meurthe	1,045	6.1	44
Nièvre	1,041	9.9	49
Seine-et-Marne	966	10.2	26
Loire-Inférieure	948	6.3	12

continued

Department	Children Employed	Children as Percentage of Work Force	Industrial Ranking of Department*
Puy-de-Dôme	873	5.1	40
Gironde	824	5.7	21
Aude	790	12.4	62
Haute-Saône	761	7.6	55
Loir-et-Cher	740	14.7	70
Allier	649	6.1	64
Haute-Garonne	639	5.1	29
Basses-Pyrénées	604	11.0	77
Meuse	557	4.1	47
Loiret	538	8.8	41
Charente	516	8.3	54
Sarthe	493	5.4	42
Ain	479	5.8	39
Deux-Sèvres	472	7.8	48
Aveyron	464	3.3	52
Indre	458	9.8	60
Creuse	457	12.2	83
Indre-et-Loire	447	9.4	56
Yonne	439	10.7	66
Eure-et-Loir	430	13.2	53
Côte-d'Or	422	3.8	32
Mayenne	404	4.4	69
Aube	402	2.0	34
Cher	401	4.6	58
Finistère	393	5.5	38
Jura	377	5.5	59
Manche	367	5.0	46
Ariège	347	6.7	75
Morbihan	327	6.6	63
Var	300	2.7	51
Lot-et-Garonne	285	5.4	45
Pyrénées-Orientales	253	4.4	79
Hautes-Alpes	235	8.6	84
Vienne	213	6.0	68
Basses-Alpes	195	9.9	82
Dordogne	191	3.6	43
Côtes-du-Nord	179	2.9	74
Charente-Inférieure	176	3.5	61
Savoie	171	5.9	85
Haute-Loire	163	4.0	72

Department	Children Employed	Children as Percentage of Work Force	Industrial Ranking of Department*
Haute-Savoie	143	3.8	86
Landes	135	3.5	71
Hautes-Pyrénées	132	3.9	78
Vendée	131	2.1	57
Corrèze	115	7.9	88
Haute-Marne	107	0.9	65
Alpes-Maritimes	101	3.4	80
Tarn-et-Garonne	99	2.8	73
Lozère	95	6.0	87
Cantal	64	6.2	89
Corse	55	1.9	81
Lot	50	2.2	76
Gers	21	1.5	67

*Determined by annual value of industrial goods produced.
Source: Statistique de la France, *Industrie: Résultats généraux de l'enquête effectuée dans les années 1861–1865* (Nancy, 1873), 850, 852.

Table 4
French Industries Employing over One Thousand Children, ca. 1865

Industry	Children Employed	Children as Percentage of Work Force	Percentage of All French Child Laborers
Textiles	69,948	10.2	59.7
Metallurgy and metal goods	7,624	4.2	6.5
Mining	7,139	6.5	6.1
Food	6,701	3.8	5.7
Construction	6,681	9.8	5.7
Ceramics	5,899	12.3	5.0
Artistic, literary, and scientific goods	4,965	9.0	4.2
Clothing and toiletries	2,937	5.4	2.5
Transportation	1,926	10.0	1.6
Chemicals	1,699	7.9	1.4

Source: Statistique de la France, *Industrie: Résultats généraux de l'enquête effectuée dans les années 1861–1865* (Nancy, 1873), xix.

late 1860s. Moreover, the conditions that French factory children had been enduring since before midcentury had changed but little. Child laborers in shops not covered by the factory law of 1841 still had to work at tedious jobs for long hours in often insalubrious environments, and even where the factory law was supposed to apply, formal restrictions often had little practical effect. This lack of improvement meant that those worried about the prevention of child labor abuse still had grounds for their concern and that child labor reform could still command the attention of paternalistic activists looking for ways to promote *moralisation* among the working classes. Indeed, by the late 1860s the campaign against child labor abuse had become symbolic of the efforts of the privileged classes to rescue the children of the poor from misery and degeneracy. Middle-class public opinion had come to view rehabilitating working children collectively as a way of assuring the future, just as it had come to see working children individually as vulnerable beings worthy of special attention.

It was clear from the commerce ministry's polling of the prefects, if it had not already been clear before the 1867 survey, that several fundamental matters would have to be addressed in any consideration of further child labor reform. First was the question of extending the applicability of child labor regulations to more shops and industrial establishments. Second was the question of redefining the minimum age for employment and the maximum length of the workday for youngsters. Third was the vexing question of how best to monitor compliance with present and future child labor regulations. As the Ministry of Commerce wrestled with these issues and began to formulate a specific proposal for new action on child labor, it turned once again for advice to the sociopolitical elite in the provinces whom it had polled on several previous occasions. The ministry wanted to assess the opinions and attitudes of this elite in a systematic fashion before proceeding with any legislative proposal.

In a circular dispatched on August 21, 1867, Forcade la Roquette directed each departmental prefect to consult with his *conseil général* and then to submit to Paris the responses of that body to four specific questions. The ministry solicited the opinions of the councils on extending the protection of the factory law to all industrial establishments except those in which only family members or apprentices were employed; it also asked for ideas about raising the minimum age for employment, reducing the workday of the youngest workers, and instituting salaried and centralized inspection. The same four issues were put before France's chambers of commerce and *chambres consultatives des arts et manufactures* in a circular of August 30, 1867, and copies of the inquiry came into the hands of some *conseils des prud'hommes*, local child labor commissions, and industrialists' societies as well. Although some of these latter bodies prepared responses to the government inquiry, it was the *conseils généraux*, the chambers of commerce, and the *chambres consultatives* that produced the bulk of the replies and that supplied officials at the Ministry of Commerce with the material they used to prepare a summary report.[9]

Under the administrative system of the late Second Empire, the *conseil général* of each department met regularly with the department's prefect and served as both a legislative and an advisory body. Each council was composed of one elected representative from each canton in the department, which meant that each *conseil général* comprised some two to three dozen members. The departmental councils, taken together, thus represented a broad cross-section of the provincial elite, and for this reason the administration was inclined to weigh their opinions carefully. Chambers of commerce and *chambres consultatives* were consulted because they represented the more narrow business and manufacturing interests. On the child labor subcommittee of the chamber of commerce of Mulhouse, for instance, several extremely important entrepreneurial families were represented: Schlumberger, Dollfus, and Mieg.[10] The opinions of bodies with members such as these were understandably of special interest to the government as it considered the matter of child labor reform.

Of the eighty-nine *conseils généraux* in France, only six failed to respond in any way to the government inquiry of August, 1867. In addition, ten other councils indicated to the Ministry of Commerce that they could not render opinions on any of the issues raised in the inquiry: the councils of several agricultural departments said they were not qualified to respond to the government's questions, and other councils claimed they lacked the time or the data that would allow them to do so. Finally, eight departmental councils submitted incomplete responses to the government inquiry. On the other side, fully sixty-five of France's *conseils généraux* (73 percent) submitted complete responses to Forcade la Ro-

9. On the 1867 inquiry, see *Renseignements et avis* and material in AN, F12–4723. At least two chambers of commerce published accounts of their deliberations over the ministerial questionnaire; see Edmond de Planet, *Travail des enfants dans les manufactures* (Toulouse, 1867), and [George Steinbach *et al.*], *Travail des enfants dans les manufactures* (Mulhouse, 1867).

10. See [Steinbach *et al.*], *Travail dans les manufactures*.

quette's inquiry regarding child labor reform. The response rate from France's chambers of commerce and *chambres consultatives* was similarly gratifying.

When the results of the 1867 inquiry were tabulated, they revealed that a substantial majority of France's provincial notables and business leaders favored the extension of the country's child labor law to cover all industrial establishments or at least more of them. As Table 5 indicates, at least 67 percent of all departmental councils favored broadening the scope of coverage, as did 91 percent of the chambers of commerce and 79 percent of the *chambres consultatives*. Adamant opposition to broadened coverage was extremely rare. The overwhelming support for extending the applicability of the factory law was, no doubt, motivated by both ideological and practical considerations. On the one hand, by the late sixties there was a tremendous interest among French opinion leaders in keeping working children from harm and allowing them a chance to develop properly, so it seemed only reasonable to them to extend the protection of the factory law to as many youngsters as possible. On the other hand, the owners of large industrial enterprises had always been concerned about the labor cost advantage held by smaller shops, which were allowed to use unrestricted child labor, and they were anxious to subject those establishments to the same limitations that were imposed on larger factories. It is little wonder that only three chambers of commerce objected to extending the purview of the factory law.

Replies to the ministerial circular also indicated a widespread belief that the minimum age established in 1841 was too low. At least 60 percent of France's *conseils généraux* wanted to see the minimum age for employment raised to ten or higher, whereas only 13 percent of departmental councils wanted to retain the minimum age of eight. About three out of every four chambers of commerce and *chambres consultatives* also favored a new minimum age of ten or higher. Here again, ideals and practical considerations pointed to the same conclusions. While raising the minimum age for industrial employment seemed to be a worthwhile humanitarian gesture, it would have almost no perceptible impact on prevailing industrial practices. By the late 1860s, there were already very few children under ten working in factories, and even restrictions on the hiring of children under twelve would probably be felt very little by French industry.

Responses to the third question posed in the government survey, the one dealing with the length of the workday for young laborers, sug-

Table 5
Responses to the Ministry of Commerce Inquiry of 1867

Question 1: Should the child labor law be extended to all industrial establishments employing children other than apprentices or family members?

Response	Conseils généraux Responding	Chambers of Commerce Responding	Chambres consultatives Responding
Do not extend law	7 (8%)	3 (5%)	8 (10%)
Extend law to more shops	3 (3%)	0 (0%)	0 (0%)
Extend law to all shops	57 (64%)	58 (91%)	64 (79%)
No opinion or no reply	22 (25%)	3 (5%)	9 (11%)

Question 2: Should the minimum age for employment be raised?

Response	Conseils généraux Responding	Chambers of Commerce Responding	Chambres consultatives Responding
Maintain minimum age at 8	12 (13%)	8 (13%)	11 (14%)
Raise minimum age to 10	45 (51%)	31 (48%)*	40 (49%)*
Raise minimum age above 10	8 (9%)	18 (28%)	19 (23%)
Vary age with conditions	4 (4%)	4 (6%)	2 (2%)
No opinion or no reply	20 (22%)	3 (5%)	9 (11%)

*One chamber of commerce and one *chambre consultative* wanted the minimum age raised only to nine.

Question 3: Should the workday of the youngest workers be reduced?

Response	Conseils généraux Responding	Chambers of Commerce Responding	Chambres consultatives Responding
Eliminate work for children under 12	6 (7%)	10 (16%)	15 (19%)
Reduce workday of children under 12	39 (44%)	12 (19%)	18 (22%)
Keep 8-hour day for children under 12	22 (25%)	20 (31%)	26 (32%)
Increase workday for some under 12	1 (1%)	15 (23%)	7 (9%)
Vary workday with conditions	1 (1%)	2 (3%)	4 (5%)
No opinion or no reply	20 (22%)	5 (8%)	11 (14%)

continued

Question 4: Should a corps of salaried inspectors be established?

Response	Conseils généraux Responding	Chambers of Commerce Responding	Chambres consultatives Responding
Maintain existing system	18 (20%)	16 (25%)	22 (27%)
Establish salaried inspection	36 (40%)	29 (45%)	30 (37%)
Have existing functionaries inspect	15 (17%)	13 (20%)	9 (11%)
No opinion or no reply	20 (22%)	6 (9%)	20 (25%)

Note: Column percentages may not equal 100% because of rounding.
Source: *Renseignements et avis recueillis en 1867 sur le travail des enfants dans les établissements industriels* (Paris, 1867), 7–34.

gested that few provincial notables and business leaders were content with the existing provisions of the factory law. Given the opportunity to respond freely, many of the bodies contacted by the Ministry of Commerce proposed new schemes for regulating the workdays of children; some of them represented major departures from the pattern established by the 1841 law. For example, the *conseil général* of the Loire-Inférieure, which had suggested a minimum age of eleven, also wanted to see a maximum workday of only six hours for all children. The *conseil général* of the Seine-et-Marne advocated a nine-hour day for children in factories where primary education was provided and a six-hour day elsewhere. The council of the Oise recommended that children under twelve work a six-hour day in winter and an eight-hour day in summer. The chamber of commerce in Amiens favored a six-hour day for youngsters who had not completed their primary schooling but a twelve-hour day for those who had, regardless of their age. The chambers of commerce of Calais and Dijon advised varying the length of children's workdays according to the work they performed, but the Roanne Chamber of Commerce and the *chambre consultative* of Avesnes wanted children to be allowed to work as long as adult laborers did each day.

Despite the fact that several of the proposed plans for regulating children's hours involved lengthening the workdays of some children under twelve, there seemed to be a general consensus that at least the very youngest children employed in industry were being overworked. About half of all the bodies responding to the 1867 inquiry wanted either to see the workday of children under twelve reduced in length (a six-hour workday for these children was the most common suggestion) or to have children under twelve barred from industrial employment altogether. Moreover, many of those who advocated retaining the eight-hour workday for children under twelve did so on the assumption that the minimum age for employment would be raised to ten or even higher. Those whose proposals allowed for the actual lengthening of children's working hours also invariably assumed that the minimum age for employment would be raised.

In proposing their various minimum age and maximum hour schemes, respondents to the ministerial circular of 1867 seem to have been attempting to formulate programs that would protect more children from premature employment but, at the same time, allow for the most efficient use of the youngsters working in the factories. A six-hour workday for children under twelve was so attractive because it would reduce the number of hours children worked but it would also facilitate the introduction of two shifts of child laborers to complement the twelve-hour workday of adults. Protecting the very young while making child labor more productive also seems to have been the motivation behind those schemes that involved raising the minimum age for factory labor but lengthening the workday of some preadolescents. Children eight or nine years old would be spared the hardships of industrial labor, but the working hours of children ten or eleven years old could be brought into conformity with those of adults. It is perhaps to be expected that schemes geared to the needs of industry were less attractive to departmental councils than they were to chambers of commerce and *chambres consultatives*, which represented business interests specifically.

Over the years, the lax enforcement of France's child labor regulations had come to be seen as a major problem, and the 1867 government inquiry made it clear that most local notables and entrepreneurs believed it was time to institute an improved system of surveillance. Among *conseils généraux*, only 20 percent favored maintaining the existing factory inspection system, based on local child labor committees serving voluntarily, whereas 40 percent wanted to see the appointment of special factory inspectors, salaried by the government. Most of the councils that favored salaried inspectors thought it proper for the national government to pay them, but a few were willing to allow departmental budgets to bear the cost. Another 17 percent of *conseils généraux* believed that special inspectors were unnecessary but wanted to see inspection improved by delegating it to existing government functionaries, such as school inspectors, inspectors of weights and measures, overseers of abandoned children, or police officials. Among the chambers of commerce, 45 percent suggested naming special salaried inspectors, and 20 percent said they were in favor of having existing functionaries take on the oversight of child labor. Other chambers of commerce expressed their desire for improved factory inspection only in general terms: the Bordeaux chamber called for a system that would be "full and reliable"; the Le Mans chamber called for "active and assiduous" surveillance. Of the *chambres consultatives,* 37 percent came out for special salaried inspectors, and another 11 percent favored charging existing functionaries with the task of oversight.

In general terms, the exhaustive inquiry of 1867 revealed widespread support among the leaders of French society and commerce for a more rigorous system of child labor controls. Of all the departmental councils, chambers of commerce, and *chambres consultatives* that actually rendered opinions on the issues raised in the Ministry of Commerce questionnaire, 91 percent favored extending the purview of the child labor law, 82 percent favored raising the minimum age for employment, 51 percent favored either prohibiting children under twelve from engaging in industrial labor or at least shortening the hours they could work, and 70 percent favored improving the system of factory surveillance. It is also significant that not a single body responding to the government inquiry raised any objection to the existing limitations on the use of child labor.

Although the majority of respondents to the government inquiry of 1867 favored more rigorous child labor measures, there was, of course, also a minority among those polled that was essentially satisfied with existing child labor restrictions. As in the responses to earlier inquiries, however, there again seemed to be no clear pattern of divergent views that could be explained by such factors as varying levels of industrialization or child labor utilization. Among the *conseils généraux* of France's fifteen most industrialized departments, for example, nine favored extending the coverage of the factory law, three opposed extension, one rendered no opinion, and two (the Eure and the Seine-Inférieure) did not even respond to the government survey. Similarly, concerning the minimum age for employment, three of these councils favored retaining a minimum age of eight, but seven favored a minimum of ten or higher. On the question of factory surveillance, seven councils wanted salaried inspectors, three wanted existing functionaries to conduct inspections, and two declared that voluntary inspection was sufficient.

An examination of the relationship between responses to the 1867 inquiry and such seemingly relevant factors as local rates of rejection for military service or local rates of illiteracy, which might have reflected the ill effects of premature employment, also suggests that the opinions on reform expressed by local notables did not conform to any general pattern.[11] In the final analysis, the attitudes of local notables in the 1860s, like the attitudes of their counterparts thirty years earlier, appear to have had little to do with the actual conditions of working children at the local level. Whether they were in the majority that favored reform or not, what the notables were responding to was their perception of child labor abuse as a national problem, regardless of its local manifestations. It was the general concern of the privileged classes with the children of the poor, both individually and collectively, that accounts for much of the support expanded factory legislation enjoyed within the French elite, and it was the declining importance of children in the work force that allowed local notables to express that support so freely. Most manufacturers and businessmen no longer viewed the curtailment of child labor as a serious threat to productivity or to entrepreneurial prerogative, and this allowed them and their associates to view the employment of children in industry as a residual national problem that could easily be solved.[12]

All of this suggests that the leaders of the child labor reform movement in the late 1860s, men such as Jules Simon, Armand Audiganne, and the founders of the Société de protection des apprentis, were having an impact on national opinion. By centralizing their propaganda efforts and by speaking always in broad national terms rather than trying to influence specific local elites through allusions to local conditions, the reform movement was gaining support. The generalized propaganda of the sixties, emanating mainly from Paris, was certainly very important in convincing the majority of France's notables to look favorably upon reform.

While the Ministry of Commerce was evaluating the results of its poll of departmental councils and chambers of commerce, it was also reviewing the results of two other recently completed surveys. One of these, conducted by Charles de Freycinet, was an extensive investigation of the child labor situation in England, where the Factory Acts Extension Act

11. See Lee Shai Weissbach, "The Child Labor Problem in the 1860s: Realities and Attitudes" (Annual Meeting of the Society for French Historical Studies, 1983). Information on departmental rates of rejection for service and of illiteracy can be found in Statistique de la France, *Mouvement de la population pendant les années 1861, 1862, 1863, 1864 et 1865* (Strasbourg, 1870), 338–39.

12. Compare Musgrove, *Youth and the Social Order*, 73–74.

and the Workshops Act, passed in 1867, had significantly expanded the protection of young British workers.[13] Whenever action on child labor was contemplated in France, either by reformers or by the administration, England's child labor policy came under close scrutiny. The other survey was one conducted by the Ministry of Public Instruction, and it provided further evidence of how unevenly the education provisions of the 1841 factory law were being enforced. The prefects contacted by the Ministry of Public Instruction reported a wide range of conditions. The prefect of the Haut-Rhin wrote that local employers were doing all that was required of them concerning schooling; the prefect of the Ardennes counted 1,820 of the 2,170 children employed in his department as literate; and the prefect of the Nord reported that the education provisions of the child labor law were "executed in a manner as satisfactory as possible, thanks to the system of salaried inspection that exists in the department and to the perseverance of the local administration." On the other side, the prefect of the Loire complained that the education provisions of the law were "unheeded" and that "children are hired in the factories without any question about their education." Similarly, the prefect of the Isère wrote that the regulations regarding schooling had "always been executed only very imperfectly," and the prefect of the Eure stated flatly that "the law seems to be generally ignored." Some prefects voiced the familiar disclaimer that the 1841 law simply did not apply in their departments.[14]

Armed with the huge amount of data it had collected and reviewed, the Ministry of Commerce was prepared by December of 1867 to submit to the Conseil d'état a proposal for a substantially new child labor law. The new bill was referred to committee, and it was reported out on November 26, 1868, almost a year after it was first taken under review. The measure placed before the Conseil d'état called for an extension of factory legislation to cover all industrial establishments regardless of size, and though it retained the minimum age of eight, the bill provided that this minimum age apply to apprentices as well as to free laborers. Further, the bill provided that factories using a continuous fire could not hire workers under ten, that neither children under thirteen nor women could be employed in mining, and that all females would be subject to child labor regulations until the age of eighteen, rather than the age of sixteen set as the limit for all child workers by the law of 1841. For the

13. See Thomas, *Young People*, 99–103; AN, F12–4721; and Charles de Freycinet, *Souvenirs 1848–1878* (Paris, 1912), 83–88.
14. Material on this inquiry is in AN, F12–4722 and F12–4723.

first time, a clear gender distinction was being proposed as part of a child labor bill. A six-hour workday for all children was stipulated in the measure, which also proposed that exemptions from half-time work could be granted only for children over thirteen. Children under thirteen would be required to attend school at least two hours a day, and under no circumstances could they be at work before 5 A.M. or after 9 P.M. Children were to be barred from performing certain hazardous jobs and banned entirely from working in a number of dangerous industries. As under the 1841 law, employers would be expected to oversee the health and morals of their young employees and to post notices of child labor regulations. The *livret* was also to be retained.

To provide for enforcement, the child labor bill called for the creation of a salaried corps of inspectors whose members would have a legal right to enter and scrutinize industrial establishments. The exact nature of the inspection corps was to be determined by the administration. A *commission supérieure* was also to be established, with its members nominated by the emperor. Where the situation warranted, local child labor commissions were to be retained and strengthened.[15]

Despite the fact that the child labor bill had been under review in committee for nearly a year, the Conseil d'état declined to take immediate action on the proposed legislation, in large part because the appointment of a new corps of inspectors involved substantial budgetary considerations.[16] The Ministry of Commerce, however, was less prepared to temporize. More intimately concerned with the matter of child labor reform, it was feeling the pressure of public opinion more directly than any other government agency. Letters with comments and suggestions began flowing into Paris as soon as the new child labor bill had been placed before the Conseil d'état, and the legislature, recently empowered with the review of ministers, was also demanding action.[17] The issue of child labor was raised in the 1867 debates on primary education and on the budget of the Ministry of Commerce; the Senate expressed a specific desire to see voluntary agents replaced with special factory inspectors.[18] Responding to these pressures, the Ministry of Commerce

15. A printed copy of the bill distributed to members of the Conseil d'état is in AN, F12–4721.

16. See Bec, *Législation de l'inspection*, 38ff.

17. See material in AN, F12–4721. See also the communication from Goldenberg, a member of the chamber of commerce of the Haut-Rhin, published in *BSPA* (1868), 129–43.

18. See, for example, the Corps législatif debate of March 11, 1867, and the Senate debate of February 28, 1868.

proceeded to take matters into its own hands: it decided on its own authority to implement a scheme that would provide an immediate amelioration of the child labor situation.

In a decree of December 7, 1868, Forcade la Roquette proclaimed that beginning on January 1 of the following year, factory surveillance would become the responsibility of government mining engineers throughout France. For the first time, there would be a centrally administered body of functionaries charged with child labor inspection. The minister also established his own *commission supérieure* to consult on the control of child labor and to issue annual reports, and he named Charles de Freycinet to coordinate factory inspection for the Direction des mines.[19]

The implementation of the ministry's new scheme for enforcing France's existing child labor law was not without its problems. The mining engineers did not like their new task, considered it a burden, and gave it low priority. Neither were they equipped with the specific knowledge and experience that would have made it possible for them to perform their new job creditably. In addition, the change in the system of enforcement caused numerous bureaucratic complications. The responsibility for child labor had to be transferred initially from the Direction de commerce interieur to the Direction des mines, and when the Ministry of Public Works was separated from the Ministry of Commerce at the beginning of 1870, the machinery of inspection became even more cumbersome. The status of locally organized inspection efforts was also put in question. Local child labor commissions, which had exerted a positive influence in some places at least, virtually ceased to exist, and factory inspectors salaried by various departments found themselves in confused circumstances.[20]

In the Seine, Barreswil had to be discharged, but Maurice, a mining engineer by training, was retained. In the Nord, Inspector Dupont was forced into retirement with an indemnity of three thousand francs after seventeen years of service. In January of 1870, the journal *L'Echo du Nord* expressed its concern over the recent relaxation of labor law enforcement and editorialized against the use of mining engineers as factory inspectors. "The mining engineer has more important things to do than examine young *rattacheurs* and *bobineurs* on their ABCs," the journal contended. When the minister of commerce inquired into the validity of the charges that had been leveled in the Nord, the prefect of the department replied: "The facts reported [in the article] are, sadly,

19. Material in AN, F12–4721.
20. See, for example, an 1869 note from Charles de Freycinet in AN, F12–4721.

all too true. Formerly child labor inspection was entrusted to a special inspector, as well as to local commissions which concerned themselves with it actively, and the law was obeyed everywhere in the department. But since the suppression of the local commissions, the industrialists think themselves freed of all surveillance and a new laxity has appeared everywhere."[21]

An inquiry conducted in January of 1870 among France's mining engineers and prefects (after the engineers had been in service as factory inspectors for about a year) revealed that on a national level their activity had left the child labor situation essentially unchanged. Those child labor restrictions to which manufacturers could easily accommodate themselves were generally honored, but other provisions of the law, such as those regarding education and limiting to eight hours the workday of children under twelve, were still often ignored. From the Seine-Inférieure came word that "factory owners never bother" with the certification of schooling and that of 5,534 factory children over the age of twelve in the department, only 648 had fulfilled the education requirements of the law. From the Haut-Rhin the prefect wrote that "despite the efforts of many influential members of the Société industrielle de Mulhouse . . . the law of March 22, 1841, is not observed completely." He attributed this laxity "to the force of inertia, to the difficulty of changing a state of affairs consecrated by prolonged practice." The prefect of the Gironde reported that the child labor law "seems completely unknown in most of those establishments in the department where it should be found in force."[22] For all the sentiment expressed by the middle classes about the fate of poor children and for all the support child labor reform enjoyed among the leaders of French society and commerce, much resistance to child labor controls obviously still existed among those most directly involved. In individual factories and workshops all over the country, ideals were being sacrificed before the exigencies of daily operation. Moreover, many of the employers who circumvented the provisions of the factory law did not believe they were harming the children they employed: they realized they had little control over factory children's school attendance, and they saw themselves as providing these children with needed income.

Many respondents to the 1870 inquiry offered suggestions for im-

21. Overbergh, *Inspecteurs*, 124–26; Report of February 26, 1869, in AN, F12–4717; H. V., "Lille et le Nord de la France," *L'Echo du Nord*, January 7, 1870; Correspondence in AN, F12–4717.

22. Correspondence in AN, F12–4718, F12–4719, and F12–4727.

proving compliance with the law. From a dozen departments, including the highly industrialized Nord, Seine-Inférieure, Pas-de-Calais, and Ardennes, came the recommendation that a corps of lower ranking officials—mine wardens—be appointed to assist the mining engineers with factory inspection. From fifteen departments came the suggestion that other functionaries be assigned to aid the engineers, and from three departments (including the Nord) came the idea of reactivating local child labor commissions. In only fourteen departments, all of them nonindustrial, did respondents express the belief that the existing inspection system was adequate. Many mining engineers and prefects also used the occasion of the 1870 inquiry to lobby once more for changes in the basic provisions of France's child labor policy. They repeatedly urged extending the control of the law to all industrial establishments and raising the minimum age for employment.[23]

Nor were those contacted by the Ministry of Commerce the only ones who found occasion to comment on the use of mining engineers and to press for improvements in France's child labor legislation. Armand de Melun, for instance, published a lengthy article in *Le Correspondant* in 1869 calling for new factory legislation, for public support of the law, and for the good will and cooperation of entrepreneurs. Melun declared that he was willing to give factory surveillance by mining engineers a fair trial, but he urged the government not to resist financing special inspection if the need for it became apparent. At about the same time, in a speech delivered to an industrialists' organization and subsequently published, a reform advocate named Paul Allard called for an improved and more explicit child labor law to replace the law of 1841. He was especially concerned that there be a well-defined system of inspection incorporated into the legislation. "The fate of any vague and ill-defined article of law," he warned, is that "it is forgotten."[24]

The ongoing discussion of the need for further reform, along with the results of the experiment in factory surveillance undertaken in 1869, prompted the recently installed minister of commerce, Charles Louvet, to reintroduce the 1867 child labor bill to the Conseil d'état in March of 1870. The bill was now slightly revised, but it still left the establishment

23. Material on this inquiry, whose primary vehicle was a circular of January 15, 1870, is in AN, F12–4727. Some of the individual responses to the inquiry are in AN, F12–4717, F12–4718 and F12–4719.

24. Armand de Melun, "Le Travail des enfants," *Le Correspondant*, June 10, 1869, esp. 859–72; Paul Allard, *Du travail des enfants et des femmes* (Rouen, 1869), esp. 5.

of a system of factory inspection to administrative fiat. Louvet himself was willing to give the mining engineers a chance to prove themselves as factory inspectors. "If they succeed, as one may hope," he wrote, "the simplest and at the same time happiest solution to this serious problem will have been found."[25] The head of the Conseil's child labor committee, Nicholas Heurtier, was less sanguine about the success of the mining engineers, however, and he presented his colleagues with a plan that would use the power granted to the administration under the proposed legislation to establish an independent factory inspectorate with four inspectors-general and sixteen divisional inspectors.[26] Avoiding a specific decision on inspection for the time being, the Conseil d'état finally approved Louvet's child labor bill and sent it forward to the Senate.

The imperial government's ultimate decision to sponsor a new child labor bill was a wise move politically, for by 1870 child labor reform commanded much support. On the one hand, it was a cause that (the view of some Social Catholics notwithstanding) appealed to the middle classes, which had provided the empire with much of its backing from the beginning. Middle-class support for new legislation was apparent both in the voluminous propaganda emanating from middle-class circles in the later 1860s and in the results of the various Ministry of Commerce surveys of that period. On the other hand, the prospect of further child labor reform also pleased at least the more articulate elements of the working classes, which the imperial government was increasingly interested in wooing. A desire to promote the welfare of the working classes and to strengthen their support of the empire was specifically articulated by Heurtier as a motive for the adoption of a new child labor measure. Speaking before the Conseil d'état in 1868, Heurtier had declared:

> As for me, *messieurs*, it is impossible not to feel satisfaction and confidence in the future when I contemplate all that the Empire has done for the working class. The worker, yesterday excluded from high society and from the bourgeoisie, has been given human dignity and the dignity of citizenship by the Empire; ... the worker, yesterday still fearing for his children, too often victims of unjust exploitation, is today reassured by the law upon which we are working. . . .
> Let us continue this fruitful series of acts . . . ; it is through them that a dynasty may root itself in the hearts of the population.[27]

25. Document in AN, F12–4721.
26. See Eugène Tallon and Gustave Maurice, *Législation sur le travail des enfants* (Paris, 1875), 53. See also Bec, *Législation de l'inspection*, 38; and Overbergh, *Inspecteurs*, 123.
27. Document in AN, F12–4721.

The child labor proposal approved by the Conseil d'état was placed before the Senate on June 28, 1870. Within three weeks, however, the matter of child labor reform was abruptly shunted aside as France declared war on Prussia. As in 1848, a national crisis and a fundamental change in France's form of government were destined to disrupt the adoption of new factory legislation and to frustrate the efforts of the child labor reform movement, at least temporarily.

TEN

The Child Labor Law of 1874

Although the Franco-Prussian War interrupted the imperial Senate's discussion of a new child labor law in the summer of 1870, the government's bureaucratic concern with child labor did not seem to wane even as the nation faced the trials of combat, defeat, and domestic upheaval. As late as August, 1870, the Ministry of Commerce issued a circular requesting data on the child labor situation throughout France. Soon after the war, while the situation in Paris occupied most of the nation's attention, the ministry dispatched memoranda seeking to complete child labor surveys that had been disrupted by the fighting.[1] Moreover, the legislative discussion of a new factory law was resumed very shortly after the Peace of Frankfurt was signed with Germany. On June 19, 1871, Ambroise Joubert, deputy from the Maine-et-Loire, introduced a child labor bill before the National Assembly. Over the next three years, the shape of France's future child labor legislation would be the subject of much debate, and before a new factory law would be enacted in 1874, the political leaders of the nation would be forced to confront many of the issues fundamental to the creation of both a welfare policy and a labor policy under the Third Republic.

The bill introduced by Joubert in 1871 was much briefer and less detailed than the child labor bill that had been under consideration when hostilities erupted in 1870. Composed of just five articles, the Joubert bill failed to specify the types of establishments to which his proposed

1. Memoranda on uncompleted surveys were dispatched on March 17 and May 28, 1871. See material in AN, F12–4706.

law would apply, left vague the responsibility of manufacturers for the schooling of their young employees, and seemed to allow nighttime work by children. The bill's provision for inspection was rather naïve, as it proposed assigning the task of factory surveillance to the nation's school inspectors. On the other hand, the legislation proposed by Joubert was in some ways more demanding than the bill that had come out of the Conseil d'état in 1870. For example, the 1870 bill had sought to retain eight as the minimum age for employment, but Joubert's bill proposed that the minimum age be raised to ten.[2] The primary importance of the Joubert bill, however, was that it served to place the child labor issue squarely before the new National Assembly in the very early months of the provisional republic and thus to preserve the momentum for reform that had been generated in the late 1860s.

Joubert's personal motives for rushing to introduce a new child labor bill before the assembly are not completely clear, but the fact that he was a graduate of the Ecole polytechnique and the head of a well-established sailcloth mill at Angers suggests that he must have been aware of and influenced by the growing child labor reform movement of the latter 1860s. In more general terms, the new assembly was inclined to undertake a consideration of child labor abuse because, even though in its character it was very different from the legislative bodies of the late Second Empire, it was concerned no less than the imperial government had been with the broad issues underlying the demands for child labor reform: moral regeneration, military preparedness, and the nurture of the nation's youth. For the predominantly Catholic and conservative deputies elected in 1871, these issues took on an added urgency in the face of France's recent defeat by Germany, an experience that seemed to pervade French thinking on nearly every issue in the early 1870s.[3] Many of the deputies believed that France's defeat resulted from her neglect of the moral and physical development of the nation's youth.[4] In addition, many of them felt a strong religious obligation to care for society's unfortunates.[5] Thus, in August of 1871, on the advice of a preliminary study commission headed by Charles Kolb-Bernard, the assembly voted

2. Notes comparing the 1870 government bill and Joubert's bill are in AN, F12–4727.
3. See, for example, Koenraad W. Swart, *The Sense of Decadence in Nineteenth-Century France* (The Hague, 1964), 123–38.
4. See, for example, Raoul Jay, *Du travail des enfants et filles mineures dans l'industrie* (Paris, 1880), 19–20.
5. See Dansette, *Religious History*, I, 324–43; Copin, *Doctrines économiques*, 114–15; and Cobban, *History of Modern France*, III, 16.

to take up consideration of a new factory act, and a fifteen-member child labor committee was established.[6]

The chairman of the assembly's child labor committee was Anatole de Melun, twin brother of the tireless child labor crusader Armand de Melun; the secretary of the committee was the lawyer Eugène Tallon. By the spring of 1872, the Melun committee had prepared its own version of a new child labor bill, and Tallon, who seems to have been the dominant member of the committee, released its report on May 11. Under the empire, Tallon had run an unsuccessful campaign for a seat in the legislature as an independent liberal, and in the National Assembly he counted himself among the Orleanists. His own political philosophy could thus be considered a moderate one, and the child labor report he presented to his colleagues in 1872 echoed the dominant attitudes toward social policy within the assembly. On the one hand, it reflected the paternalistic concern with the welfare of the lower classes that was especially strong among Legitimists but that was common among conservatives of all stripes and had also been manifested among *haute bourgeois* liberals in recent years. On the other hand, the report was sensitive to the assembly's general cautiousness on matters of social legislation (evident especially among liberal Orleanists) and to its hostility toward the working classes, recently reenforced by the revolt of the Paris Commune.[7]

Tallon's exhaustive report began with a review of the history of French child labor legislation and a comparison of France's legislation with the laws of other countries. Observing that the innovative Child Labor Law of 1841 had been designed as a very limited measure, the report argued that the industrial progress of France in recent decades and the incomplete enforcement of existing measures now made a reappraisal of the nation's factory legislation a necessity. The report assured the assembly that though the Melun committee had felt compelled to reconsider the key philosophical question nagging at the child labor reform movement since the beginning of the century, it nonetheless had readily affirmed the right of the state to interfere with parental and entrepreneurial authority in order to control child labor. What had once been the pivotal

---

6. NA, August 2, 16, 1871. Kolb-Bernard was a sugar manufacturer who had been an unusually assiduous volunteer child labor inspector in the Nord, the president of the Lille Chamber of Commerce, and a member of the imperial Corps législatif from 1859 to 1870.

7. Compare Samuel M. Osgood, *French Royalism Under the Third and Fourth Republics* (The Hague, 1960), 12–13. See also Jacques Chastenet, *Cent Ans de république* (Paris, 1970), I, 383–85; Weill, *Mouvement social*, 91; and Moon, *Labor Problem*, 172ff.

issue in the debate over child labor legislation was now no longer a point of contention. The various controversies that arose in committee concerned only the details of the bill that was being hammered out. The committee was aware of the structural factors hindering the effectiveness of child labor restrictions, and it was willing to recommend a more intrusive government policy to end the abuse of child labor once and for all.[8]

The bill that emerged from committee bore little resemblance to the original Joubert proposal. It was even more detailed and more demanding than the imperial bill of 1870, though clearly the imperial bill had served as the model for the new one. The Melun committee's bill called for a minimum age of ten and a six-hour workday for children under thirteen. Children over thirteen would be allowed to work the same hours as adults. The upper age limit of thirteen for those who would be subject to a half-time schedule had been decided on only after some haggling. Several members of the Melun committee had wanted an upper limit of only twelve, whereas others wanted an age limit as high as fourteen or fifteen. The argument over how to define the youngest category of workers was in reality an argument between those who wanted to preserve children from the hardships of full-time labor for as long as possible and those who were more concerned about the demands of industrialists for young workers and the requirements of poor families for supplementary income. Thirteen, then, was seen as a compromise age limit.

By contrast, the committee members found it easy to agree that the coverage of France's child labor legislation should be vastly extended, and their bill provided that it be applied to all those "working in factories, workshops and yards, or in general outside the family, under the direction of an employer." The primary argument advanced in support of extending the factory law was by then well established: the law's protection was most needed in small shops, where public scrutiny could be avoided and where considerations of economy often precluded attention to the welfare of young workers. That children laboring in family enterprises would not be subject to the scrutiny of the government, however, demonstrated the committee's reluctance to go so far as to permit intervention into what were still viewed as unequivocally private matters.

The committee bill stipulated a ban on work at night, on Sundays, and on holidays for all children under sixteen, with limited exemptions pos-

8. The Tallon report and the committee bill are in Tallon and Maurice, *Législation*, 15–71. See also NA, May 11, 1872.

sible only for adolescents over the age of thirteen. A ban on underground labor for children under thirteen was also proposed, as was the total exclusion of youngsters from jobs that were especially dangerous or unhealthy. The committee addressed the problem of conflicts between the factory law and the Apprenticeship Law of 1851 by providing that certain portions of the measure it had drafted be applied to apprentices as well as to free laborers: the minimum age of ten, for example, was to apply to both categories of young workers.

The provisions the Melun committee was incorporating into its factory bill were derived from the general middle-class consensus that defenseless children ought to be protected from premature exploitation, for their own sakes and, most especially, for the common good, but these provisions were among the most rigorous and far-reaching restrictions that had ever been proposed for the regulation of child labor. If French society was to be stabilized and France restored to her position of power in the world, a properly reared and physically strong working class was critical. There was no longer any significant support for the contention that hiring children for industrial labor was a private matter, and the leaders of French society in the 1870s were much more prepared than their counterparts in previous decades had been to combat the more disturbing aspects of industrial working conditions with a program of government intervention.

Indeed, the Melun committee went so far as to suggest that some limitations be placed even on the labor of adult women. The committee proposed that the factory law's prohibitions of work at night and on Sundays and holidays, as well as its ban on underground and dangerous labor, be extended to apply to all female workers, regardless of age. Because the members of the Melun committee (like the majority of their colleagues in the assembly) were still somewhat uneasy about expanding the realm of factory legislation to include adults, however, they justified their proposal to restrict female labor in the same way a similar proposal had been defended by the framers of the abortive child labor bill of 1847. The committee argued that limitations on the work of women were needed primarily to assure that children were not deprived of their mothers' attentions and to promote the survival of the working-class family. In other words, any restriction placed on women's work was to be seen not as an encroachment on the rights of adults but rather as an extension of the measures introduced to protect children and to provide for their proper upbringing. "Nothing does more to loosen the bonds of marriage, and nothing has a greater negative influence on the conduct of the worker, than the continual absence of the wife," the committee report observed; "nothing is more prejudicial to the health of the child than the removal of the mother during the hours when, under its own roof, the family gathers to rest."

A relatively strong provision for education was written into the bill presented to the National Assembly in 1872, for education was seen as a key factor in proper upbringing. However, great care was taken to separate the matter of guaranteeing minimal schooling for factory children from any mention of broader education reform. By the early 1870s, the cause of compulsory education was already closely linked with republican anticlericalism, and the monarchist majority in the assembly was sure to be wary of any measure that seemed to support the notion of enforced schooling for all.[9] Thus, in presenting his report, Eugène Tallon was careful to emphasize the distinction between a demand that an employer help oversee the schooling of his young employees and an implementation of compulsory education. Even those who in general opposed required school attendance could feel comfortable supporting the child labor bill's insistence on the education of factory children, Tallon insisted.

The proposed factory bill asked that no children under thirteen be admitted to industrial employment if they were not also attending school and that no children between thirteen and fifteen be admitted without proof that they had received a primary education. Factory owners themselves were to verify their young employees' presence in school by checking attendance records weekly, or they were to provide classes in their own shops for at least two hours a day. Employers were also asked to maintain working conditions conducive to morality and health, and the Melun committee's bill even dictated some rudimentary accident prevention measures employers were to implement.

The provisions for the law's enforcement contained in the 1872 bill demonstrated further that the members of the committee were not reluctant to adopt a relatively intrusive policy in order to subject industrial labor to uniform standards. At the heart of the committee's enforcement proposal was the creation of an inspectorate comprising two inspectors-general and fifteen divisional inspectors to be selected by the administration and salaried by the state. In addition, a *commission supérieure* was to be established to nominate inspectors, coordinate enforcement, suggest

9. See, for example, J. P. T. Bury, *Gambetta and the Making of the Third Republic* (London, 1973), 65ff, and Bertocci, *Jules Simon.*

revised legislation when necessary, and issue annual reports on the child labor law. Local child labor commissions were to be reconstituted as well. The members of local boards were to be named by prefects, and there was to be at least one commission in each *arrondissement*. Local commissions were each to consist of five to seven individuals, and where possible, they were to include local doctors, school inspectors, and mining engineers.

Obsessed with the memory of the Franco-Prussian War, those who drafted the 1872 proposal for a strong system of factory inspection obviously had in mind the need to prepare France's youth for future military confrontations (and for revenge against Germany); they argued that effective enforcement of the child labor law would serve to "marshal a multitude of robust youths under the flag of France, sheltering in its folds the hope of reawakening her grandeur." It was not only the supporters of new legislation who alluded to the recent conflict, however. Some of the opponents of a new system of factory inspection also invoked the memory of the war: when they argued against undertaking the expense of a new corps of factory inspectors, they pointed to the immense cost of the fighting and to the huge indemnity demanded by the Germans. But the objections to a corps of inspectors collapsed in the face of arguments that the nation simply could not afford to skimp where the welfare of its youth was concerned.

The first formal reading of the new child labor bill before the National Assembly took place on November 25, 1872. Ambroise Joubert, who had been a member of the Melun committee and who had apparently been won over to its comprehensive proposal, was assigned the task of explaining the provisions of the bill to his colleagues. When Joubert finished, Louis Blanc, perhaps France's most prominent advocate of state involvement in social welfare, rose to address the bill. Blanc applauded the bill as "a generous effort for good," but reiterating much of what had been said about the importance of factory legislation, he went on to express the hope that even more stringent limitations would be placed on the labor of children and that stiffer penalties would be written into the law. Tallon used the occasion of the first reading to speak once again in favor of the bill he had played such a large part in drafting, and the assembly readily voted to bring the measure back for another reading.[10]

The second reading of the new child labor bill was scheduled for January, 1873, and it occasioned an extensive and sometimes heated debate

10. For the first reading of the 1874 law, see NA, November 25, 1872.

that continued on into February. As the bill was brought forward for discussion section by section, nearly every issue that had been discussed over the past four and a half decades in connection with the limitation of child labor was revived in one form or another. The fundamental matter of the legitimacy of state intrusion in familial affairs was raised once again, for example. There was no significant objection within the traditionalist assembly to some extension of the factory law, but by the same token, the conservatism of most deputies led them to fear intervening in those employment patterns that were often essentially family relationships. Thus, the deputies found it very difficult to accept a precise and absolute definition of the industrial establishments to which the new child labor law would apply, and even at the close of debate, many of the questions raised in this connection remained unanswered.

Another matter that resurfaced at the second reading of the child labor bill was the severity of the punishment to be imposed on those who violated the factory law. Some deputies thought that the legal sanctions proposed in committee were too strict, whereas others thought they were too lenient. Emile Keller, a Social Catholic deputy from Belfort who seemingly had not lost his faith in the efficacy of government coercion, even suggested that jail sentences of up to a month be introduced to supplement the system of fines contained in the bill. The legislators, however, rejected the idea of imposing more severe punishments for infractions of the factory law. They were apparently convinced to reject the idea by Tallon's argument that judges would hesitate to convict violators of the child labor law if the sentences they would be forced to impose were perceived as too harsh.

The matter of education for factory children was debated again in early 1873 as well. As Tallon had anticipated, many deputies were reluctant to approve any measure that smacked of compulsory education, and supporters of the child labor bill had to promote it carefully so as not overly to antagonize the conservative Catholic majority. "It would be a mistake," Tallon observed, "to confuse the theory of compulsory education with the specific terms we have provided for instruction in the present law." He went on to assure his colleagues that "as for us, we respect the liberty of teaching, we respect free choice for the father of a family concerning the mode of instruction he intends to provide his children." In the end, the majority of the deputies were able to make the distinction between enforced schooling for factory children on the one hand and compulsory education on the other, and the assembly retained the rather stringent schooling requirements proposed by its child labor committee.

So comprehensive was the 1873 debate on child labor that even the matter of imposing Sunday as a day of rest for working children was not accepted without some discussion. Here it was the deputy from Metz, Edouard Bamberger, who rose to object to the assembly's insensitivity on the issue. Unlike his coreligionist and predecessor under the July Monarchy, Achille Fould, who declared that French Jews would willingly accommodate themselves to the requirements of the Child Labor Law of 1841, Bamberger protested that the Sunday rest provision was prejudicial to Jewish children, who observed the sabbath on Saturday. Still, the provision for Sunday rest was retained; too many deputies feared that allowing exemptions would create a bureaucratic nightmare and invite fraud.

Ultimately, however, all these matters—defining affected firms, determining penalties, requiring schooling, and imposing Sunday rest—occasioned much less intense controversy than did three other issues that became major points of contention. The first of these larger issues was the immediately practical one of defining a minimum age for industrial employment and a maximum workday for the youngest workers. There were some members of the assembly, such as the deputy Jules Leurent of the Nord, who argued that the minimum age for employment should be relatively high but that once children entered the work force, they should be allowed to labor as long as adults did each day. However, the idea that it was important to maintain two age categories also had its supporters. Moreover, although the advocates of a distinction between children and adolescents generally agreed that the youngest workers should be restricted to a six-hour workday, they themselves could not agree on how each of the two age categories should be defined. Most accepted the Melun committee's minimum age of ten, but many were unhappy with the upper age limit of thirteen for the younger category. Even in committee, the compromise standard of thirteen had been adopted by the narrow margin of eight votes to seven.

Partisans of an upper age limit of twelve for the younger category of factory children contended that technological advances, local labor shortages, and the wisdom of gradual change in employment practices all militated in favor of this lower age limit. Anatole de Melun, a supporter of the limit being set at twelve, even argued that in the long run, full-time employment at an earlier age could contribute to a child's health.

He suggested that because the families of unemployed or underemployed thirteen- and fourteen-year-olds often could not provide for their children, these children would be better off doing "moderate work" in industry and earning a livelihood. On the other side, those deputies who favored fourteen as the upper age limit of the younger category argued quite simply that since overwork was now understood to undermine the health and welfare of the young, the longer work was delayed, the better. No one presented the case for delaying full-time employment better than did the physician Théophile Roussel, who had an especially keen interest in protecting the young and who would soon make a lasting reputation for himself as the sponsor of an important law for the regulation of wet-nursing.[11]

Because it was so difficult for the assembly to reach a consensus on the issue of age, Tallon and Joubert, consistent advocates of compromise, continued to exhort their colleagues to adopt the Melun committee's scheme of two categories divided at the age of thirteen. In the end, the partisans of compromise did win at least a partial victory. The concept of two age categories was accepted, and the division between them at the age of thirteen was adopted for boys by a vote of 277 to 263. But the assembly also adopted an amendment introduced by Maximilien Richard (founder of France's first mechanized hemp mill at Angers) to establish for girls an upper age limit of fourteen for the younger category. Richard had argued that girls needed to be protected from full-time labor until a later age because they were weaker than boys. Tallon, who opposed the introduction of different rules for boys and girls, contended that if anything, girls were more precocious than boys, but his view did not prevail. As in the Ministry of Commerce proposal of 1867, serious consideration was now being given to gender distinctions among working children and to the imposition of different child labor standards for boys and for girls.

The second issue that occupied the assembly in protracted debate revolved around the proposal to extend the factory law's protection to adult women working in industry. Here it was the theoretical implication of the provision, rather than any practical effect it would have, that made it controversial. The bill that had come out of committee in 1872 had included a significant amount of coverage for adult female workers, but the floor debate in the assembly made it apparent that this coverage

11. See George D. Sussman, *Selling Mothers' Milk: The Wet-Nursing Business in France, 1715–1914* (Urbana, Ill., 1982), 128–29, 166.

was philosophically unacceptable to the vast majority of the deputies. "An extremely grave innovation," Pierre Clément called it. As a result, the Melun committee agreed to remove the provisions for the protection of adult women from its bill in order to better the chances of the bill's adoption. The committee asked only that a prohibition of the nighttime labor of females under the age of twenty-one be preserved.

The floor fight over the protection of women was to continue, however, for Louis Wolowski was prepared to demand at least that the prohibition of nighttime labor be extended to cover all female industrial workers. Despite his suffering from a bothersome head cold, Wolowski argued vigorously that the progress of civilization demanded women be afforded more protection than they had been in the past. He spoke with great passion, and as his authority he invoked the memory of the recently deceased Charles Dupin, the foremost champion of factory reform under the July Monarchy. But the primary argument raised in opposition to Wolowski's demand was still a very powerful one in the early 1870s. The minister of commerce himself, Pierre-Edmond Teisserenc de Bort, rose to defend the widely accepted notion that the state had no authority to interfere with the right to work of any adult. Quoting Turgot, the minister declared that "the right to work is the most sacred property of man." Ultimately, Wolowski's proposal went down to defeat by the lopsided vote of 507 to 90. The members of the Melun committee, it seems, were ahead of their time in proposing limitations on the labor of women in industry, even though they justified those limitations primarily in the name of improved conditions for children.

The third matter hotly contested in the course of the National Assembly's child labor debate was the nature of the inspection system that would be established to guarantee compliance with the factory act. The Melun committee had prepared a plan involving inspectors-general, divisional inspectors, local commissions, and a supervisory *commission supérieure*, but there were still deputies who wanted to put in a word for inspection by government functionaries already in place. "Alas!" protested the Legitimist lawyer Paulin Gillon, "we have many sicknesses, but one of the most dangerous and tenacious is assuredly the malady of offices, the appetite for positions." He suggested that instead of creating a whole new corps of inspectors, the assembly should adopt the system contained in the original Joubert bill of 1871 and entrust factory surveillance to school inspectors. The most lengthy response to Gillon came from Léon Lefébure, who had been a member of the Melun committee, but the key argument against the use of school inspectors (or any other government functionaries) was succinctly summarized by the venerable republican deputy Edmond de Tillancourt. Government functionaries in existing positions, he observed, "do not even have the time to fulfill the duties that are entrusted to them now." Gillon's proposal that factory inspection be carried out by school inspectors was defeated by voice vote.

The main concern of those opposing a new corps of child labor agents was its cost, and despite the defeat of Gillon's suggestion, the monarchist Alfred Monnet proposed that France's 220 existing overseers of abandoned children be empowered to enforce the factory law. This time it was Eugène Tallon who rose to respond. Tallon observed that almost everyone agreed there were two allocations on which it was always improper to skimp: the budget for defense and the budget for education. Since child labor legislation was designed to promote both the military preparedness and the educational advancement of French youth, Tallon continued, the proposed factory law deserved to be implemented fully, even if doing so was a costly proposition. Monnet's proposal, too, was easily defeated by voice vote.

There was one final idea to be considered in the debate over inspection. Emile Keller, who had earlier suggested jail sentences for those who violated the factory law, now proposed that factory surveillance be intensified by granting police authorities at the local level a role in it. Many deputies conceded that the factory law would be more effective with police support, but opponents of the scheme argued that police action would be inappropriate in dealing with the entrepreneurial class. Again, it was Tallon who found a middle ground. He proposed that the police be empowered, along with the factory inspectors, to enforce the child labor law but that they be denied the right of free entry into industrial establishments without a court order. Tallon's proposal was accepted, but even this was not the last amendment of the factory bill's enforcement provisions. Before completing its business, by a vote of 361 to 203 the National Assembly eliminated the posts of inspector-general from the scheme developed in committee. A majority of the deputies had become convinced that, given the existene of a *commission supérieure*, inspectors-general would be superfluous and would only cloud the authority structure of the inspection service. It was February 10, 1873, when the National Assembly at last reached accord on all the elements of a new child labor measure for France. All that was left was the formality of a third and final reading of the bill.[12]

12. For the second reading of the law, see NA, January 22–February 10, 1873.

Throughout the period of deliberation and debate over child labor in the National Assembly, the Ministry of Commerce was engaged in gathering information to aid in the formulation of new legislation. As early as September, 1871, following the introduction of the Joubert bill, the ministry had issued a call for updated information on child labor from all of the nation's prefects. However, the ministry's main fact-finding campaign of this period was initiated just after the second reading of the Melun committee's bill. On February 12, 1873, a circular went out to the nation's chambers of commerce and *chambres consultatives* seeking the opinions of these bodies on the three elements of the proposed law that had occasioned the greatest controversy in the assembly. The various chambers were asked to express their views on age categories, on the protection of females, and on factory inspection. Although they had had a chance to comment on at least two of these matters just a few years earlier, the government thought it wise to have an up-to-the-minute review of what the business and entrepreneurial elite thought about these sensitive issues. Perhaps because it realized that factory legislation had always faced some resistance from individual employers who either could not or would not comply with the more demanding of the child labor provisions, the government wanted to give at least the leaders of French commerce and industry an opportunity to express their views in advance of new legislation.

As it stood after its second reading, the child labor bill provided for a six-hour day (that is, a half-time schedule) for the youngest industrial workers: boys ten to thirteen years old, and girls ten to fourteen. When they were polled, however, only seventeen chambers of commerce and twelve *chambres consultatives* expressed a favorable view of this cumbersome arrangement. Some 79 percent of the bodies that responded opposed the measure because it would too greatly reduce the number of youngsters available for full-time employment. Opponents of the age limits incorporated in the assembly's child labor bill strongly favored allowing children to begin full workdays at the age of twelve. They thought relays of young children would be difficult to institute, and they complained that limitations on the work of children over twelve unfairly deprived those youngsters of a livelihood. Some of France's business leaders (including those in such important industrial centers as Roubaix, Tourcoing, Elbeuf, Rouen, and Saint-Etienne) were even willing to forgo although the use of youngsters under twelve, provided that those over twelve would be allowed to work full time. Twenty-four chambers of commerce and twelve *chambres consultatives* urged the assembly simply to raise the minimum age for employment and to allow children to work a twelve-hour day if they could prove that their schooling was adequate.

When asked about the child labor bill's prohibition of nighttime labor for females up to the age of twenty-one, about three-fifths of the chambers of commerce and *chambres consultatives* responding said they were dissatisfied with this provision of the bill. Again, their concern seemed to be primarily with the practical impact of the proposed limitation: the number of young women who would be barred from nighttime employment would be too great. About half of the chambers registering opposition indicated that they supported the prohibition of nighttime employment for young women in principle and that they sought only a modification of the measure being proposed. Many suggested that female workers be barred from night work only up to the age of eighteen.

Finally, responses to the commerce ministry's request for reactions to the idea of allowing local police authorities to act in concert with special factory inspectors revealed that the nation's chambers of commerce and *chambres consultatives* were divided almost evenly on this matter. Many local bodies that opposed the suggested scheme approved of special inspection but not of the use of police; some bodies wanted the police alone to enforce the factory law; yet others still wanted enforcement to be placed in the hands of present government officials, such as mining engineers or school inspectors. Some councils even suggested returning to the old system of volunteer child labor commissions. A summary tabulation prepared by a clerk at the Ministry of Commerce indicates the general breakdown of the responses to the three issues raised in the 1873 survey:

On the six-hour day for boys ten to thirteen and girls ten to fourteen:
  favorable: seventeen chambers of commerce and eighty-four *chambres consultatives*
  unfavorable: fifty-nine chambers of commerce and twelve *chambres consultatives*

On the prohibition of work at night by females up to the age of twenty-one:
  favorable: twenty-eight chambers of commerce and twenty-four *chambres consultatives*
  unfavorable: forty-one chambers of commerce and thirty-one *chambres consultatives*
  no opinion: five chambers of commerce and six *chambres consultatives*

On the use of police in child labor law enforcement:
  favorable: thirty-two chambers of commerce and twenty-five *chambres consultatives*

unfavorable: thirty-seven chambers of commerce and twenty-six *chambres consultatives*

no opinion: seven chambers of commerce and ten *chambres consultatives* [13]

On September 4, 1873, proclaiming that it wanted its data to be as current as possible in preparation for the third and final reading of the new child labor bill, the Ministry of Commerce complemented its inquiry among the chambers of commerce and *chambres consultatives* with a new survey of the nation's prefects. The results of the September study are not available, but it is safe to assume that they added little in the way of new knowledge.[14] What the Ministry of Commerce inquiries of 1873 showed most clearly, then, was that there was no more unanimity of opinion on the specifics of child labor reform among France's business and industrial leaders and among her local notables than there was among the legislators in the National Assembly at Versailles. Furthermore, the inquiries revealed once again that there was no consistent pattern that could explain the diversity of the opinions expressed about the details of French child labor policy.

By contrast, a survey of the opinions of mining engineers at about this time revealed that, for the most part, they were in agreement with the provisions of the industrial labor bill as it stood in 1873. Almost to a man, the engineers approved the extension of legislation to all industrial shops, the raising of the minimum age for employment, and the reduction of the workday of the youngest laborers to six hours. The engineers did have some reservations about the child labor bill's proposed method of factory surveillance, however. Nearly all of them believed that the inspection force in place at the time was totally inadequate, but they contended that the naming of only fifteen divisional factory inspectors would hardly be an improvement.[15]

As the proposal's third reading approached, the members of the National Assembly had available to them a tremendous amount of data on reactions to the new labor bill. Not only did they have the results of the Ministry of Commerce inquiries to assimilate, but they also had a variety of published opinions and many letters to the government to consider. Some of the communications received were concerned with specific points of the law: a sardine packer from Port-Louis wrote to ask that

13. See material in AN, F12–4727. The results of the February inquiry are also reported in Tallon and Maurice, *Législation*, 463–80.
14. See AN, F12–4706.
15. Material in AN, F12–4727.

certain additional exemptions be considered; the chamber of commerce of Troyes wrote to request that a distinction be made between night work in winter and night work in summer. Gustave Maurice, the factory inspector in the Seine, wrote concerning individual matters on at least three occasions.[16] Most of the published discussions of child labor reform were concerned with broader issues, however.

One of the recurrent themes in the reform literature that appeared while new legislation was under consideration was the fear that the intense political rivalries of the time—monarchists against republicans, Legitimists against Orleanists—would interfere with the adoption of a new industrial labor act. A writer in the journal *Le Soleil*, for instance, complained that the members of the assembly were so caught up in "political agitation" and "perpetual recriminations and accusations" that they were ignoring the plight of young workers and thus allowing the development of "a working class worse even than that which we have today." Similarly, a note addressed by a writer from Grenoble to the assembly's child labor committee urged its members not to make factory reform a partisan issue. The author of the note described a child labor law in these words: "[It] has nothing to do with politics; it is solely a philanthropic, humanitarian issue that is at the same time a matter of wise social welfare. It is neutral ground on which the most divergent parties may come together as patriots for the true good of our beloved and unfortunate Country."[17]

Politics was also on the mind of Anatole Langlois when, in a strategy reminiscent of the one employed by Charles Dupin three decades earlier, he defended the members of the heavily monarchist assembly against the charge that their partisan political concerns were retarding legislative action. In a pamphlet published in 1872, Langlois praised the past efforts of the members of the assembly to deal with the problems of the working classes and pointed to the swift attention given renewed efforts at child labor reform as proof of the good will of the legislators. In defending the need for new child labor legislation, Langlois acknowledged the opinion of Frédéric LePlay and his followers that the establishment of a society based on Christian virtue would preclude the need for state intervention. He contended, however, that such a society was still far in the future and that though individual initiatives to aid working-class youths should be encouraged, it would be foolhardy to ignore the use of legislated sanctions in the interim. Langlois was obvi-

16. *Ibid.*
17. Emile Hardouin, "Le Travail des enfants dans les manufactures," *Le Soleil*, June 29, 1873; B. Nicollet to child labor committee, February 20, 1873, in AN, F12–4727.

ously lobbying for support from across the political spectrum as he called for public opinion to be mobilized in favor of the child labor bill that was under consideration even as he wrote.[18]

A number of articles appearing in the influential liberal journal *Revue des deux mondes* in 1872 were also among the published works touching on child labor that came out while a new factory act was under discussion. In an essentially optimistic article on female factory labor, Paul Leroy-Beaulieu paid special attention to the situation of minors and discussed the value of cautiously framed factory legislation. Louis Reybaud, in an article on the need for improved training in the industrial arts, wrote of the inadequacy of the laws of 1841 and 1851. And in an article devoted specifically to the matter of child labor legislation, Eugène d'Eichthal appealed for public support of the newly proposed factory law. He was especially worried lest the free time that would accrue to factory children under the proposed law be ill spent; for this reason, he thought it important that employers, parents, and workers (both individually and through their associations) cooperate to ensure working-class youngsters would truly benefit from the law. Still, Eichthal stopped short of unequivocal support for compulsory education.[19]

The mining engineer Descottes was also heard promoting a strong factory law while opposing compulsory education. In an 1872 report on child labor reform presented before a gathering of Catholic social welfare activists and published soon thereafter, Descottes defended the concept of state intervention to prevent child labor abuse and to guarantee that time would be provided for the schooling of factory children, but he also warned against the "dangerous principle of compulsory education." He contended that "neither natural law nor Christianity authorizes the civil authorities to undermine the inviolable right of parents to see to the education of their children." Later in the year, Descottes wrote directly to the framers of the labor bill to express his concern that too heavy a reliance was being placed on local child labor commissions as agents of enforcement. He argued that local factory inspection had already been proven inadequate, and he urged the legislators to increase the number of special inspectors that were to be authorized.[20]

18. Anatole Langlois, *Le Travail des enfants dans les manufactures* (Paris, 1872), *passim*.

19. Paul Leroy-Beaulieu, "Les Ouvrières de fabrique," *RDM*, 2nd per., XCVII (1872), 630–57; Louis Reybaud, "Les Ecoles d'apprentis," *RDM*, 2nd per., XCIX (1872), 518–47; Eichthal, "Lois," 415–38.

20. Descottes, *Rapport de la section du contentieux et de législation sur les modifications à apporter à la loi du 24 mars 1841* (Paris, 1872); document of December 4, 1872 marked "Observation" in AN, F12–4727.

By the time the industrial labor bill was introduced on the floor of the National Assembly for its third reading, on May 18 and 19, 1874, the deputies were prepared for a final round of debate on its provisions and for the adoption of a law. The act that ultimately emerged reflected the collective soul searching of the deputies and their protracted pursuit of compromise. Although by the early 1870s aristocratic conservatives and bourgeois moderates alike accepted the government's basic right and responsibility to become involved in the protection of the nation's youth, many of the articles of the new law were debated up to the last minute as the deputies sought to discover the fine line that divided effective legislation from undue encroachment into private affairs.[21]

The first article of the child labor law enacted in 1874 was among the most controversial, for it was supposed to define exactly how pervasive the application of the measure was to be. Because of the sensitivity of this issue, however, even the final wording of the article left its intent quite vague. The article stipulated that "children and minor females may be employed in industrial labor in factories, mills, works, mines, yards, and shops only under the conditions set forth in the present law." The enumeration of places where the law was applicable implied that there were also establishments where it was not (such as small, family-operated workshops, perhaps), but there was no exact delineation of protected and unprotected shops. The intent of the law in this connection would remain a point of controversy for years, and as late as 1883 the *commission supérieure* established by the law could still be found debating the interpretation of "usines et manufactures."

Despite its vagueness on the issue of where the law would be in force, article one of the child labor act did resolve another serious question about the law's applicability. Throughout the deliberations over a new measure for child labor reform, there had been those who wished to exempt children who worked together with their parents from the restrictions the law imposed. Even during the final reading of the factory bill, the liberal republican deputy Nicholas Ducarre (an oilcloth manufacturer from Lyon) suggested inserting a provision that the law apply only in establishments "other than those where a parent of [the child laborer] works." The final redaction of the act indicates that the assembly declined to allow parental supervision by itself to serve as an excuse for escaping the requirements of the law. The action of the as-

21. For the third reading of the 1874 law, see NA, May 18–19, 1874. On the debates over the law in general, see also Overbergh, *Inspecteurs*, 127–40; Jay, *Travail des enfants*, 21–139; and Emile Durand, *Inspection*, 25–43.

sembly reflected its jaundiced view of the child-rearing practices of working-class parents. When Ambroise Joubert responded to Ducarre, he argued that it was often parents themselves who were most responsible for the abuse of child laborers and that where parental authority was invoked to the detriment of the child, it deserved to be restricted.

Articles two and three of the new child labor law dealt with the minimum age for employment and the length of the workday, and the wording of these articles, too, had been surrounded by controversy. In 1873, the assembly had approved a compromise proposal that provided for a minimum age of ten and a workday of six hours for boys up to the age of thirteen and for girls up to the age of fourteen. By the time the factory bill was introduced for its final reading, however, a majority of the deputies were no longer satisfied with this arrangement. The Ministry of Commerce, in its recent inquiry, had found that more than half of the nation's chambers of commerce and *chambres consultatives* also had serious reservations about the system approved in 1873. Thus, the assembly had to deal anew with the issue of age and hours in 1874. The deputies considered one plan, proposed by Théophile Roussel, that France adopt the German model and impose a minimum age of twelve and a six-hour workday for children under fourteen, but this scheme was rejected, along with several others, on the first day of final debate. It was only during the overnight recess between May 18 and 19 that the assembly's child labor committee finally came up with a proposal acceptable to the majority. Adopting a concept that had been discussed previously by business leaders in the provinces, the committee proposed the age of twelve as the minimum for employment and a twelve-hour day for all children of that age and above. At the same time, however, it provided for administrative rulings to designate certain industries in which children would be allowed to work a six-hour day from the age of ten.

The fourth article of the 1874 law, adopted without much controversy, stipulated that children under sixteen could not work between 9 P.M. and 5 A.M. The same limitation was applied, in addition, to females between the ages of sixteen and twenty-one who were employed in large factories or mills. Only in cases where time was lost due to an unanticipated and unavoidable work stoppage were exemptions from the ban on nighttime labor to be granted and then only for children over twelve. Articles five and six of the law prohibited work on Sundays and holidays by boys under sixteen and girls under twenty-one, but again there were to be exceptions. As long as no one under twelve would be asked to work and as long as there would be no interference with religious obligations, administrative rulings could release some youngsters to labor on Sundays and holidays in establishments that depended on a continuous fire. Edouard Bamberger's final appeal that special consideration be given Jewish workers, bolstered by a petition from the Jewish *consistoire*, had again fallen victim to Melun's rather inconsistent argument that the law "must be of a general character" and could abide no exceptions.[22] The law's seventh article, adopted in the form it had taken in 1873, forbade children under twelve, as well as all women, to work underground, and it stipulated that children between twelve and sixteen could work there only in compliance with specific administrative rulings.

The eighth and ninth articles of the law concerned primary education. With surprisingly little last-minute opposition, the National Assembly voted to require that all working children under twelve attend school at least two hours a day in their free time and to demand that their attendance be verified weekly by their employers. Further, the assembly voted that no children under fifteen could work more than six hours a day unless they produced a certificate attesting to their completion of a primary education.

The next six articles of the 1874 law dealt with matters of health, safety, and worker welfare. Employers were required by the law to keep a log of their young employees, to record the period of each child's employment in his or her *livret*, and to post a copy of the child labor law and of relevant administrative rulings. This section of the law also granted the administration the power to limit or forbid child labor in those industries it considered dangerous. In anticipation of more specific rulings, the law from the outset barred children under sixteen from labor in the most obviously dangerous shops, such as those where explosives or corrosives were employed or those where the polishing of various substances presented hazards. Finally, this section called for workplaces to be clean and well ventilated and for machinery to be shielded. It also made entrepreneurs responsible for overseeing the moral behavior of their young employees.

The four articles that constituted the next section of the law defined the inspection system that was to be instituted. This section provided for fifteen divisional inspectors to be chosen by the government and paid by the state. It also set down the basic qualifications for nomination to the

22. Compare Simon Bloch, "La Loi sur le travail des enfants," *Univers israélite* (1874), 591–94.

corps of inspectors and outlined the powers inspectors were to have. Agreement upon a system of factory surveillance had not come easily. The nature of the inspection system had been the single most hotly contested issue in the deliberations over child labor reform; even on the final day of debate, there were still some deputies who felt compelled to put in one last word for some alternative system of surveillance. Citing both financial considerations and his respect for the police authorities, Alfred Giraud, monarchist deputy from the Vendée, once more proposed that the local police, in lieu of special inspectors, be placed in charge of factory law enforcement. Giraud was answered by both Anatole de Melun and Ambroise Joubert, who again observed that entrusting factory surveillance to the police would unnecessarily antagonize factory owners. Joubert did not want the law to be seen primarily "as one of repression," and he added that the police had neither the training nor the inclination to inspect factories.

Not deterred by the response to Giraud, Charles Pernolet, a Parisian coal magnate and a consistent opponent of factory legislation, proposed leaving all factory surveillance to voluntary local child labor commissions. However, an emotional outcry from the deputy Achille Testelin finally silenced the opposition to centralized, salaried inspection. "*Messieurs*, you have just discussed at length, on three different occasions, a law of the greatest importance," Testelin reminded his colleagues. "All of its articles have been weighed, determined and refined by the most capable men, and now what is proposed to you? To suppress the only article that can make the law work." Testelin added that funds for a salaried inspectorate could certainly be found by an assembly that had just recently voted some six million francs for the Paris Opera. There were no further challenges to salaried inspection.

Testelin not only staunchly defended the need for centralized inspection in the final debate on the child labor law, but he also proposed that in the interest of even more complete enforcement, individual departments be granted the prerogative of naming their own salaried inspectors. This idea was adopted and embodied in the section of the 1874 factory law that outlined the constitution of local child labor commissions. Although most of the legislators in the assembly had accepted the need for a national factory inspectorate, they were still somewhat wary of placing too much power in the hands of agents of the central government, and they welcomed the prospect of leaving some control over child labor surveillance in the hands of local notables. Moreover, many deputies believed that a partial reliance on voluntary commissions would help keep down the cost of enforcing the factory law.[23] The concept of local commissions had remained unchallenged since the initial presentation of the child labor bill in 1872, and in the final version of the law, those bodies took the form suggested in the Tallon report.

The next section of the new labor law established a *commission supérieure* of nine members charged with overseeing the implementation of child labor regulations and preparing regular reports to the legislature. Yet another section of the law set out the penalties for violating the new legislation. Employers were made liable to fines of sixteen to fifty francs for each count of breaching the law, and in cases of a second infraction within twelve months of the first, the fine rose to as much as two hundred francs for each count. As an added deterrent, convictions were to be publicized. There was one escape clause written into this section of the law, however, despite the last-minute efforts of the republican deputy René Goblet to have it deleted. Employers could avoid prosecution if they could show that their violation of the child labor law was based on false documentation presented to them by others.

The final section of the law brought apprentices under the protection of the new legislation, though it did not abrogate those sections of the 1851 apprenticeship law with which there was no conflict. This portion of the law also allowed children already employed under the less demanding proscriptions of the 1841 factory law to remain at work, and it delayed implementation of the new legislation entirely for one year.

Like the Child Labor Law of 1841, the 1874 industrial labor act was an important milestone in the history of French social legislation. Its importance lay partly in that it completed the work, begun under the July Monarchy, of offering children employed in industry basic protection from abuse. By extending the compass of factory legislation to all industrial workplaces and by providing for a centrally administered corps of salaried child labor inspectors, the 1874 law corrected two of the most serious faults of the pioneer legislation of 1841. The law was seen as a great benefit for working-class children and was greeted with joy by the child labor reform movement. It was also seen as an essential element in the hoped-for development of a skilled and stable working class that would conform to the image the privileged orders had projected for French labor. The law was hailed as a boon to family life and as an integral part of France's postwar recovery.[24] "Our country is in such need of

23. See Bec, *Législation de l'inspection*, 53.
24. See, for example, Audiganne, *Nouvelle Loi*.

regeneration that a law such as that which has just been enacted can play a great role in promoting the increase of its force and its grandeur," proclaimed Eugène Tallon and Gustave Maurice.[25]

The law had more far-reaching implications as well. For one thing, the Child Labor Law of 1874 signaled the advent of a whole program of legislation designed to preserve the health and safety of French children in a comprehensive way. In large measure because of the impact of the defeat at the hands of Germany, the leaders of France in the final decades of the nineteenth century set out to assure the future harvest of French youth much more determinedly than they had ever done before. By the 1870s, many of France's social and political leaders were acutely aware of the relative slowness of France's population growth. They were all the more troubled by this demographic disadvantage because they also believed the Franco-Prussian War had revealed a laxity in the physical, moral, and intellectual preparation of French youth for future responsibility. Although the monarchists who dominated the legislature in the early 1870s differed with the republicans who succeeded them over the nature of the reform that was needed, both factions seemed to agree that the nation's youth was crucial to its future. Thus, the factory act of 1874 was soon followed by such measures as the Roussel Law for the protection of nurslings (December, 1874), the various republican-sponsored education reforms of the period 1879–1886, and the law depriving unfit parents of their parental authority (1889). In the minds of some proponents of protective legislation, the various child welfare and social control measures of the turn of the century were directly associated with the pathbreaking child labor laws of previous years, and they cited those laws as precedents for new ones.[26]

The factory act of 1874 was significant in yet another sense, for it marked the transition from an older-style, cautious social legislation, sponsored by conservative paternalists and humanitarian liberals, to the increasingly aggressive type of social legislation that would be promoted by the more broadly based political forces emerging in the late nineteenth century. In rejecting a provision for the exclusion of adult women even from nighttime labor, the legislation of 1874 looked backward to the essentially laissez-faire liberalism of the July Monarchy. In inaugu-

25. Tallon and Maurice, *Législation*, 5.
26. Compare Armengaud, "Attitude," 306–307; Donzelot, *Policing*, esp. 78–79; and Mary Lynn McDougall, "Protecting Infants: The French Campaign for Maternity Leaves, 1890s-1913," *French Historical Studies*, XIII (Spring, 1983), 84–86.

rating a system of factory inspection by agents of the national government, however, it foreshadowed the frankly interventionist labor laws of
the turn of the century—laws such as the Factory Act of 1892, the ten-
hour measures of 1900 and 1904, and the 1906 law making Sunday rest
obligatory for all.[27] That the Child Labor Law of 1874 had a tremendous
theoretical and symbolic importance was, however, no guarantee that
it would be any more enthusiastically welcomed by ordinary factory
owners and working-class parents than was the 1841 law it superseded.
Indeed, the implementation of the new measure was to be a complex
affair.

27. Compare Judith F. Stone, *The Search for Social Peace: Reform Legislation in France,
1890–1914* (Albany, N.Y., 1985), esp. Chap. 6; Carlton J. Hayes, *A Generation of Materialism,
1871–1900* (New York, 1941), 209 ff; and Cobban, *History of Modern France*, III, 68–69.

ELEVEN

The Impact of New Legislation and Child Labor Reform in Eclipse

The legislators of 1874, like those of 1841, left to the administration the refinement and the implementation of several crucial aspects of the child labor law they had enacted. In the years after 1841, the Ministry of Commerce had failed in large measure to carry out its trust. Most notably, it had declined to utilize its power to establish an effective system of factory law enforcement. With the 1874 legislation, however, the administration was to play a much more active role. Almost immediately after the new child labor law was adopted, the Ministry of Commerce charged its Comité consultatif des arts et manufactures with the preparation of the various administrative rulings called for in the legislation. To deal with these matters, the Comité consultatif in turn appointed a subcommittee, among whose members were the industrial engineer and educator Michel Alcan, the radical republican textile manufacturer E. P. Bérard, the head of the Direction de commerce interieur Dumoustrier de Frédilly, and Charles de Freycinet, who had been in charge of factory inspection when it was in the hands of government mining engineers.

The first responsibility of the newly formed subcommittee was the delineation of the fifteen factory inspection districts into which the country was to be divided. In approaching this task, the subcommittee considered the rail transportation networks of various regions, the physical and political geography of France, and the number of child laborers employed in each department. For information on the extent of child labor throughout France, it relied primarily on the exhaustive industrial census completed in 1865 and secondarily on a report from France's mining engineers, prepared in 1869. The 1865 industrial census (apparently still quite accurate a decade later) showed that there were some 117,000 children theoretically subject to the 1874 factory law.[1] The 1869 mining engineers' report added the information that 56,823 of France's young workers labored in shops with more than twenty employees.[2] The child labor subcommittee submitted its report concerning the creation of inspection districts on December 2, 1874, and in a decree of February 15, 1875, the administration announced the composition of the various districts. Table 6 shows the definition of the original divisions.

While the child labor subcommittee of the Comité consultatif was concerning itself with the matter of inspection districts, it had also begun preliminary work on the other administrative decisions demanded in the 1874 law. At the end of August, 1874, the subcommittee had dispatched a circular inviting chambers of commerce, *conseils des prud'hommes*, individual industrialists, former child labor inspectors, and any others who had an interest in the matter to render their opinions on the various questions that the administration would have to decide in order to implement the new labor law fully. Respondents were given the opportunity to suggest which industries should be allowed to hire ten-year-olds and which should be granted exemption from the ban on employing children at night and on Sunday. They were also asked to suggest what conditions should surround the employment of children in mines, which industries should be closed to children, and in which industries the labor of children should be subject to special conditions.

There were a large number of responses to the August circular in a very short time, and by the beginning of 1875 the child labor subcommittee was able to start preparing its own suggestions for administrative rulings. The subcommittee's various reports became the basis for a series of decrees issued by the Ministry of Commerce between March and May of 1875.[3] The first of these decrees, issued March 27, legalized the hiring of ten-year-olds in ten specific industries connected with textile production, as well as in glassmaking and paper production. The second of the decrees, issued May 12, established an eight-hour day for children aged

1. The 1865 census did not count child laborers in Paris, in Lyon, or in government-operated establishments. An 1872 mining engineers' survey (apparently ignored by the child labor subcommittee) reported 124,054 child laborers in the country; see Tallon and Maurice, *Législation*, 461–62.

2. See material in AN, F12–4727, and Overbergh, *Inspecteurs*, 141.

3. On the first administrative rulings on child labor, see AN, F12–4727 and F12–4729; and Tallon and Maurice, *Législation*, 554–92. The initial set of rulings was modified slightly in 1877.

Table 6
Inspection Districts Established in 1875

District Number	Departments Included	Inspector's Residence	Number of Protected Children in District	Children in Shops of over 20 Workers
1	Seine	Paris	7,600	3,307
2	Cher	Orléans	4,823	2,910
	Loiret			
	Loir-et-Cher			
	Eure-et-Loir			
	Indre			
	Seine-et-Marne			
	Seine-et-Oise			
3	Yonne	Dijon	4,894	2,753
	Côte-d'Or			
	Jura			
	Ain			
	Saône-et-Loire			
	Nièvre			
	Allier			
4	Vosges	Nancy	7,658	5,794
	Doubs			
	Meurthe-et-Moselle			
	Saône (Haute-)			
	Marne (Haute-)			
5	Aisne	Reims	8,024	3,782
	Ardennes			
	Marne			
	Meuse			
	Aube			
6	Pas-de-Calais	Lille	19,353	6,863
	Nord			
7	Somme	Rouen	15,453	10,708
	Oise			
	Seine-Inférieure			
8	Eure	Caen	9,505	2,830
	Calvados			
	Manche			
	Orne			
9	Mayenne	Rennes	4,999	1,776
	Sarthe			

continued

District Number	Departments Included	Inspector's Residence	Number of Protected Children in District	Children in Shops of over 20 Workers
10	Côtes-du-Nord Ille-et-Vilaine Maine-et-Loire Loire-Inférieure Morbihan Finistère Vendée Vienne Indre-et-Loire Creuse Vienne (Haute-) Charente Charente-Inférieure Sèvres (Deux-)	Limoges	3,598	1,815
11	Corrèze Dordogne Lot-et-Garonne Gironde Landes Gers Pyrénées (Basses-) Pyrénées (Hautes-) Lot Tarn-et-Garonne	Bordeaux	2,355	1,046
12	Cantal Aveyron Tarn Garonne (Haute-) Ariège Aude Pyrénées Orientales	Toulouse	4,117	1,330
13	Ardèche Lozère Gard Hérault	Nîmes	8,238	4,135
14	Drôme	Avignon	5,584	5,181

District Number	Departments Included	Inspector's Residence	Number of Protected Children in District	Children in Shops of over 20 Workers
15	Alpes (Hautes-) Alpes (Basses-) Alpes-Maritimes Vaucluse Bouches-du-Rhône Var Corse Rhône Loire Loire (Haute-) Puy-de-Dome Isère Savoie Savoie (Haute-)	Lyon	7,989	2,593

Source: Table compiled by the child labor subcommittee of the Comité consultatif des arts et manufactures and preserved in AN, F12–4727 (revised to show changes made before February 15, 1875).

twelve to sixteen who were employed in underground labor, and it defined certain functions that these children were forbidden to fulfill. The next two decrees, issued May 13 and 14, respectively, defined several tasks that children would not be allowed to perform and specified the industries from which children would be barred entirely, out of regard for their health and safety. Among the tasks forbidden to youngsters were greasing, cleaning, or repairing machines in motion, carrying heavy loads, feeding circular saws, and controlling steam valves.

The final decree in the initial series of administrative rulings, issued May 22, concerned exemptions from the ban on nighttime and Sunday labor. In response to its circular of August, 1874, the child labor subcommittee had received fifty-three communications favoring exemptions in metal works, fifty-two favoring exemptions in glassworks, and twenty-seven each favoring exemptions in sugar refineries and in paper mills. The administration decided to allow these four industries to employ children over twelve at times when their labor would normally have been forbidden, but it denied requests for exemptions in twenty-two other industries regarding which petitions had been received. Although the various administrative rulings of 1875 had the positive effect of clarifying the provisions of the country's new child labor law, they also revealed the persistence of the tendency to allow practical considerations to take precedence over idealistic goals. When the administration decided to honor the requests of industrialists for leniency and to allow such practices as the employment of ten-year-olds in textile mills and of thirteen-year-olds in glassworks all night long, much of the force of the 1874 labor law was dissipated.

As the Ministry of Commerce wasted no time in preparing its first set of administrative rulings on child labor, so the president of the republic hastened to appoint the first members to the Commission supérieure which was established by the new factory law. In July, 1874, he appointed J. B. Dumas as president of the commission, the comte de Melun as vice-president, and seven other prominent figures as members. The deputies Ambroise Joubert and Eugène Tallon were named to the commission, as were the former minister of commerce Alfred Deseilligny, the president of the Paris Chamber of Commerce Eugène Gouin, the secretary-general of the commerce ministry Jules Ozenne, the abbé Auguste de Broglie, and the director of domestic commerce Dumoustrier de Frédilly. When Deseilligny died, he was replaced by another former minister of commerce, Louis Grivart. At the outset, the commission spent much of its time screening requests from various industrial interests for special consideration in light of the country's new labor law, but its most important early task was preparing a list of candidates from which the central government's first factory inspectors would be chosen.[4]

The selection of inspectors to fill the fifteen posts created in 1874 involved the successive narrowing of a list of candidates until for each available position the Commission supérieure had three people to suggest to the administration. The selection process used suggests that the commission had a rather clear idea of the kinds of individuals it was seeking to be the first professional child labor inspectors appointed by the national government. It wished them to be well-established men of the middle classes with some practical experience that would prove useful in their work. It also wanted them to be persons who could relate easily to the manufacturers, managers, and shop owners with whom they

4. Tallon and Maurice, *Législation*, 553; correspondence in AN, F12–4727.

would be in constant contact. If the transition to serious labor law enforcement was to be made smoothly, it was important to have child labor inspectors who would not unduly antagonize those whom they would have to confront. Starting with an exhaustive list of candidates who had either nominated themselves or been suggested by others, the commission narrowed the number of prospects to seventy-six men by January, 1875. Of these seventy-six, nearly half came with a background in engineering of one kind or another. Ten of the candidates claimed experience as either departmental or local child labor inspectors, and ten had been active in industry as either owners or directors of manufacturing firms. Several of the prospects brought with them experience in the military or in public service. Among the candidates were four mine wardens, two inspectors of weights and measures, a teacher, a physician, and an architect. Half the candidates still under consideration after January, 1875, were in their thirties, but there was also a twenty-five-year-old, a couple of sixty-five-year-olds, and three individuals whom the commission eventually dismissed as simply "too old."

In a second round of elimination, the list of seventy-six potential factory inspectors was trimmed to forty-nine, and it was from this list that France's first divisional inspectors were chosen. Gustave Maurice, who had earlier survived the change from inspection by departmental agents to inspection by mining engineers, again lasted through a bureaucratic transition. He was appointed factory inspector at Paris for the first district. Also surviving the transition to central inspection was Théodore Nadeau, departmental inspector in the Nord since 1872; he was assigned as divisional inspector at Lille. Although Nadeau was already sixty-one years old at the time of his appointment, he would remain in the inspection service until 1887. Both Maurice and Nadeau were given the rank of inspector first class, as were three other newly appointed divisional inspectors: Doll, a former diplomat and one-time child labor inspector at Mulhouse, who was assigned to Reims; Colombier, a manufacturer, assigned to Rouen; and Gauthier, another manufacturer, assigned to Lyon.

Ten inspectors second class were also named. They were D'Estienne d'Orves at Orléans, de Villenaut at Dijon, Plassiard at Nancy, Aubert at Caen, Dechaille at Rennes, Blaise at Limoges, Jacquemart at Bordeaux, Delaissement at Toulouse, Estelle at Nîmes, and Linarès at Avignon. Five of these inspectors second class were civil engineers, two had backgrounds in mining, one had been a school inspector, and one had been a postmaster. Perhaps the most exceptional of the new inspectors second class was Jacquemart. At twenty-eight, he was the youngest of the child labor inspectors appointed in 1875, but like Nadeau and Doll, he was a *chevalier* of the Legion of Honor, having earned that distinction during the siege of Paris.[5]

At the time the 1874 child labor law came into effect, a number of departments also appointed their own salaried child labor inspectors, to be supervised by the divisional inspectors as the new law provided. By the mid-1880s, there were locally appointed inspectors in nineteen departments, including the Nord, the Seine-Inférieure, the Pas-de-Calais, the Rhône, the Seine-et-Marne, and the Seine-et-Oise. The Department of the Seine was the most deeply involved in local child labor surveillance. As early as 1879, the department had fourteen child labor inspectors, both male and female, and in 1881 the number of agents was raised to eighteen and an *inspecteur principal* was named.[6] At least in some cases, however, positions as departmental inspectors were filled by patronage, and the individuals appointed may not have been the best available. When he was passed over for an inspectorship in the Seine in 1879, one F. Gouillon published a three-page attack on the patronage system, insisting that it was undemocratic.[7]

At first glance, it might appear that the new corps of salaried child labor inspectors appointed to enforce the 1874 labor law would not have had a very difficult task before it. The specific limitations imposed by the new measure, though more rigorous than those imposed by the 1841 law, were by no means extreme, and the administrative rulings of 1875 had softened their impact on several key industries even further. Moreover, the number of children who came under the protection of the law for the first time after 1874 was quite limited. The prefects' reports of 1867 had revealed that some 79 percent of all French child laborers under the age of sixteen were already subject to the factory act of 1841, and a survey of mining engineers in 1872 had suggested that 88 percent of the children working in industry were already protected. Still, there were thousands of young women aged sixteen to twenty-one (some 86,948 by 1884) who were brought within the purview of the factory law for the first time in 1874, and there were some new norms for dealing with children that the central government's factory inspectors were ex-

5. On the appointment of the first child labor inspectors, see AN, F12–4773; and "Département de l'agriculture et du commerce," in *Almanach national* (Paris, 1875).

6. See Overbergh, *Inspecteurs*, 154; the responses to a circular of June 21, 1887, in AN, F12–4773; and Tallon and Maurice, *Législation*, 481–502.

7. See Overbergh, *Inspecteurs*, 168, and Emile Durand, *Inspection*, 62–85. For F. Gouillon's publication, see AN, F12–4773.

pected to enforce.[8] Furthermore, in the early years of the republic even the long-established standards of 1841 were not yet universally accepted. As late as 1872, the mining engineers charged with factory inspection had encountered 5,784 children between the ages of eight and twelve working over eight hours a day, 23,690 child laborers without *livrets*, and fully 44,157 working children between twelve and sixteen who did not have certificates of primary education. In only 1,657 of the 6,823 establishments visited by mining engineers in 1872 was a copy of the 1841 law posted as required.[9] An 1872 study published by the Société de protection des apprentis asserted that in only half of the sixty departments with a significant level of child labor was the 1841 law generally obeyed.[10]

The lingering problem of noncompliance with child labor regulations in the 1870s stemmed from the fact that those who had made the law and those who were asked to abide by it still viewed the restriction of child labor from opposing perspectives, as they had for several decades. For the child labor reformers and for the legislators of the early republican period, the fundamental issues that underlay labor reform were still humanitarian and ideological. These reformers and lawmakers were, after all, trying to solve a broadly conceived *question sociale* and, especially after 1871, to prepare the nation for a glorious recovery of its grandeur. For those who lived day to day with the reality of child labor, however, the fundamental issues were still the practical ones. Even though the normative bourgeois attitude toward children was now different from what it had been earlier in the century, this attitude was not always reflected in the actions of the individual entrepreneurs who were asked to abide by child labor restrictions or the local commissioners and bureaucrats who were charged with overseeing their implementation. Although these people were probably thinking about childhood in a more modern way and though they were probably more nurturing and protective of their own children, nonetheless when it came to the practical matter of complying with labor law restrictions, structural factors intervened. Confronted with the difficulty of altering long-standing practices in their shops in order to comply with the limitations on child labor, local entrepreneurs often allowed inertia to overcome sentiment.

So, too, even as the fourth quarter of the nineteenth century began,

8. Ministère du commerce et de l'industrie, *Rapport sur l'application de la loi du 19 mai 1874 pendant l'année 1885* (Paris, 1886), 30.

9. See Tallon and Maurice, *Législation*, 461–62.

10. See Eichthal, "Lois," 428.

many working-class parents were still reluctant or unable to allow their children to delay entry into the work force, and they resented the intrusion of the government into their familial decisions. In Paris during the 1876–1877 school year, for example, only 42 percent of boys and 34 percent of girls aged twelve to thirteen were enrolled in school, and of the children who were in school, the vast majority assumed that they would go to work when they completed their primary education at the age of fourteen. In the provinces, the percentage of children attending school was probably even smaller. The main reason that children entered the work force early in their lives in the years after 1874 was the same as it had always been: their contributions to the family budget were critical. One child leaving school at the age of fourteen in 1877 explained in response to a government survey: "I would like to have continued my studies, in the end to become a teacher. But I am not the only child in my family and it is necessary that I work."[11] Faced with the continuing refusal of many businessmen and parents to change their practices simply to comply with a law they saw as irrelevant at best, France's first Inspecteurs du travail des enfants faced a considerable challenge as they began their service.

When he embarked on his duties in 1875, for example, Inspector Aubert, based at Caen, still found some seven-year-olds working twelve hours a day, and in 1876 the prefect of the Loire was still complaining of the "ill will of employers and children." He reported that local child labor commissioners faced a situation that "discourages them and causes daily resignations." In the same year, the prefect of the Isère wrote that the lure of financial reward was motivating both entrepreneurs and workers to evade the law. Moreover, even in some places where the new factory law was well received by nearly everyone in principle, it was not necessarily observed. Expressing his hope that the divisional inspector would visit his department more frequently, the prefect of the Tarn wrote in 1876: "The [local] industrialists and heads of factories have shown much good will and are in general eager to conform to the provisions of the law. There remains much to do nonetheless, to insure its serious execution." As late as 1880, Inspector Doll, based at Reims, still had to report that the child labor law was completely ignored in 34 percent of the 693 shops he visited that year. In only 19 percent of the shops he inspected was the law observed in its totality.[12]

11. See John W. Shaffer, "Family, Class, and Young Women: Occupational Expectations in Nineteenth-Century Paris," *Journal of Family History*, III (Spring, 1978), 62–77, esp. 68.
12. Reports in AN, F12–4743, F12–4771, and F12–4736.

Certain specific provisions of the 1874 law were routinely and blatantly ignored. The imposition of a half-time schedule for children under twelve, for instance, proved impractical, unpopular, and unenforceable. Within a few years of the passage of the 1874 law, several divisional inspectors were calling for a reappraisal of the half-time system, and as late as 1886 reports showed that the requirement that children under twelve work only six hours a day was generally overlooked. So, too, was little attention paid to conditions of hygiene in small shops, and certification of schooling was often accomplished with little concern for a child's true record of school attendance or achievement. Some manufacturers who claimed to be offering schooling for their own employees deceived factory inspectors who visited in the morning by telling them that classes were held in the afternoon. If inspectors came in the afternoon, they were told that classes were held in the morning. Moreover, the various exemptions written into the factory law opened the door to widespread fraud; the leeway given shops with continuous fires, for example, was constantly abused.[13]

Although the central government's new factory inspectors embarked upon their task of enforcement with a general seriousness of purpose, it was apparent from the start that their numbers were insufficient for a truly effective monitoring of the child labor situation in France. A complete implementation of all the regulations was retarded also because the inspectors themselves tempered their enforcement efforts in the hope that gentle persuasion would do more good than legal action.[14] Even the most committed and experienced of the inspectors allowed illegal suspensions of the factory law at times. Théodore Nadeau was overly tolerant regarding the education provisions of the law.[15] Gustave Maurice became embroiled in a serious controversy with the press and with the Ministry of Commerce when a letter showing that he had agreed to allow several manufacturers some limited infractions of night work and Sunday work restrictions was leaked to the newspapers.[16] Moreover, both

13. On problems with the half-time system, see, for example, reports of 1880 to 1883 from the third, seventh, tenth, twelfth, and fifteenth child labor districts in AN, F12–4729 and F12–4755. Evidence of problems with school certification is in AN, F12–4765: see circulars of July 20, 1875, February 20, 1877, November 21, 1879, and May 20, 1882. See also Ministère du commerce, *Rapport*, and Louis, *L'Ouvrier devant l'état*, 224–27.

14. The policy of reliance on gentle persuasion apparently continued into the twentieth century; see Donald Reid, "Putting Social Reform into Practice: Labor Inspectors in France, 1892–1914," *Journal of Social History*, XX (Fall, 1986), 68–87.

15. Report in AN, F12–4739.

16. Material in AN, F12–4731, including a newspaper clipping from *La Révolution* of

Nadeau and Maurice are known to have allowed some children whose labor was limited by law to six hours a day to work eight hours. Similarly, in 1878, the factory inspector for the eighth district confessed that "the honest intentions manifested by the vast majority of industrialists, and the existence of diverse material obstacles that still interfere with the complete execution of the law, have caused me on numerous occasions to allow a certain tolerance."[17] Despite its problems, however, the system of central inspection instituted by the factory act of 1874 was far better than the earlier local volunteer service.

The vast superiority of the new system was confirmed when the reconstitution of local child labor committees was undertaken, as mandated by the 1874 law. The relative swiftness and efficiency with which the divisional inspectors began their work contrasts sharply with the protracted and only partially successful process of establishing new local commissions. In July, 1874, a circular was sent to all of France's prefects explaining to them their responsibility for establishing local child labor committees before the new factory law was to take effect in June of 1875. The response to this communication was apparently so limited, however, that the Ministry of Commerce had to circulate reminders in November and again in December, 1874, and finally as late as May, 1875.[18]

Six months after the 1874 child labor law took effect, the administration inquired of the nation's prefects concerning the effectiveness of the local child labor commissions, which presumably had been installed in each *arrondissement*. The responses of the prefects indicate that in many places the voluntary commissions had not yet begun to operate. The prefect of the Ardennes reported that the local boards in his department were awaiting the appearance of the divisional inspector, Doll, before initiating their activity. Inspector Doll in the meantime had begun his rounds in two other departments of the district, and the minister of commerce had to prod the local committees to begin functioning on their own. The prefect of the Nord confessed that he had no idea where to tell his local inspectors to begin their work and that both he and they were waiting idly for further instructions. Such was still the case in March of 1876, when the minister of commerce finally told the prefect to rely on his own judgment and delay no further in setting factory inspection in motion.

November 17, 1876, and a letter of November 29, 1876, from Gustave Maurice to the minister of commerce.
17. Documents in AN, F12–4765; report in AN, F12–4743.
18. Documents in AN, F12–4767.

From the Seine-Inférieure came a report that "of all the local commissions instituted in the department, only the two that operate in the *arrondissement* of Le Havre have truly and usefully set to work." From the Calvados came word that all the local commissions there, save that at Caen, were inactive, despite the efforts of the prefect and the subprefects to "stimulate" their activity. In April of 1876, the prefect of the Finistère complained: "From day to day I await the reports that the local commissions are supposed to address to me. . . . The five local commissions that now exist in the department convened for the first time last August when *Monsieur* the Divisional Inspector passed through. Only two of these commissions . . . have met on their own since. . . . As for the other three, they appear to give no sign of their existence."[19]

Many local commissions that did begin functioning in 1875 abandoned their activities over the next few years, and when the five-year terms of their members expired, the boards were not restaffed. The members of the local commission in the most industrial *arrondissement* of the Pyrénées-Orientales resigned en masse because their demands for payment would not be met. One compilation of data revealed that in 1884 at least six departments had not a single local child labor commission. Even those voluntary commissions that did remain active were not necessarily useful. In 1878, Inspector Aubert at Caen wrote that the local commissions in his district "have not rendered the services the legislature expected of them at all." In 1883, a communication from the fifteenth child labor district reported: "The departmental inspectors . . . in agreement with their divisional inspector, are unanimous in recognizing that the local commissions, with very rare exceptions, render no service whatsoever—even when they manage to avoid being a hindrance to the execution of the law."[20]

The one major exception to this pattern was the situation in the Department of the Seine. Twenty-eight local child labor commissions were established there in 1876, and they grew in number and activity over the years. By 1884 there were eighty local commissions in the Seine, forty concerned with male workers and forty with female workers.[21] Even in the Seine, however, some knowledgeable observers were dissatisfied with

19. Reports in AN, F12–4771.

20. Documents in AN, F12–4771, F12–4767, F12–4743, and F12–4755.

21. On the Seine commissions, see AN, F12–4731 and F12–4770; Louis, *L'Ouvrier devant l'etat*, 225–27; Villate-Lacheret, *Les Inspectrices du travail en France* (Paris, 1919), 22–28; and F. Malapert, "De l'application des lois sur le travail des enfants," *JE*, 4th ser., XXXII (1885), 238–43. Malapert was a member of the departmental *commission supérieure* for child labor and wrote very positively about local inspection. Other places where local

the work of the local boards. Inspector Maurice once lamented that "many of the commissions do nothing, a few do something useful, and others are harmful." Maurice's successor, Laporte, penned similar complaints in the 1880s.[22]

Many factors contributed to the general failure of local inspection. As under the 1841 factory law, volunteer agents could devote neither much time nor much energy to their tasks, and they were constantly fearful lest they offend their industrialist neighbors. Prominent entrepreneurs could and sometimes did use their positions to escape compliance with the demands of local child labor inspectors. In the Isère, for example, the manufacturer and civic leader Rochat fought allegations for over a year that he was guilty of several infractions of the child labor law, but the charges against him were finally dropped (on orders from the minister of commerce) because of "his position and his influence."[23] Local inspection was impeded also because factory owners' longstanding opposition to the surveillance of their shops was reenforced after 1874 by the fear of industrial espionage, whose proportions grew as technology advanced. After all, reasoned industrialists, most voluntary inspectors were themselves involved with manufacturing in one way or another and they would be anxious to learn about innovations in technology and factory procedures.[24]

Moreover, under the new factory law, employers were theoretically subject to visits by two authorities. This circumstance they especially disliked because at times divisional inspectors and local commissioners gave contradictory advice and made conflicting demands in the same cases.[25] That the relationship between the local commissions and the divisional inspectors was never fully clarified did not help matters. Article twenty of the Child Labor Law of 1874 stated that the local commissions were

---

commissions apparently functioned well were the cities of Rouen, Marseilles, Aix, and Albi, and the Department of the Gard; see Overbergh, *Inspecteurs*, 156.

22. See AN, F12–4731 for Gustave Maurice's reports, F12–4730 for Laporte's.

23. See AN, F12–4755.

24. On the fear that local commissioners would engage in industrial spying, see, for example, an 1886 letter from Thiebaud, Kister, et Cie. in AN, F12–4770. See also Overbergh, *Inspecteurs*, 146, 170. There are quite complete lists of the members of local commissions that existed at least on paper in the late 1870s and early 1880s in AN, F12–4757, F12–4768, and F12–4769. See also Dolfus-Francoz, *Essai historique*, 64ff.

25. See, for example, reports of conflicts over enforcement between Inspector Nadeau and a local commission in 1876 in AN, F12–4770, and between Inspector Blais and a local commission in 1883 in AN, F12–4770.

"to control the inspection service," but they were clearly in no position to do so. In response to many demands for a clarification of this phrase, Ambroise Joubert, as a member of the Commission supérieure for child labor, attempted an explanation: "It is a question of moral control, and never did it enter the minds of the legislators that the Divisional Inspector should be subordinate to the local commissions."[26] What generally happened in reality was that the divisional inspectors usurped nearly all responsibility for child labor inspection, while the local boards, for their part, were glad to be unburdened.

The major problems with the Child Labor Law of 1874 were clearly those related to its provisions for inspection, but the measure had other shortcomings as well, many of which stemmed from the fact that the law remained vague on a number of issues where clarity was demanded. The imprecise definition of establishments in which child labor regulations applied and the confusing description of the relationship between salaried and volunteer child labor inspectors are but two examples. There was also a problem with the use of the term "rest periods" in the text of the law: since it was not clear what was meant by "rest periods," it was impossible to determine the exact limitations placed on the workday of children. Neither had there been a clarification of whether the maximum workday stipulated in the law applied to the time of actual labor or to the time of presence in the shop. The time spent in cleaning machines traditionally had not been counted as part of the workday, and the question of having it counted remained open after 1874. There was also some vagueness on the issue of a child laborer's time in school. It took a circular of July 10, 1876, to affirm the policy that factory inspectors need concern themselves not with seeing that children went to school but only with verifying that they were not in the shop longer than was allowed.[27]

Many of the problems with the factory act of 1874 were recognized very soon after its passage, and an attempt was made to address some of them promptly. For example, supplementary measures to mitigate the confusion over where child labor measures applied came under discussion frequently. A new law of December 7, 1874, barred youngsters un-

---

26. Minutes of the Commission supérieure for July 21, 1875, in AN, F12–4767.

27. See divisional inspectors' reports of the 1880s and other documents in AN, F12–4729. See also Malapert, "Application," 235–37. For one work that recognized immediately that many aspects of the 1874 law would need further interpretation, see A. Blondel, *Le Travail des enfants et des femmes dans les manufactures* (Paris, 1874).

der sixteen from street trades, such as acrobatics, unless they were supervised by their parents, and a decree of October 31, 1882, forbade the hiring of children to work on rooftops. The Department of the Seine decided on its own to extend application of the child labor law specifically to butcher shops and bakeries. On the other side of the issue, a court ruling of 1881 exempted welfare institutions from surveillance by child labor inspectors. Because welfare institutions themselves existed for the benefit of children, the court reasoned, it did not make sense to subject them to child protection legislation. The proponents of policing welfare institutions observed that some of these agencies were known to set children as young as four laboring in their workshops and to leave children of seven and eight at their workbenches for eleven hours at a time, but their protests were ignored.[28]

There is also evidence that the Ministry of Commerce sought to facilitate implementation of the child labor law by having the Ministry of Public Instruction ensure adequate school facilities would be available to factory children, especially those working half-time schedules.[29] Another sign of concern was that the administrative rulings related to the 1874 law were under constant review. In 1885, for example, the number of factory inspection districts and divisional inspectors was increased from fifteen to twenty-one. There was also talk of entirely new legislation to correct the various faults of the child labor law, some of it heard even before the decade of the 1870s had ended. As early as 1879, a proposal for a new factory law was put forward by the Radical deputy Martin Nadaud (the Icarian stonemason exiled under the Second Empire), and a report on the subject was prepared in 1880 by Richard Waddington, who, like Nadaud, was a member of the Commission supérieure for child labor. In the early 1880s, the issue of new legislation was raised by the conservatives Albert de Mun and Charles Freppel (royalist bishop of Angers), by the moderate future president of the republic Félix Faure, and by the socialist deputies Zéphirin Camelinat (a bronze worker) and Emile Basly (a miner).

Obviously, there were a variety of difficulties that inhibited the total implementation of the Child Labor Law of 1874 in the years following its enactment, and in the 1880s there were still factories and workshops where, for reasons of expediency or out of sheer habit, the abuse of child labor continued. There can be no question, however, that the child labor situation in France was improving markedly by the eighties. The latest

28. Louis, *L'Ouvrier devant l'état*, 224.
29. Correspondence of 1880–82 in AN, F12–4765.

factory law did provide something of a check on conditions in industrial establishments, and the various economic and technological factors that had already been acting to reduce the number of youngsters in industrial labor under the Second Empire were continuing to effect a decline in the exploitation of these children. The total number of working children under the age of twelve, for example, decreased dramatically in the years after 1874: whereas the mining engineers charged with factory inspection encountered 14,876 child laborers under the age of twelve in 1872, the divisional inspectors of 1884 encountered only 1,775. In the first inspection district, the number of laboring children aged ten to twelve dropped from 2,009 to 275 in only two years. In the sixth district, which included the Nord, the inspector reported finding 859 working children under the age of twelve in 1876; in 1881 there were only 268. In the eighth district, the number of very young workers went from 430 in 1876 to 183 in 1880. It is possible that inspectors' reports were not completely accurate, and inspectors did have an interest in showing that their presence made a difference, but it is unlikely that their accounts were so biased as to misrepresent what was actually happening. By the mideighties, children under twelve represented less than 1 percent of all youngsters protected by the factory act.

The educational level of young workers seems to have improved significantly as well. Here the education laws of 1879–1886 had the effect of reenforcing the intent of the child labor law. In 1879, only 29 percent of the child laborers encountered by factory inspectors possessed the school certificates required by law; in 1881, 54 percent had them. By 1884, 68 percent of the working children aged twelve to fifteen encountered by factory inspectors had certificates. Futhermore, in 1885, the official report of the Commission supérieure on child labor observed that the number of children with certificates underrepresented the true number of literate child laborers, and it asserted that "the intellectual level of the young workers in industry is tending to rise each year."[30] By the mid-1880s, then, the abuse of factory children no longer seemed to be the urgent matter it had been in the preceding decades, and the child labor reform movement was on the wane. Moreover, by the time the republic entered its second decade, the era of mass politics had arrived and a new genre of reformism—one not preoccupied with the child labor problem—was on the ascent.

30. On the improving child labor situation of the 1880s, see reports in AN, F12–4730, F12–4739, and F12–4743; Ministère du commerce, *Rapport*; and E. Levasseur, *Questions ouvrières et industrielles en France sous la Troisième République* (Paris, 1907), 436n.

As the end of the nineteenth century approached, developments such as the confirmation of government accountability in the *seize mai* crisis and the legalization of trade unions in 1884 were encouraging both the Radical republicans and the emerging socialists to demand that more concerted attention be paid to social legislation. As the working classes became increasingly assertive and politically influential in the final years of the century, they demanded that labor dictate its own priorities and that the welfare of all workers, not just of children, be protected. At the same time, those who hoped to stabilize the bourgeois-dominated society of the late nineteenth century also came to place increasing faith in comprehensive social legislation. In the 1881 debates over a proposed ten-hour day for all workers, moderate republican deputies were still arguing that factory legislation covering adults was too gross an attack on liberty and thus an open invitation to socialism, but increasingly this attitude was being challenged by supporters of broader social legislation.

More specifically, the new generation of social activists of the late nineteenth century rejected the view that factory reform should attack only the specific problem of child labor abuse and thus attempt to preserve a system of laissez-faire liberalism. By the mideighties, problems such as industrial safety ceased to be viewed primarily from the perspective of young employees and became matters related to the protection of all workers. Before long, the central government's Inspecteurs du travail des enfants were assigned the task of enforcing the twelve-hour day decreed in 1848 for all industrial workers, and in 1889 they became known as Inspecteurs du travail dans l'industrie. To the extent that a concern with improving the lot of child laborers remained in the minds of late nineteenth-century reformers, it tended to become more and more closely associated with the protection of working women and often to be subsumed within even broader social programs. Reflecting the amalgamation of child labor with other issues of industrial society in the 1880s was contemporary literature, whose interest in working children had tended to ebb and flow together with the intensity of the child labor reform movement throughout the nineteenth century. When the matter of child labor surfaced in one of the greatest novels of the late 1800s, Emile Zola's *Germinal*, published in 1884, it was almost an incidental concern, overshadowed by several other labor issues. Moreover, many of the abusive conditions Zola described had long been modified.[31]

31. Overbergh, *Inspecteurs*, 144; Emile Zola, *Germinal*, trans. Leonard Tancock (Harmondsworth, Eng., 1954), *passim*.

The broadened understanding of factory reform, as well as the increasing acceptance of government intervention for the protection of all workers, was very much in evidence in an inquiry conducted in 1884 by the Ministry of Commerce, then under Charles Hérisson. When the ministry asked departmental councils, chambers of commerce, local child labor commissions, and similar bodies to comment on the state of factory legislation, it found not only that there was a strong desire among French notables to amend the child labor law that had been enacted ten years earlier but also that they were now thinking of labor legislation as something that should encompass more than just the protection of children. The 1884 inquiry revealed that only 138 of 525 respondents were satisfied with the basic minimum age for employment being set at twelve and that 308 wanted to see it raised to thirteen. This change would put the factory law more in line with the recently enacted legislation on compulsory education. Only 122 respondents favored allowing some exemptions from the minimum age provision of the factory law, whereas 239 respondents suggested they be ended. On a third question, 98 respondents liked the use of a half-time system for very young workers, but 226 were for its abolition.

Even more significantly, however, the 1884 inquiry revealed a new willingness to legislate a prohibition of all nighttime labor by adult women: 321 respondents were in favor of such a measure, and only 151 were against it. A majority of those expressing an opinion were even willing to see a further limitation placed on the labor of adult males: 170 respondents favored the twelve-hour workday then in force, 104 wanted to see it lowered to eleven hours, and 119 wanted it reduced to ten hours. Only 88 respondents still believed that any regulation of adult labor was improper.[32]

Ultimately, when the next important industrial labor law was enacted in France in 1892, it not only corrected some of the faults of the Child Labor Law of 1874 but it moved ahead to treat the protection of an important segment of the adult work force as well. The 1892 law raised the minimum age for employment to thirteen and allowed exemptions only to qualified twelve-year-olds. It lowered the workday of all children under sixteen to ten hours and imposed a maximum workday of eleven hours on youths between the ages of sixteen and eighteen. The law also

32. See César Caire, *La Législation sur le travail industriel des femmes et des enfants* (Paris, 1896), 65–74; Villate-Lacheret, *Inspectrices*, 35–37; Overbergh, *Inspecteurs*, 185; Emile Durand, *Inspection*, 87ff; and Dolfus-Francoz, *Essai historique*, 65–66.

replaced local child labor commissions with departmental bodies, made child labor restrictions applicable in nearly every shop in France, and revamped the hierarchy of the factory inspection service. It provided for eleven divisional inspectors and ninety-two departmental inspectors, all salaried by and under the direction of the central government.

The law also restricted the workday of adult women. They were no longer allowed to work over eleven hours a day, nor could they labor at night. With the labor of young people and of women thus restricted, the right of adult male workers to labor twelve hours a day under conditions of total liberty became little more than a legal fiction. Seldom could men continue to work when women and children left the factory or shop, and there is no doubt that this de facto limitation of all adult labor was a calculated side effect of the 1892 legislation.[33] By 1900, all women and children in industry were limited to a ten-hour day.

Clearly, factory reform was no longer synonymous with child labor reform in the minds of late nineteenth-century social activists. Indeed, these reformers sometimes overlooked the issue of child labor entirely. This seems to have been the case even among the advocates of education reform, which had become the foremost child-centered social issue as republicanism came to dominate government and society from the late 1870s onward. When the Ferry education laws were enacted during the period 1879–1886, the existence of a corpus of child labor law was virtually ignored. The new republican advocates of mass education seem to have been so out of touch with the early industrial issue of child labor that their measures actually contradicted the labor act of 1874 in several important respects.

The most basic discrepancy between the legislation on education and that on child labor resulted from the fact that the education law of March 28, 1882, extended compulsory education to cover children up to the age of thirteen, whereas the factory law allowed youngsters of twelve to begin full-length workdays. Other discrepancies existed as well, and each raised the question of priority. Under the 1874 labor law, children of twelve needed certification of their schooling in order to enter the work force on a full-time basis, but the 1882 education law allowed for such certification to be granted some qualified students at the age of eleven. Were children to be allowed full workdays then at a younger age?

33. Overbergh, *Inspecteurs*, 202–208; Louis, *L'Ouvrier devant l'état*, 227–31; and Mary Lynn McDougall, "The Meaning of Reform: The Ban on Women's Night Work, 1892–1914," in *Proceedings of the Annual Meeting of the Western Society for French History*, X (1982), esp. 404.

Under the 1874 law, children between the ages of twelve and fifteen were allowed only half-time labor if they had not completed their schooling, but the 1882 law stated that "all scholastic obligations cease at age thirteen." What was to be done with adolescent workers?

Throughout 1883 and 1884, the Ministry of Commerce and the Ministry of Public Instruction argued at length over whether the child labor law or the education law took precedence. At first, it appeared that the Commission supérieure for child labor would defer to the Ministry of Public Instruction and declare that the 1882 law superseded that of 1874, but at the end of 1885 the Ministry of Commerce, with the approval of the Ministry of Public Instruction, issued to its factory inspectors guidelines confirming the applicability of all aspects of the 1874 law.[34] Although the provisions of the child labor law were upheld, it was nonetheless clear that the positivist republican politicians who now determined French legislation considered public education the key to molding the future of the nation's children and that these politicians viewed further controls on the working conditions of the young as a secondary issue at best.[35] Even where the deteriorating state of apprenticeship training continued to be discussed, it was addressed more often than not in terms of improving formal technical education within the school system.[36]

The eclipse of the child labor issue by other issues of social reform was, in the final analysis, due to a combination of factors. First of all, the early factory reform movement had been relatively successful. The most flagrant abuses of children working in industry had all but disappeared, and by the 1880s a program of child labor restrictions was a permanent feature of French social and economic life, administered by its own bureaucracy and overseen by a corps of salaried inspectors. The decline of child labor reform as a prominent social action issue must also be attributed to the diminution of the political power of those groups in French

34. There is extensive correspondence in AN, F12–4765, on the problems raised by the 1882 law; see especially the Ministry of Commerce circular of December 16, 1885. Child labor inspectors were often concerned with this matter as well; see, for example, reports from the Seine in AN, F12–4730 and F12–4731. On education reform in general, see Félix Ponteil, *Histoire de l'enseignement en France* ([Tours?], 1966), 283–90.

35. Compare Sanford Elwitt, *The Making of the Third Republic: Class and Politics in France, 1868–1884* (Baton Rouge, 1975), 170ff, and Bertocci, *Jules Simon*, 192–211. A similar shift of emphasis from factory reform to education reform occurred in England in the late nineteenth century; see Thomas, *Young People*, 126–31.

36. See the report of an 1877 inquiry into the state of apprenticeship in AN, F12–4831. See also Octave Gréard, *Des écoles d'apprentis: Mémoire adressé à Monsieur le préfet de la Seine* (Paris, 1872).

society that had most forcefully promoted child labor legislation. As the relative sociopolitical strength of religious traditionalists and of laissez-faire liberals declined in the era of republican entrenchment, the focus of demands for welfare legislation shifted away from such relatively narrow issues as child labor and toward such matters as education reform and the protection of the national labor force in its entirety. For the new generation of political activists, legislators, and bureaucrats that was emerging by the 1880s, the legitimacy of government interventionism was no longer a significant ideological question; the members of this generation assumed that an ultimate solution to the nation's lingering *question sociale* would depend on comprehensive programs of reform legislation.[37]

37. On the new type of reformism that emerged late in the nineteenth century, see Sanford Elwitt, *The Third Republic Defended: Bourgeois Reform in France, 1880–1914* (Baton Rouge, 1986). See also Stone, *Search for Social Peace*.

Conclusion

The decline of child labor reform as a fundamental social and political concern marked the end of the era of early industrial reformism in France. For over half a century, the campaign to control child labor had been one of the key reform movements in France, reflecting the world view of an important segment of the nation's sociopolitical elite and exemplifying one of the major forms of social activism in the early industrial period. Many social problems had been created or exacerbated by the emergence of industrial society—problems such as pauperism, sexual promiscuity, drunkenness, urban squalor—but the problem of child labor abuse was the first to be attacked in a systematic fashion with a program of legislation. The abuse of young workers directly affected the most vulnerable of the nation's citizens, France's children, and it was seen as a radically new evil growing directly out of the formation of industrial society. It was a problem linked both to the *question sociale*, which troubled so much of the French elite, and to the new middle-class concern with family life and the experience of childhood. Many observers of early industrial society saw in the deplorable conditions of laboring children a glaring symptom of the breakdown of working-class family life, and this breakdown, as some very important recent scholarship has demonstrated, was perhaps the central concern of nineteenth-century social critics.[1]

Because the dominant classes in France saw children as the hope of

1. Donzelot, *Policing*, is the most influential work dealing with this theme. See also Lynch, *Family, Class, and Ideology*, which includes a perceptive critique of Donzelot's work.

the future, the defenders of the homeland, the guarantors of industrial progress, and the custodians of the national morality, the protection of the young received the highest priority. The goal of the child labor reform movement was to protect laboring children from the worst sorts of abuses, to shelter them from the most corrupting influences, and to provide them with at least a minimal education. Child labor reformers wanted to make of working-class children healthy and productive (albeit deferential) workers and sturdy defenders of the motherland. In short, they wanted to protect the nation's seedlings in order to assure the future harvest.

Throughout the period of its prominence, the child labor reform movement in France had been dominated by a coalition of convenience between religious traditionalists and paternalistic middle-class liberals.[2] Although these two highly influential groups often differed on questions of social policy, it was the attitudes and concerns they shared that brought reformers from the two groups together on the issue of child labor. Both religious traditionalists and liberal philanthropists envisioned an ideal society controlled by an elite that enjoyed a privileged position but that also felt bound to concern itself with the welfare of subordinate social classes. Both these groups were interested in securing the physical safety and the material prosperity of France, from which the dominant classes benefited most. Both these groups recognized that in order to perpetuate social stability, they would have to influence the youth of the working classes.

The key to the emergence of a coherent reform movement was that both the religious traditionalists and the liberal paternalists who concerned themselves with the condition of working children recognized the need for national legislation to impose controls on child labor in a uniform fashion. Moreover, they agreed that government intervention was acceptable as a tool of social policy only as long as it was not too intrusive; the restrictions on child labor demanded by reformers were always judicious. Throughout the period of their campaign, virtually all advocates of reform continued to hope that noncoercive measures could be found to cope with the problems of working-class misery and depravity, and they viewed government intervention as neither particularly desirable nor sufficient in and of itself. They saw interventionist legisla-

2. In Donzelot's terms, this was also a coalition between "Christian political economists" and "social economists"; in Lynch's terms, this was a coalition between Social Catholics and "moral economists." See Donzelot, *Policing*, 62–63; and Lynch, *Family, Class, and Ideology,* Chap. 1.

tion not as a basis for a sweeping national policy but only as a limited remedy for specific problems.

Given their position within early industrial society, the child labor reformers of the middle decades of the nineteenth century found it possible to lobby effectively at the highest levels of government for the kinds of programs they favored. At first, the champions of child labor legislation had been few in number, but eventually their movement developed a significant following and met with some success. Although progress on child labor reform was unavoidably subject to the political vicissitudes of nineteenth-century France, the sort of limited but definitive national laws that the child labor crusaders desired were eventually enacted. The legislative successes of the child labor reform movement reflected both the pervasiveness of the assumptions made by early industrial reformers and the efficacy of their political strategy.

Success in the legislature, however, was no guarantee that even the minimal restrictions on child labor sponsored by reformers would be enforced. Those who lobbied for child labor laws—progressive industrialists, comfortable intellectuals and philanthropists, idealistic legislators—were insulated for the most part from the direct impact of the measures they demanded. On the other side, those whose economic interests would be most disrupted by child labor restrictions—factory owners, craft shop masters, working-class parents—often resisted their effective implementation, and because the inspection provisions of France's early child labor laws were seriously flawed, some abuses of child labor and apprenticeship continued throughout the nineteenth century. The actual conditions of working children in French factories and workshops ultimately depended as much on the practical considerations of their families and their employers as it did on the wishes of reformers from the privileged classes. Still, the condition of child laborers did improve over the decades, both because a body of child labor law was on the books and because of advances in industrial technology and changes in popular attitudes toward childhood and education. Many of the jobs youngsters had done in factories and shops had been so transformed by the end of the nineteenth century that young children could no longer do them, and under the Third Republic there appeared both an increased popular appreciation of formal education and a legal requirement that it be provided to all children.

Child labor reform in the middle decades of the nineteenth century had been a movement dominated by paternalists who could bring their influence to bear on policy makers in an essentially authoritarian political system. As such, the movement could not survive the changes wrought within French society and politics at the end of the century. The cautious reformism of the early industrial period eventually had to give way before the triumph of republicanism, the development of mass politics, and the established acceptability of government interventionism. By the 1880s, new issues were occupying the limelight, and new approaches to promoting change were being adopted. The most prominent advocates of reform in the final decades of the nineteenth century had an agenda quite different from that of the men who had engineered the passage of France's first child labor law in 1841, of the men who had pressed for further legislation in the forties, fifties and sixties, or of those who had insured the passage of a new industrial labor act in 1874.

By the time the Third Republic was firmly established, France's apprenticeship in the politics of reform was over, and the nation was prepared for a new era of social legislation. The cautious reformers of the early industrial period, driven by a sense of religious or philanthropic obligation and seeking also to protect their own interests, considered social legislation as a tool with only limited applicability, but their movement had served as one of the main vehicles by which the leaders of French society learned to grapple with such issues as the regulation of family life in modern society and the management of labor relations under industrialization. The attention commanded by the problem of industrial child labor forced the dominant classes to confront the complex task of forging a new relationship between liberty and social welfare. Ultimately, by legitimating the principle of government interventionism, the child labor controls adopted in France during the early industrial era facilitated the introduction of intrusive family policies and labor regulations in the late nineteenth and early twentieth centuries.

The child labor laws of 1841 and 1874 were not conceived in the same way as were later measures that sought to regulate some very intimate aspects of family life and industrial management. By the time these more stringent measures were enacted under the entrenched Third Republic, the kind of reformers who had championed child labor legislation had been overshadowed on the social and political scene, and their concept of the appropriate role of government was no longer predominant. The legacy of France's early industrial reformers remained, however, for it was the child labor legislation of the midnineteenth century that laid the foundation for the myriad laws subsequently passed for the protection of children, the policing of families, and the regulation of industrial labor.

Appendix A
The Child Labor Law of 1841

Article 1: Children may be employed only under the conditions established by the present law:

1. In factories, works, and workshops that employ mechanical power or a continuous fire, and in their annexes;

2. In any factory employing more than twenty workers assembled in the shop.

Article 2: Children must be at least eight years old to be admitted to employment.

Between the ages of eight and twelve, they may not be employed in actual labor more than eight hours out of twenty-four, divided by rest periods.

Between the ages of twelve and sixteen, they may not be employed in actual labor more than twelve hours out of twenty-four, divided by rest periods.

This labor may take place only between five o'clock in the morning and nine o'clock in the evening.

The children's age shall be verified by a certificate supplied, on non-stamped paper and free of charge, by the registrar of the civil authority.

Article 3: All labor performed between nine o'clock in the evening and five o'clock in the morning is considered night work.

All night work is forbidden to children under thirteen years of age.

If it is required as a consequence of the stoppage of a hydraulic motor or of urgent repairs, children over the age of thirteen may labor at night,

·between nine o'clock in the evening and five o'clock in the morning, with two working hours counted as three.

Night work by children over thirteen, likewise calculated, will be tolerated if it is recognized as indispensable in establishments employing a continuous fire whose operation cannot be suspended during the course of the twenty-four-hour day.

Article 4: Children under sixteen years of age may not be employed on Sundays and holidays recognized by the law.

Article 5: No child under twelve may be admitted to employment unless his parents or guardian prove that he is presently attending one of the public or private schools in the locality. Every child admitted to employment must attend a school until the age of twelve.

Children over twelve will be exempt from attending school if they have a certificate, provided by the mayor of their place of residence, attesting that they have received an elementary primary education.

Article 6: Mayors are directed to provide to his father, mother, or guardian a *livret* showing the age, the surname, the name, the place of birth, and the place of residence of the child, and the period during which he received his primary education.

The heads of establishments shall write:

1. In the *livret* of each child, the date of his entry into the establishment and that of his departure.

2. In a special register, all the information mentioned in the present article.

Article 7: Rulings of the administration may:

1. Extend the application of the provisions of the present law to factories, works, or shops other than those mentioned in article one;

2. Raise the minimum age and reduce the length of the workday delineated in articles two and three, with regard to those types of industries or labors of children that exceed their physical ability or compromise their health;

3. Specify those factories where, because of dangers or unhealthy conditions, children under sixteen may not be employed at all;

4. Forbid children to perform certain types of dangerous or harmful tasks in those shops to which they are admitted;

5. Rule on indispensable labor on the part of children to be tolerated on Sundays and holidays in works employing a continuous fire;

6. Rule in cases of night work covered in article three.

Article 8: Rulings of the administration should:

1. Attend to the measures necessary for the execution of the present law;

2. Assure the maintenance of moral behavior and public decency in shops, works, and manufactures;

3. Assure the primary education and the religious instruction of children;

4. Prevent, with regard to children, all maltreatment and abusive punishment;

5. Assure conditions of cleanliness and of safety necessary for the life and health of children.

Article 9: Heads of establishments should see that the internal regulations that they are asked to prepare in order to assure the execution of the present law are posted in each shop, along with the law itself and the administrative rulings relative to it.

Article 10: The government will institute inspections to oversee and assure the execution of the present law. Inspectors may, in each establishment, demand to see the registers relative to the execution of the present law, the internal regulations, the *livrets* of children and the children themselves; they may also bring with them a physician commissioned by the prefect or the subprefect.

Article 11: In case of a violation, the inspectors will prepare a report, which shall be considered as proof until proven otherwise.

Article 12: In case of a violation of the present law or of administrative rulings prepared for its execution, the proprietors or operators of the establishments [involved] shall be brought before the justice of the peace of the canton and punished with a police fine that may not exceed five francs.

Those violations that result either in the admission of underage children or in an excessive workday shall occasion as many fines as there are children improperly admitted or employed, as long as all the fines taken together do not exceed two hundred francs.

If there is a repeated offense, the proprietors or operators of the establishments [involved] shall be brought before the police court and punished with a fine of sixteen to one hundred francs. In those cases covered by the second paragraph of the present law, the total fines may never exceed five hundred francs.

A repeated offense shall have been committed when an offender has

been convicted of a first violation of the present law or of the administrative rulings it authorizes in the twelve months previous to the new
offense.

Article 13: The present law shall go into effect only six months after
its promulgation.

Source: *Documents relatifs au travail des enfants et des femmes* (Brussels, 1871), 300–302.

Appendix B
The Apprenticeship Law of 1851

TITLE ONE
THE APPRENTICESHIP CONTRACT

Section One
The Nature and Form of the Contract

Article 1: A contract of apprenticeship is that by which a manufacturer, a foreman, or a worker obliges himself to teach the practice of his profession to another person who, in return, obliges himself to work for him; all this under the conditions and for the duration agreed upon.

Article 2: An apprenticeship contract is concluded by public document or by private contract. It may also be made verbally; but oral evidence about it is admissible only in conformity with the title "Concerning Contracts and Contractual Obligations in General" of the Civil Code. Notaries, secretaries of *conseils des prud'hommes*, and clerks of the justice of the peace may accept the apprenticeship document. This act is to be submitted for registration at the fixed cost of one franc, even though it may contain obligations for transferable sums or shares, or receipts. The honorarium payable to the public officials [involved] is fixed at two francs.

Article 3: The apprenticeship document shall contain: 1) The surname, names, age, profession, and residence of the master; 2) The surname, names, age, and residence of the apprentice; 3) The surname, names, profession, and residence of his father and mother, of his guardian, or of the person authorized by his parents and, in their absence, by the magistrate of the peace; 4) The date and the duration of the contract; 5) The conditions of lodging, of board, of remuneration, and all other agreements between the parties. It shall be signed by the master and by the representatives of the apprentice.

Section Two
Conditions of the Contract

Article 4: No one may take on an apprentice unless he is at least twenty-one years of age.

Article 5: No master, if he is a bachelor or a widower, may provide lodging for minor girls as apprentices.

Article 6: Disqualified from taking on apprentices are: individuals who have been convicted of a crime; those who have been convicted of a breach of morals; those who have been sentenced to more than three months imprisonment for offenses covered in articles 388, 401, 405, 406, 407, 408, or 423 of the penal code.

Article 7: A disqualification resulting from the provisions of article 6 may be lifted by the prefect, on the advice of the mayor, if the convicted has resided in the same commune for at least three years after the expiration of his sentence. In Paris, the disqualifications are to be lifted by the prefect of police.

Section Three
Obligations of Masters and Apprentices

Article 8: The master must conduct himself toward his apprentice as a good father of a family, oversee his conduct and his morals, both at home and outside, and inform his parents or their representative of any grave faults he might commit or any penchants for vice he might exhibit. He must also apprise them without delay in case of illness, of absence, or of any event that would motivate their intervention. He shall employ the apprentice only in labors and services that are connected to the practice of his profession, unless there is an agreement to the contrary. He shall never employ him in those [labors] that would be unhealthy or beyond his physical capacity.

Article 9: The duration of actual work may not exceed ten hours a day for apprentices under the age of fourteen. For apprentices fourteen to sixteen years of age, it may not exceed twelve hours. No night work may be imposed on apprentices under sixteen years of age. All work performed between nine in the evening and five in the morning is considered night work. Apprentices may in no case be kept by their masters at any labor in their profession on Sundays and on recognized or legal holidays. In a case where the apprentice is obliged, pursuant to agreements or in conformity with custom, to clean the workshop on the days indicated above, this work may not be prolonged beyond ten in the morning. Action contrary to the provisions contained in the first three [clauses] of the present article is permitted only by a decree produced by the prefect, on the advice of the mayor.

Article 10: If an apprentice under sixteen years of age does not know how to read, write, and calculate, or if he has not yet completed his primary religious education, the master is directed to allow him the time and the liberty necessary for his instruction, during the workday. However, this time may not exceed two hours a day.

Article 11: The apprentice owes his master fidelity, obedience, and respect; he must help with his labor, to the extent his ability and his strength allow. He is directed to replace, at the end of his apprenticeship, the time he was unable to work due to sickness or an absence of more than fifteen days.

Article 12: The master must teach the apprentice, progressively and completely, the art, the craft, or the particular profession that was the object of the contract. He shall present him, at the end of his apprenticeship, with a discharge permit or a certificate attesting to the fulfillment of the contract.

Article 13: Any manufacturer, foreman, or worker convicted of having lured an apprentice away from his master in order to employ him as an apprentice or as a worker may be liable for all or part of the indemnity decreed in favor of the abandoned master.

Section Four
Cancellation of a Contract

Article 14: The first two months of an apprenticeship contract are considered a trial period during which the contract may be annulled if either party desires. In this case, no indemnity shall be assessed against either party, without express agreements [to the contrary].

Article 15: The apprenticeship contract may be dissolved without need of sanction: 1) By the death of the master or of the apprentice; 2) If the apprentice or the master is called to military service; 3) If the master or the apprentice becomes subject to one of the condemnations covered in article 6 of the present law; 4) For minor females, in case of the death of the wife of the master or of any other woman in the family who directed the household during the period of the contract.

Article 16: The contract may be dissolved at the request of the parties or of one of them: 1) In cases where one of the parties fails [to fulfill] the stipulations of the contract; 2) On account of grave or habitual infractions of the requirements of the present law; 3) In cases of habitual misconduct on the part of the apprentice; 4) If the master moves his permanent residence to a commune other than that which he inhabited at the time the contract was made. However, a request for a dissolution of contract based on this reason is admissible for three months only, counting from the day on which the master changed his residence. 5) If the master incurs or the apprentice incurs a sentence carrying with it imprisonment for more than a month; 6) In the case where an apprentice proceeds to contract a marriage.

Article 17: If the time agreed upon for the duration of the apprenticeship exceeds the maximum duration sanctioned by local custom, the time may be reduced or the contract dissolved.

TITLE TWO
JURISDICTION

Article 18: All requests for exceptions from or dissolution of the contract shall be judged by the *conseil des prud'hommes* that has jurisdiction over the master and, in its absence, by the justice of the peace of the canton. The charges that may be directed against third parties by virtue of article 13 of the present law shall be brought before the *conseil des prud'hommes* or before the justice of the peace of their place of residence.

Article 19: In the various cases of cancellation provided for in section four of title one, the indemnities or the restitutions that may be due to one or another of the parties shall be set, in the absence of express stipulations, by the *conseil des prud'hommes* or, in cantons where no *conseil des prud'hommes* has jurisdiction, by the justice of the peace.

Article 20: All violations of articles 4, 5, 6, 7, 8, 9, or 10 of the present law shall be prosecuted before the police tribunal and punished with a fine of five to fifteen francs. For violations of articles 4, 5, 9 and 10, the police tribunal may, in the case of a repeat offense, pronounce a sentence, besides the fine, of imprisonment for one to five days. In the case of a repeat offense, the violation of article 6 shall be prosecuted before the correctional tribunals and punished with imprisonment for fifteen days to three months, without prejudice to the fine, which may be as high as fifty to three hundred francs.

Article 21: The provisions of article 463 of the Penal Code are applicable to the matters provided for in the present law.

Article 22: Articles 9, 10, and 11 of the law of 22 Germinal, Year XI, are abrogated.

Source: *Documents relatifs au travail des enfants et des femmes* (Brussels, 1871), 367–70.

Appendix C
The Child Labor Law of 1874

SECTION ONE
MINIMUM AGE—WORKDAY LENGTH

Article 1: Children and minor females may be employed in industrial labor in factories, mills, works, mines, yards, and shops only under the conditions set forth in the present law.

Article 2: Children may not be hired by employers or admitted to factories, works, shops, or yards before the age of twelve years.

Nevertheless, they may be employed from the age of ten years in those industries specially designated by a ruling of the administration, prepared with the consent of the Commission supérieure instituted below.

Article 3: Children, until they are twelve years old, may not be subjected to a work period of more than six hours per day, divided by a rest period.

From the age of twelve, they may not be employed more than twelve hours per day, divided by rest periods.

SECTION TWO
NIGHT, SUNDAY, AND HOLIDAY LABOR

Article 4: Children may not be employed in any night work until the age of sixteen years.

The same prohibition applies to the employment of minor females aged sixteen to twenty-one years, but only in works and factories.

All labor between nine in the evening and five in the morning is considered night work.

Nonetheless, in case of an absolutely necessary work stoppage resulting from an accidental interruption, the above prohibition may be temporarily suspended for a fixed period by the local commission or the inspector instituted below, but without allowing children under twelve years of age to be employed.

Article 5: Children under sixteen, and minor females under twenty-one may not be employed by their employers at any work on Sundays and holidays recognized by the law, even in the cleaning of the shop.

Article 6: Nonetheless, in works with a continuous fire children may be employed at indispensable tasks at night or on Sundays and holidays.

The labor to be tolerated and the amount of time during which it can be performed shall be determined by administrative rulings.

This labor shall, in any case, be authorized only for children at least twelve years old.

They must be allowed, moreover, the time and the liberty necessary for them to fulfill their religious obligations.

SECTION THREE
UNDERGROUND LABOR

Article 7: No child may be admitted to work in underground labors in mines, pits, and quarries before the age of twelve.

Girls and women may not be admitted to these labors.

The special conditions pertaining to the labor of children aged twelve to sixteen in underground galleries shall be determined by administrative rulings.

SECTION FOUR
PRIMARY EDUCATION

Article 8: No child less than twelve years old may be hired by an employer without his parents or guardian proving that he is presently attending a public or private school.

Every child admitted to labor in a shop before the age of twelve must, until that age, attend classes in a school during the time he is free from work.

If a special school is attached to the industrial establishment, the child must receive at least two hours of instruction.

School attendance shall be verified by means of an attendance sheet, prepared by the instructor and given to the employer each week.

Article 9: No child under the age of fifteen may be admitted to labor more than six hours per day unless he proves that he has acquired an elementary primary education by producing a certificate from the instructor or the school inspector, countersigned by the mayor.

This certificate shall be provided on free paper and gratis.

SECTION FIVE
SURVEILLANCE OF CHILDREN—POLICE OF SHOPS

Article 10: Mayors are directed to provide to the father, mother, or guardian, a *livret* containing the surname and name of the child, the date and place of his birth, his domicile, and the period of his school attendance.

Foremen or employers shall write in the *livret* the date of his entry into the shop or establishment and that of his exit. They must also keep a register in which shall be entered all the information set forth in the present article.

Article 11: Employers or foremen are directed to post the stipulations of the present law and administrative rulings relative to its execution in every shop.

Article 12: Administrative rulings shall determine the different types of labors presenting dangers or exceeding their strength, which will be forbidden to children in the shops to which they are admitted.

Article 13: Children may be employed in factories and shops indicated on the official table of unhealthy or dangerous establishments only under the special conditions determined by an administrative ruling.

This prohibition shall be applied generally to all operations where the worker is exposed to functions or emanations prejudicial to his health.

In anticipation of the publication of this ruling, it is forbidden to employ children under sixteen:

1. In shops where explosive materials are handled, or where detonating mixtures such as powder, fulminates, etc., or any others detonated by shock or by contact with flame are manufactured;

2. In shops involved in the preparation, in the distillation, or in the manipulation of corrosive or poisonous substances or those which give off harmful or explosive gases.

The same prohibition applies to dangerous or unhealthy tasks, such as:

Dry polishing or sharpening metal objects and glass and crystal;

Dry scraping or beating carbonized leads in ceruse factories;

Dry scraping lead oxide based enamel in so-called muslin glassworks;

Mercury tinning of glass;

Mercury gilding.

Article 14: Shops must always be kept in a state of cleanliness and be well ventilated.

They must exhibit all the conditions of safety and cleanliness necessary for the health of children.

In works with mechanical motors, the wheels, belts, gears, or any other apparatus, where it is shown that they present a danger, shall be separated from the workers in such a manner that they may be approached only to be serviced.

Pits, trap doors, and stairwells must be enclosed.

Article 15: Employers or foremen must, further, see to the maintenance of good morals and to the observance of standards of public decency in their shops.

SECTION SIX
INSPECTION

Article 16: To assure the execution of the present law, fifteen divisional inspectors shall be appointed. The government shall name the inspectors from a list prepared by the Commission supérieure, instituted below, and bearing three candidates for each available post.

These inspectors shall be paid by the state.

Each divisional inspector shall reside in and exercise his surveillance in one of fifteen territorial divisions defined by a ruling of the administration.

Article 17: Candidates who hold the title of state engineer or a civil engineering diploma shall be admissible to the inspectorate, as well as graduates of the Ecole centrale des arts et manufactures and of the Ecole des mines.

Those who have already served as child labor inspectors for at least three years or who prove that they have directed or overseen an industrial establishment of at least one hundred workers for at least five years shall also be admissible.

Article 18: The inspectors have the right to enter all manufacturing establishments, shops, and yards. They shall examine the children; they may have presented to them the register called for in article 10, the *livrets*, the school attendance sheets, and the internal regulations.

Violations shall be set forth in reports of the inspectors, which shall be considered as proof until proven otherwise.

When it is a matter of underground labor, violations will be verified by the inspectors or by the mine wardens concurrently.

Reports shall be prepared in duplicate, one copy of which shall be sent to the prefect of the department and the other of which will be deposited with the Parquet court.

However, when inspectors have recognized that a cause of danger or insalubrity exists in an establishment or shop, they shall seek the opinion of the local commission instituted below about the state of the danger or of the insalubrity, and they shall record that opinion in a report.

The above provisions do not detract in any way from the rules of common law with regard to the verification and the prosecution of infractions of the present law.

Article 19: The inspectors shall, each year, address reports to the Commission supérieure instituted below.

SECTION SEVEN
LOCAL COMMISSIONS

Article 20: Local commissions, their work performed gratis, shall be established in each department and charged: 1) To see to the execution of the present law; 2) To control the inspection service; 3) To address to the prefect of the department reports on the state of the service and the execution of the law, which shall be transmitted to the minister and communicated to the Commission supérieure.

For this purpose, the local commissions shall visit industrial establishments, works, and yards; they may be accompanied by a physician when they judge that to be useful.

Article 21: The *conseil général* shall determine in each department the number and the territory of the local commissions. It shall establish at least one in each *arrondissement*. Further, it shall establish others in the principal industrial or manufacturing centers where that is judged necessary.

The *conseil général* may also name a special inspector salaried by the department; this inspector must, however, act under the direction of the divisional inspector.

Article 22: The local commissions shall be composed of at least five members, and not more than seven, appointed by the prefect from a list prepared by the *conseil général.*

Where possible, a state engineer or civil engineer, an inspector of primary education, and in mining regions a mining engineer should be included on each commission.

The commissions shall be renewed every five years: outgoing members may be called to serve again.

SECTION EIGHT
COMMISSION SUPÉRIEURE

Article 23: A Commission supérieure composed of nine members serving without pay is established under the minister of commerce; this commission is appointed by the president of the republic; it is charged:

1. To see to the uniform and vigilant application of the present law;

2. To give its advice on rulings to enact and, in general, on the various matters touching upon the protected workers;

3. Finally, to prepare the lists of candidates for appointment as divisional inspectors.

Article 24: Each year, the president of the Commission supérieure shall address to the president of the republic a general report on the results of inspection and on matters relative to the execution of the present law.

This report shall be published in the *Journal officiel* in the month of its delivery.

The government shall report to the National Assembly each year on the execution of the law and on the publication of administrative rulings designed to complement it.

SECTION NINE
PENALTIES

Article 25: Manufacturers, directors or managers of industrial establishments, and employers who have violated the stipulations of the present law and of the administrative rulings relative to its execution shall be prosecuted before the correctional tribunal and punished with fines of from sixteen to fifty francs.

The fine shall be assessed as many times as there were persons employed under conditions contrary to the law, as long as the total amount does not exceed five hundred francs.

Nevertheless, the penalty shall not be applied if the manufacturers, directors, or managers of industrial establishments or the employers establish that the infraction was the result of an error originating from the production of birth certificates, *livrets* or [other] certificates containing false statements or prepared for another person.

The stipulations of articles 12 and 13 of the law of June 22, 1854, concerning workers' *livrets* shall be applicable, in this case, to the authors of the falsifications.

The heads of industries are civilly responsible for judgments made against their directors or managers.

Article 26: If there is a repeated offense, the manufacturers, directors, or managers of establishments and the employers are liable to fines of from fifty to two hundred francs.

The total of the combined fines may not exceed one thousand francs, however.

A repeated offense shall have been committed when an offender has been convicted of a first violation of the present law or of the administrative rulings relative to its execution in the twelve months previous to the new offense.

Article 27: The posting of the judgment may be ordered by the court of petty sessions, depending on the circumstances and only in the case of a repeated offense.

The court may also order, in the same case, that the judgment be inserted in one or several of the newspapers of the department, at the expense of the convicted person.

Article 28: Proprietors of industrial establishments and employers who interfere with the duties of inspectors, members of commissions, or physicians, engineers, or experts delegated to make a visit or an inquiry shall be punished with a fine of from sixteen to one hundred francs.

Article 29: Article 463 of the Penal Code is applicable to sentences passed by virtue of the present law.

The proceeds from the fines resulting from these sentences shall be deposited with the primary education subsidy fund, in the public instruction budget.

Appendix C

SECTION TEN
SPECIAL PROVISIONS

Article 30: Articles 2, 3, 4, and 5 of the present law are applicable to children placed in apprenticeship and employed in an industrial labor.

The provisions of articles 18 and 25 above are applicable in the said case, in that they modify the jurisdiction and the amount of fines indicated in the first paragraph of article 20 of the law of February 22, 1851.

The said law shall continue to be executed in its other provisions.

Article 31: As a transitional measure, the provisions proclaimed by the present law shall be applicable only one year after its promulgation.

Nevertheless, in the said period, children already legally admitted to shops shall continue to be employed in them under the conditions specified in article 3.

Article 32: At the expiration of the delay indicated above, all provisions contrary to the present law shall be and shall remain abrogated.

Source: Eugène Tallon and Gustave Maurice, *Législation sur le travail des enfants* (Paris, 1875), 445–53.

Bibliography

Reference Works

Annales de l'Assemblée nationale. 45 vols. Paris, 1871–76.
Biographie universelle (Michaud) ancienne et moderne. 45 vols. Paris, 1854–65.
Dictionnaire de biographie française. 16+ vols. Paris, 1933–.
Jeanneney, J.-M., and Marguerite Perrot, eds. *Textes de droit économique et social français, 1789–1957.* Paris, 1957.
La Grande Encyclopedie, inventaire raisonné des sciences, des lettres et des arts. 31 vols. Paris, 1886–1902.
Larousse, Pierre, ed. *Grand Dictionnaire universelle.* 17 vols. Paris, 1865–90?.
Mavidal, Jérôme, *et al.*, eds. *Archives parlementaires de 1787 à 1860.* 2nd ser. 127 vols. Paris, 1862–1913.
Moniteur universel. Paris, 1810–68.
Nouvelle Biographie générale. 46 vols. Paris, 1855–70.
Procès-verbaux des séances de la Chambre des députés. Paris, 1840–47.
Robert, Adolphe, Edgar Bourloton, and Gaston Cougny, eds. *Dictionnaire des parlementaires français.* 5 vols. Paris, 1889–91.

Archival Material at the Archives nationales, Paris

F12–4704. Appeals for legislation, 1837–41; inquiries of 1837 and 1840.
F12–4705. Responses to the 1837 inquiry.
F12–4706. Implementation of the 1841 law.
F12–4707. Enforcement of the 1841 law; preparation of the 1847 bill.
F12–4708. Appointment of child labor inspectors after 1841.
F12–4709 to F12–4714. Correspondence regarding enforcement of the 1841 law.
F12–4715. Violations of the 1841 law.
F12–4716. Child labor in other countries; correspondence between ministries *ca.* 1870.

F12–4717. Enforcement in the 1860s and early 1870s.

F12–4718 and F12–4719. Correspondence with departmental officials in the 1860s and early 1870s.

F12–4720. Responses to the circular of June 25, 1859, and others.

F12–4721. Enforcement 1867–70; the role of the mining engineers; the preparation of the 1870 bill.

F12–4722 and F12–4723. Responses to the inquiry of 1867.

F12–4724 to F12–4726. Responses to the inquiry among mining engineers *ca.* 1869.

F12–4727. Preparation of the 1874 law and its initial implementation.

F12–4728 and F12–4729. Responses to the circular of August 31, 1874, concerning implementation of the 1874 law.

F12–4730 to F12–4732. Enforcement of the child labor law in the Department of the Seine, 1875–89.

F12–4733 to F12–4764. Enforcement of the child labor law in the second through fifteenth inspection districts, 1875–92.

F12–4765 and F12–4766. Enforcement of the education provisions of the 1874 law; court cases involving violations of the 1874 law.

F12–4767 to F12–4769. Appointment and organization of local child labor commissions after 1874.

F12–4770. Local child labor commissions in the Department of the Seine after 1874.

F12–4771. Reports about and from local child labor commissions after 1874.

F12–4772. Correspondence with persons other than divisional inspectors concerning enforcement of the 1874 law.

F12–4773A. The 1858 plan for inspection; inspection personnel.

F12–4773B. Personnel files.

F12–4830 to F12–4833. The preparation and enforcement of the 1851 apprenticeship law.

Printed Primary Sources

STATISTICAL STUDIES

Chambre de commerce de Paris. *Statistique de l'industrie à Paris ... 1847–48.* Paris, 1851.

Ministre de l'agriculture et du commerce. *Statistique de la France,* series 1. Vols. X–XIII. Paris, 1847–52.

Moreau de Jonnès, Alexandre. *Statistique de l'industrie de la France.* Paris, 1856.

Statistique de la France. *Industrie: Résultats généraux de l'enquête effectuée dans les années 1861–1865.* Nancy, 1873.

———. *Mouvement de la population pendant les années 1861, 1862, 1863, 1864 et 1865.* Strasbourg, 1870.

BOOKS

Audiganne, Armand. *La Nouvelle Loi sur le travail des enfants et la famille ouvrière depuis 35 ans.* Paris, 1874.

———. *Les Ouvriers d'à present.* Paris, 1865.

————. *Les Ouvriers en famille.* Paris, 1866.

————. *Les Populations ouvrières et les industries de la France.* 2 vols. Paris, 1860.

Bères, Emile. *Les Classes ouvrières.* Paris, 1836.

Blanc, Louis. *Organisation du travail.* Paris, 1841.

Blanqui, Jérôme-Adolphe. *Cours d'économie industrielle, 1838–1839.* Paris, 1839.

————. *Des classes ouvrières en France pendant l'année 1848.* Paris, 1849.

————. *History of Political Economy in Europe.* Translated by Emily J. Leonard. New York, 1880.

Bosquet, Amélie [Emile]. *Le Roman des ouvrières.* Paris, 1868.

Buret, Eugène. *De la misère des classes laborieuses en Angleterre et en France.* 2 vols. Paris, 1840.

Cabet, Etienne. *Voyage en Icarie.* Paris, 1848.

Chevalier, Michel. *Lettres sur l'organisation du travail.* Brussels, 1850.

Daudet, Alphonse. *Jack.* Translated by Marian McIntyre. Boston, 1900.

Desvernay, Arnould, ed. *Rapports des délégations ouvrières.* 3 vols. Paris, 1869.

The Doctrines of Saint-Simon: An Exposition—First Year, 1828–1829. Translated by George G. Iggers. Boston, 1958.

Ducpétiaux, Edouard. *De la condition physique et morale des jeunes ouvriers.* 2 vols. Brussels, 1843.

Dunoyer, Charles. *De la liberté du travail.* 3 vols. Paris, 1845.

Dupin, Charles. *Avantages sociaux d'un enseignement publique appliqué à l'industrie.* Paris, 1824.

————. *Du travail des enfants qu'emploient les ateliers, les usines et les manufactures.* Paris, 1840.

Dupuynode, Gustave. *Des lois du travail.* Paris, 1845.

————. *Des lois du travail et de la population.* 2 vols. Paris, 1860.

Duvergier, J. B. *Lois principales de 1841.* Paris, ca. 1842.

Fix, Théodore. *Observations sur l'état des classes ouvrières.* Paris, 1846.

Frégier, H. A. *Des classes dangereuses de la population dans les grandes villes.* 2 vols. Paris, 1840.

Freycinet, Charles de. *Souvenirs 1848–1878.* Paris, 1912.

Froment, Mathilde [Mme. Bourdon]. *Marthe Blondel ou l'ouvrière de fabrique.* Paris, 1863.

Gérando, Joseph-Marie de. *De la bienfaisance publique.* 2 vols. Brussels, 1839.

————. *Des progrès de l'industrie dans leurs rapports avec le bien-être physique et morale de la classe ouvrière.* Paris, 1845.

————. *The Visitor of the Poor.* Translated by Elizabeth Palmer Peabody. Boston, 1832.

Hayem, Julien. *Histoire de l'apprentissage.* Paris, 1868.

Hayem, Julien, and Jules Périn. *Traité du contrat d'apprentissage.* Paris, 1878.

Horner, Leonard. *On the Employment of Children in Factories and Other Works in the United Kingdom and in Some Foreign Countries.* London, 1840.

Hugo, Victor. *Les Misérables.* Translated by Charles E. Wilbour. New York, 1964.

Jay, Raoul. *Du travail des enfants et filles mineures dans l'industrie.* Paris, 1880.

LePlay, Frédéric. *La Réforme sociale en France.* 3 vols. Paris, 1867.

Lorain, P. *Tableau de l'instruction primaire en France . . . à la fin de 1833.* Paris, 1837.

Michelet, Jules. *The People.* Translated. London, 1846.

Moreau-Christophe, Louis. *Du problème de la misère.* 3 vols. Paris, 1851.
Nadaud, Martin. *Discours de Martin Nadaud.* Paris, 1884.
Say, Jean-Baptiste. *Cours complet d'économie politique.* 2 vols. Paris, 1840.
Simon, Jules. *L'Ouvrier de huit ans.* Paris, 1867.
————. *L'Ouvrière.* Paris, 1867.
Sismondi, Jean Simonde de. *Nouveau Principes d'économie.* 2 vols. Paris, 1819.
Sue, Eugène. *The Mysteries of Paris.* Translated. London, n.d.
Symons, Jelinger C. *Arts and Artisans at Home and Abroad.* Edinburgh, 1839.
Tallon, Eugène, and Gustave Maurice. *Législation sur le travail des enfants.* Paris, 1875.
Véron, Eugène. *Les Institutions ouvrières de Mulhouse et des environs.* Paris, 1866.
Villeneuve-Bargemont, Alban de. *Economie politique chrétienne.* 3 vols. Paris, 1834.
Villermé, Louis. *Tableau de l'état physique et moral des ouvriers.* 2 vols. Paris, 1840.
Wing, Charles. *Evils of the Factory System.* 1837; rpr. New York, 1967.
Zola, Emile. *Germinal.* Translated by Leonard Tancock. Harmondsworth, Eng., 1954.

PAMPHLETS AND REPORTS
(AN notation indicates availability at the Archives nationales, Paris)

Allard, Paul. *Du travail des enfants et des femmes.* Rouen, 1869. (AN, F12–4719).
Barreswil. *Deuxième Rapport sur la situation des enfants employés dans les manufactures du département de la Seine.* Paris, 1866. (AN, F12–4717).
————. *Rapport sur la situation des enfants employés dans les manufactures du département de la Seine.* Paris, 1865. (AN, F12–4717).
Blondel, A. *Le Travail des enfants et des femmes dans les manufactures.* Paris, 1874.
Bourcart, Jean-Jacques. *Du travail des jeunes ouvriers.* Paris, 1840. (AN, F12–4704 and F12–4705).
Bugniot, C.-F. *Les Petits Savoyards.* Châlon-sur-Saône, 1863. (AN, F12–4830).
Carnot, Hippolyte-Lazare. *Lettre à Monsieur le Ministre de l'Agriculture et du Commerce sur la législation que règle, dans quelques états de l'Allemagne, les conditions du travail des jeunes ouvriers.* Paris, 1840. (AN, F12–4704).
Curnier, Léonce. *Rapport sur la nouveau projet de loi relatif au travail des enfants.* Nîmes, 1848.
Descottes. *Rapport de la section du contentieux et de législation sur les modifications à apporter à la loi du 24 mars 1841.* Paris, 1872. (AN, F12–4727).
Durassier, Léon. *Etude sur l'inspection du travail dans l'industrie.* Paris, 1888.
Fichet, César. *Mémoire sur l'apprentissage et sur l'education industrielle.* Paris, 1847.
Gillet. *Quelques réflexions sur l'emploi des enfans dans les fabriques et sur les moyens d'en prévenir les abus.* Paris, 1840.
Gréard, Octave. *Des écoles d'apprentis: Mémoire adressé à Monsieur le préfet de la Seine.* Paris, 1872.
Langlois, Anatole. *Le Travail des enfants dans les manufactures.* Paris, 1872.
[Legrand, Daniel]. *Appel respectueux d'un industriel de la vallée des Vosges . . . adressé aux gouvernements de la France, de l'Angleterre, de la Prusse, des autres états de l'Allemagne, et de la Suisse dans le but de provoquer des lois particulières et une loi internationale. . . . .* Strasbourg, 1848. (AN, F12–4707).
————. *Lettre d'un industriel des montagnes des Vosges à M. le Baron Charles Dupin*

. . . *suivie de plusieurs lettres et adresses.* Strasbourg, 1841. (AN, F12–4704 and F12–4705).

———. *Lettre d'un industriel des montagnes des Vosges à Monsieur Legentil . . . suivi de deux lettres adressées à Monsieur Guizot.* [Strasbourg?], 1847.

———. *Nouvelle Lettre d'un industriel des montagnes des Vosges à M. François Delessert.* Strasbourg, 1839. (AN, F12–4704).

———. *Projet de loi sur le travail et l'instruction des enfants.* . . . Strasbourg, 1840. (AN, F12–4704 and F12–4705).

Mallet. *Travail des enfans.* Saint-Quentin, 1840. (AN, F12–4704).

Melun, Armand de. *De l'intervention de la société pour prévenir et soulager la misère.* Paris, 1849.

———. *Rapport à la Société d'économie charitable sur le projet relatif au travail des enfants.* [Paris?], 1847. (AN, F12–4707).

Ministère du commerce et de l'industrie. *Rapport sur l'application de la loi du 19 mai 1874 pendant l'année 1885.* Paris, 1886.

Morel, Octavie. *Essai sur la vie et les travaux de Marie-Joseph Baron de Gérando.* Paris, 1846.

Penot, Achille. *Observations sur le projet de loi.* . . . . Mulhouse, 1840. (AN, F12–4704).

———. *Rapport de la commission chargée d'examiner la question relative à l'emploi des enfans dans les filatures de coton.* Mulhouse, 1837. (AN, F12–4704).

Planet, Edmond de. *Travail des enfants dans les manufactures.* Toulouse, 1867. (AN, F12–4722).

Rapport du Bureau des manufactures sur les réponses à la circulaire du 31 juillet relative à l'emploi des enfants dans les fabriques. Paris, 1837. (AN, F12–4704).

Renseignements et avis recueillis en 1867 sur le travail des enfants dans les établissements industriels. Paris, 1867. (AN, F12–4721 and others).

Sismondi, Jean Simonde de. *Du sort des ouvriers dans les manufactures.* Paris, 1834.

Société industrielle de Mulhouse. *Documens relatifs au travail des jeunes ouvriers.* Mulhouse, ca. 1841. (AN, F12–4704).

[Steinbach, George, et al.]. *Travail des enfants dans les manufactures.* Mulhouse, 1867.

Villeneuve-Bargemont, Alban de. *Discours prononcé à la Chambre des députés . . . dans la discussion du projet de loi sur le travail des enfans dans les manufactures.* Metz, ca. 1841.

Villermé, Louis. *Discours sur la durée trop longue du travail des enfants dans beaucoup de manufactures.* Paris, 1837. (AN, F12–4704).

Waziers van der Crusse, L. de. *Projet de règlement d'administration publique.* Paris, 1855. (AN, F12–4706).

Wolowski, Louis. *Le Travail des enfants dans les manufactures.* Paris, 1868.

ARTICLES

Barrois, T. Report. *Les Revoltes logiques,* III (1976), 45–58.

Bastiat, Frédéric. "Sur les questions soumises aux conseils généraux de l'agriculture, des manufactures et du commerce." *Journal des économistes,* XIII (December, 1845).

Bloch, Simon. "La Loi sur le travail des enfants." *Univers israélite* (1874).

Bonald, Louis de. "De la famille agricole, de la famille industrielle." In *Oeuvres complètes de M. de Bonald*, Vol. I. Paris, 1859.

Bourcart, Jean-Jacques. "Proposition . . . sur la nécessité de fixer l'âge et de réduire les heures de travail des ouvriers des filatures." *Bulletin de la Société industrielle de Mulhouse*, I (1827–28).

Caux, Paul de. "Patronage des apprentis et jeunes ouvriers." *Annales de la charité*, XIV (1858).

"Conférence du Révérend Père Hyacinthe." *Bulletin de la Société de protection des apprentis et des enfants des manufactures* (1867).

Coulonge, Christian de. "Etudes sur les oeuvres de patronage." *Bulletin de la Société de protection des apprentis et des enfants des manufactures* (1867).

"Cour de Cassation (14 mai, 1846): Travail des enfants. . . ." *Mémorial du commerce et de l'industrie*, X (1846).

Delamarre, Ludovic. "Exécution de la loi du 22 mars 1841 sur le travail des enfants dans les manufactures et de la loi du 4 mars 1851 sur le contrat d'apprentissage." *Annales de la charité*, XIV (1858).

Délerot, E. "Avant-propos." *Bulletin de la Société de protection des apprentis et des enfants des manufactures* (1867).

"Département de l'agriculture et du commerce." In *Almanach national*. Paris, 1875.

"Des enfans et des jeunes ouvriers employés dans les fabriques." *Bulletin de la Société industrielle de Mulhouse*, VIII (1834–35).

[Dollfus, Emile]. "Lettre . . . sur l'inobservance de la loi sur le travail des enfants. . . ." *Bulletin de la Société industrielle de Mulhouse*, XXVIII (May, 1857).

[Dumas, J. B.]. "Séance d'inauguration: Exposé de M. le Président." *Bulletin de la Société de protection des apprentis et des enfants des manufactures* (1867).

"Du travail des enfants dans les manufactures." *Journal de l'industriel et du capitaliste*, VIII (January, 1840).

"Du travail des enfants dans les manufactures." *Mémorial du commerce et de l'industrie*, III (1839).

Eichthal, Eugène d'. "Les Lois sur le travail des enfans." *Revue des deux mondes*, 2nd per., C (1872).

"Execution de la loi sur le travail des enfants dans les manufactures." *Annales de la charité*, XV (1859).

Faucher, Léon. "Le Travail des enfans à Paris." *Revue des deux mondes*, n.s., VIII (1844).

Goldenberg. "Lettre de M. Goldenberg." *Bulletin de la Société de protection des apprentis et des enfants des manufactures* (1868).

G. S. "Revue mensuelle des travaux de l'Académie des sciences morales et politiques." *Journal des économistes*, XII (September, 1845).

Hardouin, Emile. "Le Travail des enfants dans les manufactures." *Le Soleil*, June 29, 1873.

H. V. "Lille et le Nord de la France." *L'Echo du Nord*, January 7, 1870.

Kestner-Rigau, Charles. "Rapport fait au nom de la commission spéciale chargée d'examiner les questions relatives au travail des jeunes ouvriers des fabriques." *Bulletin de la Société industrielle de Mulhouse*, VI (1832–33).

Leroy-Beaulieu, Paul. "Les Ouvrières de fabrique." *Revue des deux mondes*, 2nd. per., XCVII (1872).

L. V. "Revue mensuelle des travaux de l'Académie des sciences morales et politiques." *Journal des économistes*, X (December, 1844).

Malapert, F. "De l'application des lois sur le travail des enfants." *Journal des économistes*, 4th ser., XXXII (1885).

Melun, Armand de. "Courrier des oeuvres: Oeuvre des apprenties et des jeunes ouvrières." *Revue d'économie chrétienne: Annales de la charité*, n.s., IV (1863).

———. "Le Travail des enfants." *Le Correspondant*, June 10, 1869.

Penot, Achille. "Rapport de la commission chargée d'examiner la question relative à l'emploi des enfans dans les filatures de coton." *Bulletin de la Société industrielle de Mulhouse*, X (1836–37).

———. "Rapport fait au nom d'une commission, . . . dans le séance du 25 janvier 1843, sur la loi du 22 mars 1841. . . ." *Bulletin de la Société industrielle de Mulhouse*, XVI (1842–43).

———. "Rapport présenté . . . dans la séance du 29 avril, 1847 . . . sur diverses modifications à apporter à la loi du 22 mars 1841. . . ." *Bulletin de la Société industrielle de Mulhouse*, XX (1847).

———. "Rapport sur un projet de loi réglant le travail des enfants dans les ateliers; lu à la séance du 29 décembre 1847. . . ." *Bulletin de la Société industrielle de Mulhouse*, XXI (1848).

"Règlement de la société." *Bulletin de la Société industrielle de Mulhouse*, I (1827–28).

Reybaud, Louis. "Les Ecoles d'apprentis." *Revue des deux mondes*, 2nd per., XCIX (1872).

Saveney, Edgar. "Les Délégations ouvrières à l'exposition univerśelle de 1867." *Revue des deux mondes*, 2nd per., LXXVII (1868).

Simon, Jules. "L'Apprentissage des jeunes ouvriers dans la petite industrie." *Revue des deux mondes*, 2nd per., LV (1865).

———. "L'Ouvrier de huit ans." *Revue des deux mondes*, 2nd per., LIV (1864).

"Statutes provisoires." *Bulletin de la Société de protection des apprentis et des enfants des manufactures* (1867).

Thouvenin, Jean-Pierre. "De l'influence que l'industrie exerce sur la santé des populations." *Annales d'hygiène publique et de médecine légale*, XXXVI (1846) and XXXVII (1847).

[Zickel]. "Rapport de la commission spéciale, concernant la proposition de M. Jean-Jacques Bourcart." *Bulletin de la Société industrielle de Mulhouse*, I (1827–28).

Secondary Sources

BOOKS

Aftalion, Albert. *L'Oeuvre économique de Simonde de Sismondi*. Paris, 1899.

Anderson, R. D. *Education in France, 1848–1870*. Oxford, 1975.

Ariès, Philippe. *Centuries of Childhood*. Translated by Robert Baldick. New York, 1962.

Artz, Frederick. *Reaction and Revolution, 1814–1832*. New York, 1934.

Aynard, Joseph. *Justice ou charité? Le Drame sociale et ses temoins de 1825 à 1845*. Paris, 1945.

Bacquié, Franc. *Les Inspecteurs des manufactures sous l'ancien régime: 1669–1792.* In *Mémoires et documents pour servir à l'histoire du commerce et de l'industrie,* 11th ser., edited by Julien Hayem. Paris, 1927.

Bardoul, Emerand. *Essai sur l'apprentissage industriel en France.* Paris, 1919.

Beau de Loménie, E. *Les Responsabilités des dynasties bourgeoises.* Vol. I of 4 vols. Paris, 1948.

Bec, Benjamin. *La Législation de l'inspection du travail.* Rennes, 1907.

Bénet, Jacques. *Le Capitalisme libéral et le droit au travail.* 2 vols. Neuchâtel, 1947.

Bertocci, Philip A. *Jules Simon: Republican Anticlericalism and Cultural Politics in France, 1848–1886.* Columbia, Mo., 1978.

Béziers, Simone. *La Protection de l'enfance ouvrière.* Montpellier, 1935.

Bonzon, Jacques. *La Législation de l'enfance.* Paris, 1899.

Bron, Jean. *Histoire du mouvement ouvrier français.* Vol. I of 3 vols. Paris, 1968.

Brush, Elizabeth Parnham. *Guizot in the Early Years of the Orleanist Monarchy. University of Illinois Studies in the Social Sciences,* Vol. XV. [Urbana?], Ill., *ca.* 1927.

Bry, Georges. *Cours élémentaire de législation industrielle.* Paris, 1909.

Bury, J. P. T. *Gambetta and the Making of the Third Republic.* London, 1973.

Caire, César. *La Législation sur le travail industriel des femmes et des enfants.* Paris, 1896.

Calvet, Jean. *L'Enfant dans la littérature française.* 2 vols. Paris, 1930.

Campbell, Stuart L. *The Second Empire Revisited.* New Brunswick, N.J., 1978.

Caron, François. *An Economic History of Modern France.* Translated by Barbara Bray. New York, 1979.

Cazamian, Louis. *A History of French Literature.* Oxford, 1955.

Charléty, Sébastian. *La Monarchie de juillet.* Paris, 1921. Vol. V of Ernest Lavisse, *Histoire de France contemporaine.* 10 vols.

Chastenet, Jacques. *Cent Ans de république.* Vol. I of 9 vols. Paris, 1970.

Chevalier, Louis. *Classes laborieuses et classes dangereuses à Paris pendant la première moitié du XIXe siècle.* Paris, 1958.

Cobban, Alfred. *A History of Modern France.* Vols. II and III of 3 vols. Baltimore, 1965.

Cole, G. D. H. *Robert Owen.* Boston, 1925.

Coleman, William. *Death is a Social Disease: Public Health and Political Economy in Early Industrial France.* Madison, 1982.

Collins, Ross William. *Catholicism and the Second French Republic.* New York, 1923.

Colmart, A. *De l'inspection du travail en France.* Paris, 1899.

Colomès, André. *Les Ouvriers du textile dans la champagne troyenne.* Paris, 1943.

Copin, Albert. *Les Doctrines économiques et les débuts de la législation ouvrière en France.* Lille, 1943.

Crubellier, Maurice. *L'Enfance et la jeunesse dans la société française, 1800–1950.* Paris, 1979.

D'Allemagne, Henry-Réné. *Les Saint-Simonians, 1827–1837.* Paris, 1930.

D'Andigné, Amédée. *Un Apôtre de la charité: Armand de Melun.* Paris, 1961.

Daniel-Rops, H. *The Church in an Age of Revolution, 1789–1870.* Translated by John Warrington. London, 1965.

Dansette, Adrien. *Religious History of Modern France.* Vol. I of 2 vols. Translated by John Dingle. New York, 1961.

Deslandres, Maurice, and Alfred Michelin. *Il y a cent ans.* Paris, 1939.

Dicey, A. V. *Lectures on the Relation Between Law and Public Opinion in England During the Nineteenth Century.* London, 1920.

Documents relatifs au travail des enfants et des femmes. Brussels, 1871.

Dolfus-Francoz, Eugène. *Essai historique sur la condition légale du mineur, apprenti, ouvrier d'industrie, ou employé de commerce.* Paris, 1900.

Dondo, Mathurin. *The French Faust, Henri de Saint-Simon.* New York, 1955.

Donzelot, Jacques. *The Policing of Families.* Translated by Robert Hurley. New York, 1979.

Driver, Cecil. *Tory Radical: The Life of Richard Oastler.* New York, 1946.

Duby, Georges, and Armand Wallon, eds. *Histoire de la France rurale.* 4 vols. Paris, 1975–76.

Dunlop, O. Jocelyn. *English Apprenticeship and Child Labour.* London, 1912.

Dupuy, Aimé. *Un Personnage nouveau du roman français, l'enfant.* Tunis, 1931.

Durand, Emile. *L'Inspection du travail en France de 1841 à 1902.* Paris, 1902.

Duroselle, Jean-Baptiste. *Les Débuts du Catholicisme social en France.* Paris, 1951.

Duval-Arnould, Louis. *Essai sur la législation français du travail des enfants.* Paris, 1888.

Duveau, Georges. *La Pensée ouvrière sur l'education pendant la Second Republic et le Second Empire.* Paris, 1948.

Duvoir, Léon. *Recherche des tendances interventionnistes chez quelques économistes libéraux français de 1830 à 1850.* Paris, 1901.

Elwitt, Sanford. *The Making of the Third Republic: Class and Politics in France, 1868–1884.* Baton Rouge, 1975.

———. *The Third Republic Defended: Bourgeois Reform in France, 1880–1914.* Baton Rouge, 1986.

Evans, David Owen. *Social Romanticism in France, 1830–1848.* Oxford, 1951.

Festy, Octave. *Le Mouvement ouvrier au début de la Monarchie de juillet.* Paris, 1908.

Finer, S. E. *The Life and Times of Sir Edwin Chadwick.* London, 1952.

Forrester, R. B. *The Cotton Industry in France.* Manchester, 1921.

Fournier, Pierre-Léon. *Le Second Empire et la législation ouvrière.* Paris, 1911.

Fournière, Eugène. *Le Règne de Louis Philippe.* Paris, ca. 1906. Vol. VIII of Jean Jaurès, *Histoire socialiste, 1789–1900.* 13 vols.

Frambourg, Guy. *Le Docteur Guépin.* Nantes, 1964.

Fuchs, Rachel G. *Abandoned Children: Foundlings and Child Welfare in Nineteenth-Century France.* Albany, N. Y., 1984.

Gélis, Jacques, Mireille Laget, and Marie-France Morel. *Entrer dans la vie: Naissances et enfances dans la France traditionnelle.* [Paris?], 1978.

Gillis, John R. *Youth and History.* New York, 1981.

Gooch, G. P. *The Second Empire.* 1960; rpr. Westport, Conn., 1975.

Gossez, A.-M. *Le Département du Nord sous la deuxième République.* Lille, 1904.

Grant, Elliott Mansfield. *French Poetry and Modern Industry, 1830–1870.* Cambridge, Mass., 1927.

Gray, Alexander. *The Socialist Tradition.* London, 1946.

Halévy, Elie. *England in 1815.* Translated by E. I. Watkin and D. A. Barker. New York, 1961.

Hammond, J. L., and Barbara Hammond. *Lord Shaftsbury.* New York, 1923.

Harrison, J. F. C. *The Early Victorians, 1832–1851.* New York, 1971.

Hayes, Carlton J. *A Generation of Materialism, 1871–1900.* New York, 1941.

Henderson, William Otto. *The Industrial Revolution in Europe, 1815–1914.* Chicago, 1961.

Herbertson, Dorothy. *The Life of Frédéric LePlay.* Ledbury, Eng., 1950.

Heywood, Colin. *Childhood in Nineteenth-Century France: Work, Health, and Education Among the Classes Populaires.* Cambridge, Eng., 1988.

Hutchins, B. L., and A. Harrison. *A History of Factory Legislation.* London, 1926.

International Labour Office. *Factory Inspection: Historical Development and Present Organization in Certain Countries.* Geneva, 1923.

Johnson, Christopher. *Utopian Communism in France: Cabet and the Icarians, 1839–1851.* Ithaca, 1974.

Kahan-Rabecq, Marie-Madeleine. *La Classe ouvrière en Alsace pendant la Monarchie de juillet.* Paris, 1939.

Kent, Sherman. *Electoral Procedure Under Louis-Philippe.* New Haven, 1937.

Kindleberger, Charles P. *Economic Growth in France and Britain: 1851–1950.* New York, 1964.

Labracherie, Pierre. *Michel Chevalier et ses idées économiques.* Paris, 1929.

Landes, David S. *The Unbound Prometheus.* Cambridge, Eng., 1969.

Lequin, Yves. *Les Ouvriers de la région lyonnaise (1848–1914).* Vol. II of 2 vols. Lyon, 1977.

Leuilliot, Paul. *L'Alsace au début de XIXe siècle.* 3 vols. Paris, 1959.

Levasseur, E. *Histoire des classes ouvrières et de l'industrie en France de 1789 à 1870.* 2 vols. Paris, 1903–1904.

―――. *Questions ouvrières et industrielles en France sous la Troisième République.* Paris, 1907.

Lhomme, Jean. *La Grande Bourgeoisie au pouvoir (1830–1880).* Paris, 1960.

Louis, Paul. *L'Ouvrier devant l'état.* Paris, 1904.

Lynch, Katherine A. *Family, Class, and Ideology in Early Industrial France: Social Policy and the Working-Class Family, 1825–1848.* Madison, 1988.

Manuel, Frank E. *The Prophets of Paris.* New York, 1962.

Mao-Lan Tuan. *Simonde de Sismondi as an Economist.* New York, 1927.

Marini, Lina. *L'Inspection du travail.* Paris, 1936.

Martin, Pierre. *Le Travail des enfants en Allemagne.* Paris, 1911.

Merlet, Paul. *Les Lois sur l'apprentissage et leurs consequences économiques et sociales.* Paris, 1912.

Mitchell, B. R., with Phyllis Deane. *Abstract of British Historical Statistics.* Cambridge, Eng., 1962.

Mitterauer, Michael, and Reinhard Sieder. *The European Family.* Translated by Karla Oosterveen and Manfred Hörzinger. Chicago, 1982.

Moody, John. *Les Idées sociales d'Eugène Sue.* Paris, 1938.

Moon, Parker Thomas. *The Labor Problem and the Social Catholic Movement in France.* New York, 1921.

Musgrove, Frank. *Youth and the Social Order.* Bloomington, Ind., 1965.

Neufville, Agnès de. *Le Mouvement social protestant en France depuis 1880.* Paris, 1927.

O'Brien, Patrick, and Caglar Keyder. *Economic Growth in Britain and France, 1780–1914.* London, 1978.

Osgood, Samuel M. *French Royalism Under the Third and Fourth Republics.* The Hague, 1960.

Overbergh, Cyr. van. *Les Inspecteurs du travail.* Paris, 1893.

Palmade, Guy P. *French Capitalism in the Nineteenth Century.* Translated by Graeme Holmes. New York, 1972.

Parker, Clifford Stetson. *The Defense of the Child by French Novelists.* Menasha, Wisc., 1925.

Perrot, Michelle. *Enquêtes sur la condition ouvrière en France au 19e siècle.* Paris, 1972.

Pic, Paul. *Les Lois ouvrières.* Paris, 1903.

Pinchbeck, Ivy, and Margaret Hewitt. *Children in English Society.* Vol. II of 2 vols. London, 1973.

Ponteil, Félix. *Histoire de l'enseignement en France.* [Tours?], 1966.

Postman, Neil. *The Disappearance of Childhood.* New York, 1982.

Pournin, Marcel. *L'Inspection du travail.* Paris, 1903.

Price, Roger. *The French Second Republic: A Social History.* Ithaca, 1972.

Ralston, David B. *The Army of the Republic: The Place of the Military in the Political Evolution of France, 1871–1914.* Cambridge, Mass., 1967.

Reddy, William M. *The Rise of Market Culture: The Textile Trade and French Society, 1750–1900.* Cambridge, Eng., 1984.

Riasanovsky, Nicholas V. *The Teachings of Charles Fourier.* Berkeley, 1969.

Rigaudias-Weiss, Hilde. *Les Enquêtes ouvrières en France.* Paris, 1936.

Ring, Mary Ignatius. *Villeneuve-Bargemont, Precursor of Modern Social Catholicism.* Milwaukee, 1935.

Roberts, David. *Victorian Origins of the British Welfare State.* New Haven, 1960.

Salis, Jean-R. de. *Sismondi.* Paris, 1932.

Scelle, G. *Précis élémentaire de législation industrielle.* Paris, 1927.

Scott, Joan Wallach. *The Glassworkers of Carmaux: French Craftsmen and Political Action in a Nineteenth-Century City.* Cambridge, Mass., 1974.

Sewell, William H., Jr. *Work and Revolution in France: The Language of Labor from the Old Regime to 1848.* Cambridge, Eng., 1980.

Shorter, Edward. *The Making of the Modern Family.* New York, 1975.

Smelser, Neil J. *Social Change in the Industrial Revolution.* Chicago, 1959.

Snyders, Georges. *Il n'est pas facile d'aimer ses enfants.* Paris, 1982.

Stearns, Peter N. *Paths to Authority: The Middle Class and the Industrial Labor Force in France, 1820–1848.* Urbana, Ill., 1978.

Stone, Judith F. *The Search for Social Peace: Reform Legislation in France, 1890–1914.* Albany, N. Y., 1985.

Sussman, George D. *Selling Mothers' Milk: The Wet-Nursing Business in France, 1715–1914.* Urbana, Ill., 1982.

Swart, Koenraad W. *The Sense of Decadence in Nineteenth-Century France.* The Hague, 1964.

Thomas, Maurice W. *Early Factory Legislation.* Leigh-on-sea, Eng., 1948.

———. *Young People in Industry, 1750–1945.* London, 1945.

Thompson, E. P. *The Making of the English Working Class.* New York, 1963.

Tilly, Louise A., and Joan W. Scott. *Women, Work, and Family.* New York, 1978.

Tolédano, A. D. *La Vie de famille sous la Restauration et la Monarchie de juillet.* Paris, 1943.

Touren, Suzanne. *La Loi de 1841 sur le travail des enfants dans les manufactures.* Paris, 1931.

Tudesq, André-Jean. *Les Grands Notables en France (1840–1849).* 2 vols. Paris, 1964.
Vidler, Alexander Roper. *A Century of Social Catholicism, 1820–1920.* London, 1964.
Villate-Lacheret. *Les Inspectrices du travail en France.* Paris, 1919.
Villey, Edmond. *L'Oeuvre économique de Charles Dunoyer.* Paris, 1899.
Ward, J. T. *The Factory Movement, 1830–1855.* London, 1962.
Weber, Eugen. *Peasants into Frenchmen.* Stanford, 1976.
Weill, Georges. *Histoire du mouvement social en France, 1852–1924.* Paris, 1924.
Weiss, Raymond. *Daniel Le Grand.* Paris, 1926.
Wright, Gordon. *France in Modern Times.* New York, 1981.
Zeldin, Theodore. *France, 1848–1945.* 2 vols. Oxford, 1973–77.

ARTICLES AND PAPERS

Ariès, Philippe. "Le XIXe Siècle et la révolution des moeurs familiales." In *Renouveau des idées sur la famille,* edited by Robert Prigent. Paris, 1954.
Armengaud, André. "L'Attitude de la société à l'égard de l'enfant au XIXe siècle." *Annales de démographie historique* (1973).
Berlanstein, Lenard R. "Vagrants, Beggars, and Thieves: Delinquent Boys in Mid-Nineteenth Century Paris." *Journal of Social History,* XII (Summer, 1979).
Bezucha, Robert J. "The Moralization of Society: The Enemies of Popular Culture in the Nineteenth Century." In *The Wolf and the Lamb: Popular Culture in France,* edited by Jacques Beauroy, Marc Bertrand, and Edward Gargan. Palo Alto, 1977.
Boxer, Marilyn J. "Women in Industrial Homework: The Flowermakers of Paris in the Belle Epoque." *French Historical Studies,* XII (Spring, 1982).
Darnton, Robert. "Workers Revolt: The Great Cat Massacre of the Rue Saint-Séverin." In *The Great Cat Massacre and Other Episodes in French Cultural History,* by Robert Darnton. New York, 1984.
Douailler, Stéphane, and Patrice Vermeren. "Les Enfants des hospices, remède contre l'instabilité des ouvriers." *Les Révoltes logiques,* III (1976).
Drescher, Seymour. "Two Variants of Anti-Slavery: Religious Organization and Social Mobilization in Britain and France, 1790–1870." In *Anti-Slavery, Religion, and Reform,* edited by Christine Bolt and Seymour Drescher. Folkstone, Eng., 1980.
Droulers, Paul. "Des évêques parlent de la question ouvrière en France avant 1848." *Revue de l'Action populaire,* No. 147 (April, 1961).
Durand, Marion. "One Hundred Years of Illustrations in French Children's Books." *Yale French Studies,* XLIII (1969).
Festy, Octave. "Le vte. Alban de Villeneuve-Bargemont et la condition des ouvriers français aux environs de 1830." *Revue des sciences politiques,* XLII (1919).
Gay, Peter. "On the Bourgeoisie: A Psychological Interpretation." In *Consciousness and Class Experience in Nineteenth-Century Europe,* edited by John M. Merriman. New York, 1979.

Gueneau, Louis. "La Législation restrictive du travail des enfants: La Loi du 1841." *Revue d'histoire économique et sociale*, XV (1927).

Heywood, Colin. "Education and the Industrial Labour Force in Nineteenth-Century France." Typescript in possession of Colin Heywood, Nottingham, Eng., 1980.

———. "The Impact of Industrialization on the Health of Children in Nineteenth-Century France." Typescript in possession of Colin Heywood, Nottingham, Eng., 1982.

———. "The Market for Child Labour in Nineteenth-Century France." *History*, No. 216 (1981).

Hufton, Olwen. "Women and the Family Economy in Eighteenth-Century France." *French Historical Studies*, IX (Spring, 1975).

Jan, Isabelle. "Children's Literature and Bourgeois Society in France since 1860." *Yale French Studies*, XLIII (1969).

Johnson, Christopher H. "Economic Change and Artisan Discontent: The Tailors' History, 1800–1848." In *Revolution and Reaction*, edited by Roger Price. London, 1975.

Kanipe, Esther S. "Hetzel and the Bibliothèque d'education et de récréation." *Yale French Studies*, XLIII (1969).

Landes, David S. "Religion and Enterprise: The Case of the French Textile Industry." In *Enterprise and Entrepreneurs in Nineteenth and Twentieth Century France*, edited by Edward C. Carter, Robert Forster, and Joseph Moody. Baltimore, 1976.

Lequin, Yves. "Apprenticeship in Nineteenth-Century France: A Continuing Tradition or a Break with the Past?" In *Work in France: Representations, Meaning, Organization, and Practice*, edited by Steven Laurence Kaplan and Cynthia J. Koepp. Ithaca, 1986.

"Les Enfants du capital." *Les Révoltes logiques*, III (1976).

Lynch, Katherine A. "The Problem of Child Labor Reform and the Working-Class Family in France during the July Monarchy." In *Proceedings of the Annual Meeting of the Western Society for French History*, V (1977).

Mataja, Victor. "Les origines de la protection ouvrière en France." *Revue d'économie politique*, IX (June, August-September, 1895) and X (March, April, 1896).

McDougall, Mary Lynn. "The Meaning of Reform: The Ban on Women's Night Work, 1892–1914." In *Proceedings of the Annual Meeting of the Western Society for French History*, X (1982).

———. "Protecting Infants: The French Campaign for Maternity Leaves, 1890s–1913." *French Historical Studies*, XIII (Spring, 1983).

———. "Working-Class Women During the Industrial Revolution, 1780–1914." In *Becoming Visible: Women in European History*, edited by Renate Bridenthal and Claudia Koonz. Boston, 1977.

Moch, Leslie Page, and Louise A. Tilly. "Joining the Urban World: Occupation, Family, and Migration in Three French Cities." *Comparative Studies in Society and History*, XXVII (1985).

Perrot, Michelle. "A Nineteenth-Century Work Experience as Related in a Worker's Autobiography: Norbert Truquin." In *Work in France: Representations*,

Meaning, Organization, and Practice, edited by Steven Laurence Kaplan and Cynthia J. Koepp. Ithaca, 1986.

———. "The Three Ages of Industrial Discipline in Nineteenth-Century France." In *Consciousness and Class Experience in Nineteenth-Century Europe*, edited by John M. Merriman. New York, 1979.

Pierrard, P. "Le Patronat et le travail des enfants en 1848." *Economie et humanisme*, XVIII (1959).

Pollard, Sidney. "Factory Discipline in the Industrial Revolution." *Economic History Review*, 2nd ser., XVI (December, 1963).

Reddy, William M. "Family and Factory: French Linen Weavers in the Belle Epoque." *Journal of Social History*, VIII (Winter, 1975).

Reid, Donald. "Putting Social Reform into Practice: Labor Inspectors in France, 1892–1914." *Journal of Social History*, XX (Fall, 1986).

Rolley, J. "La Structure de l'industrie textile en France, en 1840–1844." *Histoire des entreprises*, IV (November, 1959).

Scott, Joan W. "Statistical Representations of Work: The Politics of the Chamber of Commerce's *Statistique de l'Industrie à Paris, 1847–48*." In *Work in France: Representations, Meaning, Organization, and Practice*, edited by Steven Laurence Kaplan and Cynthia J. Koepp. Ithaca, 1986.

Shaffer, John W. "Family, Class, and Young Women: Occupational Expectations in Nineteenth-Century Paris." *Journal of Family History*, III (Spring, 1978).

Smelser, Neil J. "Sociological History: The Industrial Revolution and the British Working-Class Family." *Journal of Social History*, I (Fall, 1967).

Strumingher, Laura S. "The Artisan Family: Traditions and Transition in Nineteenth-Century Lyon." *Journal of Family History*, II (Fall, 1977).

Tudesq, André-Jean. "Comment le grand patronat considère le travail des enfants en 1840." In *VIIIe colloque d'histoire sur l'artisanat et l'apprentissage*. Aix-en-Provence, 1965.

"Une Politique de la force de travail." *Les Révoltes logiques*, III (1976).

Weissbach, Lee Shai. "Artisanal Responses to Artistic Decline: The Cabinetmakers of Paris in the Era of Industrialization." *Journal of Social History*, XVI (Winter, 1982).

———. "The Child Labor Problem in the 1860s: Realities and Attitudes." Paper presented at the Annual Meeting of the Society for French Historical Studies, 1983.

———. "Entrepreneurial Traditionalism in Nineteenth-Century France: A Study of the Patronage industriel des enfants de l'ébénisterie." *Business History Review*, LVII (1983).

———. "*Oeuvre industrielle, oeuvre morale*: The *Sociétés de patronage* of Nineteenth-Century France." *French Historical Studies*, XV (Spring, 1987).

Index